BREAKING ROCKS

DISLOCATIONS

General Editors: August Carbonella, *Memorial University of Newfoundland, Don Kalb, University of Utrecht & Central European University, Linda Green, University of Arizona*

The immense dislocations and suffering caused by neoliberal globalization, the retreat of the welfare state in the last decades of the twentieth century, and the heightened military imperialism at the turn of the twenty-first century have raised urgent questions about the temporal and spatial dimensions of power. Through stimulating critical perspectives and new and cross-disciplinary frameworks that reflect recent innovations in the social and human sciences, this series provides a forum for politically engaged and theoretically imaginative responses to these important issues of late modernity.

For a full volume listing, please see back matter

BREAKING ROCKS

Music, Ideology and Economic Collapse, from Paris to Kinshasa

Joe Trapido

berghahn
NEW YORK · OXFORD
www.berghahnbooks.com

First published in 2017 by
Berghahn Books
www.berghahnbooks.com

Library of Congress Cataloging-in-Publication Data
Names: Trapido, Joe, author.
Title: Breaking rocks : music, ideology and economic collapse, from
    Paris to   Kinshasa / Joe Trapido.
Other titles: Dislocations ; v. 19.
Description: New York : Berghahn Books, 2017. | Series: Dislocations ;
    volume   19 | Includes bibliographical references and index.
Identifiers: LCCN 2016053211 | ISBN 9781785333989 (hardback : alk. paper)
Subjects: LCSH: Popular music--Economic aspects--Congo (Democratic
    Republic) | Popular music--Social aspects--Congo (Democratic Republic) |
    Music   patronage--Congo (Democratic Republic) | Congolese (Democratic
    Republic)--Europe--Social conditions.
Classification: LCC ML3503.C68 T73 2017 | DDC 781.63096751--dc23 LC record
    available at https://lccn.loc.gov/2016053211

British Library Cataloguing in Publication Data
A catalogue record for this book is available from the British Library

Printed on acid-free paper

ISBN 978-1-78533-398-9 (hardback)
ISBN 978-1-78920-794-1 (paperback)
ISBN 978-1-78533-399-6 (ebook)

CONTENTS

This book is dedicated to Antoinette Trapido, Alexandra Trapido and Barbara Trapido, with love.

ACKNOWLEDGEMENTS

Writing a book is a hard thing to do and I could not have done it without the help of very many people.

First of all, thank you everyone at Berghahn. You have been very patient and encouraging. I would also like to thank Don Kalb and the other editors on the *Dislocations* series. I am very lucky to count Patrick Neveling as my friend, thank you for nudging me in this direction.

Mike Kirkwood's suggestions on my manuscript were incredibly valuable, as were his views on everything else, including cricket.

Susan Watkins and Daniel Finn at the *New Left Review,* and Professor Ian Phimister at the University of the Free State had nothing to do with this book, but having such intellectually impressive people take me seriously and offer encouragement to my wider work helped my morale enormously.

I was lucky to study at University College London's department of Anthropology, I am still profoundly grateful for the opportunity they gave me. Professors Michael Rowlands and Daniel Miller there deserve especial thanks.

At SOAS, Professor Richard Fardon made very important intellectual suggestions about this work, but he has also given me a host of other kinds of help: attentive proofreader, application reviser, and sympathetic ear. I am amazed that a scholar who has produced so many highly regarded publications and with so many other responsibilities could find the time do this.

At the Universty of Pretoria I was given much support and intellectual assistance. Professors Charles Van Onselen, John Sharpe, and Inocent Pikirayi, and Drs Detlev Krige, Fraser Mcneill, Jason Sumich, Juliana Braz-Diaz and Mallika Shakya all contributed to an enjoyable, stimulating and productive two years in South Africa.

Others I would like in particular to thank for their help are:

Kalaho Mayombo, Eric Tshimpaka, Gloria Turkhadio, Celezino, Jhimmy, Professeur Kibens, Cellulaire, Mi, Smith, Kams, Balzac, Mandela Atala, Innocent, Yves, Eboa, Maika Munan, Sec Bidens, Theo Bidens, Polistar, Lassa, Tony and Jean Mark.

Professor Filip De Boeck met me in Brussels to discuss my then very unformed project and was very generous with his time. Professor Nancy Rose Hunt has also been incredibly kind, generous and helpful. My connection to both of these eminent scholars has been a source of encouragement and intellectual inspiration.

In Kinshasa, Marc who let me stay in his house when he was away, and everyone at the premier rue, especially Mimi and Diaz. Just down the road, John at studio Mek'o was very kind. Later on I got to know the wonderful Baby, Leon and Nanou Silikani, Diji, Pitshou Imbole, Armando, Nancy, Bijou, Elko, Jimmy (and family), Vieux Tout Kin, everyone at Londres bar and Kadafi spot, what a joy you all are and how I miss all of you.

At the start of my stay in Kinshasa I was very lucky to be invited to a conference organized by Professor Nancy Rose Hunt and Professor Sabakinu. The colleagues I met via this conference changed my work very dramatically. Thank you Nancy for inviting me. Kristien Geenen gave the best paper I have ever heard, illustrated with her wonderful photographs. She also showed me how to get around the city and her approach to everything made me into a far less timid kind of researcher than I would otherwise have been. I was honoured to present a paper at the conference with Leon Tsambu (now Professor). We became friends, Leon knows more than anyone about Congo music, and he is a brilliant theorist of cultural life. I would also like to thank Yolande, Leon's wife, for being so hospitable despite children and studies of her own to manage.

Via Leon I have got to know many people working at the University of Kinshasa. Among the senior staff Professor Mutamba and Professor Obotela were especially kind. The friendship and assistance of all the people who work at the University of Kinshasa's *Centre D'Etudes Politiques* has been especially valuable – Dede Watchiba, Willy Kalala, José Bazonzi, Jules Kassay, Célestin Tshimande, Delphin Kayembe and Professor Jean Omasombo. The centre produces a huge amount of exciting work on social and political questions in the Congo, and is one of the most exciting social science research centres that I have visited.

I was also very lucky to meet and make friends with Pitshou Mangbanga, and via him with Saint José Inaka. They shared their deep knowledge of their city in a way that combined an insider's grasp with a sociological and analytical turn of mind. I also had a lot of fun in their company.

Via Saint José I got to know the entire Inaka Family. All of them have helped me to understand and feel at home in Kinshasa. I would especially like to mention Pascal, Mama Marthe, Landry, Laroche, Clotilde, Marie-Therese, Marie-Fidel, Coco, Leticia and Rebecca.

Last but not least I would like to thank my father Stanley (now dead alas), my mother Barbara, my wife Antoinette and little Alexandra.

INTRODUCTION

❧

It is 2001 and I am at a concert at the Brixton Academy given by the Congolese pop star Koffi Olomide. The concert is, as ever, extremely late in starting. The audience is extraordinary; gold leaf biker jackets, beautifully tailored suits in four colours with Andy Warhol screen-prints, fur coats, knee-high crocodile skin boots and kilts. Later on, one after another of these well-dressed men – there are few women in the audience – comes on stage and presses bank notes on to the sweat-ing forehead of Koffi, the lead singer. This is not small change. Most of the notes are fifties and each patron slaps down at least four or five notes, some patrons handing over more than a thousand pounds. As I would later learn, such prestations, called *mabanga*, are part of a wider system – the focus of this book – in which music, reputation and control of social reproduction are negotiated in an economy of prestige that links Europe and Kinshasa.

Towards the end of the 1970s, the Zaïrian state (since 1997 once again the Democratic Republic of Congo – DRC) [1] began a down-ward slide from which it would not recover. A collapse in commod-ity prices, inflation, structural adjustment and predation by the elite destroyed the formal sectors of the economy. The society began to reorganize itself into a more diffuse set of political arrangements that, though they remained authoritarian and violent, were based on much more personalized and informal kinds of clientelism.

These violent social changes also relate to the title of this book, *Breaking Rocks*, a phrase that has recurred in the region throughout the precolonial, colonial and postcolonial worlds. I believe that the various usages of the phrase – meaning initially violent chief, then leviathan colonial state, then, as a verb, in its current meaning as the act of aggressively wresting a living from a hostile world – illustrate some of the implications of these shifting political economies and how they are experienced by people, and exhibited in action and in cul-tural production (see Chapter 2). Be that as it may, as living standards collapsed in Zaïre and hard currency income became crucial, a tide of migration quickened.

Europe has long had an economic importance for the Congolese that is also quasi-mystical. In a song he wrote in 1969, 'Mokolo Nakokufa' ('The Day I Die', Ley 1970/1997), the singer Tabu Ley imagines various members of society at the moment of death. While the prostitute thinks of her wig and the drunkard of his glass of beer, the rich man thinks of the children he has sent to Europe. Wyatt MacGaffey (1986) suggests that in the late nineteenth century, Bakongo peoples thought Europeans were Kaolin-covered ancestors, returned from the land of the dead, while in contemporary 'confessions' of witchcraft, children have recounted travelling to Europe in aeroplanes made from the bones of their sacrificial victims (De Boeck and Plissart 2004).

From the 1980s, the *parisien*, the *mikiliste* and the *sapeur* became conspicuous figures in the urban culture of Kinshasa. For the young, designer clothes, strongly associated with a pilgrimage to Europe, became a mark of access to the metropole and a source of prestige that circulated as a quasi-currency. Returning, these pilgrims made prestations of clothes to musicians, in exchange for which their names were mentioned on records. This patronage, or *mabanga*, created a cast of celebrities based in Europe who 'performed' at concerts, with recorded music telling those back in Kinshasa of the good life they were leading, while prestations made by members of this cast became the stuff of legend. Before the decade was out, cash had become a more common form of payment for a mention on a record, with a set of roughly established prices. New production techniques allowed more names to be included or added and, throughout the 1990s, younger sections of the political elite, migrants to London and diamond dealers operating out of Angola or the interior all began to 'buy into' this system of prestige, until records became a kind of strange social almanac.

Conceiving the Study

At the outset of this project, I knew a certain amount about Congolese music from a fan's point of view. From a theoretical angle, I had an interest in Marxism. This pointed to a study that considered how aesthetic production and political economy intersected. A passing acquaintance with the performance of contemporary Congolese music reveals the importance of *mabanga*. Reading Waterman's (1990) ethnography of Nigerian *Jújù* music also pointed me in the direction of music patronage as a useful focal point around which to undertake an ethnographic study.

I conjectured that focusing on patronage payments would allow me to make connections between political economy and aesthetics, and also between cultural producers and audiences. I had already picked up from my MA dissertation (Trapido 2005) that the list of patrons was fairly 'interesting' – combining a collection of petty criminals, fraudsters and gangsters in the diaspora with diamond dealers and senior politicians in Kinshasa. It seemed apparent that a focus on patronage would also mean a focus on the individuals who made patrimonial payments. Thus, it appeared evident that biographical methods would be important in the study and that a major research aim would be to find life histories for a representative sample of the most significant patrons. Conversations with a number of Congolese informants, notably several members of Wenge BCBG (one of the most popular *orchestres* in the DRC), who were in London for an extended period in 2005–06, convinced me that Paris was the most important site for patronage and was, along with Kinshasa, the centre of the Congolese recording industry. This determined the choices of Paris and Kinshasa as the main field sites (see below).

Understanding the motivation for patronage also meant comprehending something of the haunts and habits of the wider audience in which patrons moved and from whence they emerged. If patronage was paying for prestige, an interest in patrons implied an understanding of the different sorts of audiences that they wanted to impress, including the various kinds of 'retinue' in Kinshasa. It was evident that Europe-based patrons were bestowing their patronage predominantly upon musicians who could give them maximum exposure in the Congolese capital. In addition, a significant number of patrons were based in Kinshasa. All this persuaded me that it would be necessary to include a substantial period of fieldwork in Kinshasa.

Methods

The various methods used in this study have been employed within an overall context of participant observation. 'Hanging out' was by far the most important method I used. Nevertheless, during the period of fieldwork, I also conducted over seventy interviews.

The themes of the interviews varied. A large number were general life-history interviews with patrons. Many of these concerned subjects related to *mayuya* – various kinds of illegal practices undertaken in the diaspora, such as prostitution, human trafficking, drug dealing, the trade in bad cheques or the marketing of stolen clothing. Many were with musicians and combined life histories with some questioning on the subject of patronage. Others were about diamond dealing and the migration to Lunda Norte in Angola. Several were conducted with members of *mutualités* – female rotating credit associations – and were on the subject of these societies (and, in a rather circumspect way, the courtesans who participate in them). Numerous interviews were conducted with music producers about their productions. More were with arrangers and studio engineers. I made an effort to conduct interviews in various parts of Kinshasa, trying to select informants with different educational profiles in Limeté, Lemba and Masina. In Limeté I interviewed *shege* – street children. Broadly, these were group interviews on the subject of music patrons and, in particular, on the interviewees' experiences with and attitudes towards patrons based in Europe.

A second kind of semistructured interview (or interview-like practice) was organized around music. I would play a piece of music and elicit both translations and comments from one or several informants about what a song meant and how they interpreted it. Such song interviews were helpful in several ways. First, it was a useful way of building my Lingala vocabulary as songs were translated for me. Once my Lingala became proficient enough for me to get the gist of songs for myself, the interviews became important as one way to gain contextual understandings of Congolese popular music. What a song 'says' and what it 'means' are often very different, and the meanings I imputed to songs were often somewhat removed from the senses given by informants, even where I had been correct about the words in a literal sense. Finally, these sessions helped me to gain an overview of which patrons were associated with particular *orchestres* and, from further questioning, to get a rough idea as to who these patrons were and where they lived. These discussions – there were many such – provided a steady flow of field notes and entries in my journal.

It has been said of interviews that they impose the researcher's concerns on the subject of the interview (Coplan 1997: 29). While this was surely a factor at times, I frequently encountered the opposite problem. Many of my interviewees interpreted the interview form via the filter of music television in Kinshasa. Once a recording device was turned on, they would employ the highly rhetorical forms of speech used in such interviews: lying extravagantly, praising themselves and their comrades in exaggerated fashion, and – ignoring my introductory spiel about anonymity – exhorting the *bana Kin* (people from Kinshasa) to mark well what they had to say. Often they would ask me to play back the interview and would want to do it again if they felt they had not expressed themselves with sufficient aplomb.

As a researcher, the information I gleaned from these interviews was not what I had expected. My primary interest became – in place of facts about lives or careers – the forms of rhetoric they contained, and the emic understanding of the media and of audience that such performances revealed.

But, as I say, interviews were never more than an adjunct to participant observation. On many subjects, such as patronage payments, extended observation led me to conclusions substantially different from those I would have reached through verbal reports alone. Likewise, my best information about music and other media was gleaned in informal settings – from conversation about songs, for example, and observation of their effects as they were played in a bar. On occasions I have included extended reports from interviews, but this does not imply that greater weight is given to the interview form (or verbatim transcripts) in comparison with other kinds of evidence. Rather, this simply presents the most tangible form of evidence for readers who were not there. In fact, I tended to accord rather less importance to formal interviews – only believing this kind of 'on the record' verbal report if it was substantiated by other evidence. Most of the time, interviews were simply an excuse for meeting people or for being in certain places. Often people would start talking in earnest only once the recorder was switched off and I would never have obtained the extensive data about clandestine practices contained in the book had I been primarily reliant on this kind of formal, recorded conversation.

The research for this book was conducted in the languages that predominate in Kinshasa and in the Congolese communities in Western Europe – French and Lingala, languages in which I am a proficient, though obviously non-native, speaker. Lingala is a western Bantu language. Initially a lingua franca along the middle Congo River, the language has become the primary language of Kinshasa and is the main communication vehicle for the western DRC.[2] Lingala is also strongly associated with Congolese music. The association with music accounts for the fact that Lingala is understood by a large number of people in the in the east of the DRC, where Swahili is the main lingua franca. At first, my Lingala was poor and I used it as a sideline that convinced informants of my interest in all things Congolese. About halfway through the project, I gained sufficient mastery of the language to conduct interviews and exchanges entirely in Lingala and from then on it was probably the main vehicle for research communication. No research assistants were employed for this project.

Much discussion has been engendered in the social sciences by the question of the perspective or 'positionality' of the ethnographer. While such discussions are often posed as 'critiques of Western rationality' or some such, in fact, they exemplify all the most problematic aspects of this tradition. Founded in Descartes' obsession with defeating scepticism as a precondition of knowledge – the endemic confusion of epistemology and ontology to which this leads causes scholarship to veer drunkenly between positivist certainties and sceptical panic attacks. Better to start with a more plausible assumption – that we are all fallible and we have all got an angle, but if we try our best to be scrupulous and rigorous, we can probably know something. Somewhat related to this, I make reference to my presence when relevant, but I have deliberately avoided the common ethnographic convention of putting myself into the frame at every juncture or making myself the centre of ethnographic narration. Problems about my position as a researcher will not be solved by hand-wringing or ostentatious markers of my presence; let the reader judge what I have written unimpeded by such get-out clauses.

Samples and Sites

The considerations discussed above established the kinds of samples I was interested in – I would be trying to obtain information about the people who paid to be cited on record and the financial backers of musical productions. I would also be trying to obtain information about the various people, from musicians and arrangers to studio engineers, who were involved in making music. And I would be trying to find information about wider audiences, both those in Paris and those in Kinshasa.

I had several friends in London who put me in touch with relatives in Paris. There I ate meals, attended concerts and drank in *ngandas* (Congolese bars) with this outer circle of contacts, trusting that they would put me in touch with various musicians and producers. Reliance on this kind of snowball/chain referral sample initially proved slow going. When I did make contact with a musician, a patron or a producer, finding ways of sustaining these relationships towards prolonged 'hanging out' was a further challenge. Then my efforts were taken in hand by a key informant, Rameses, who listened to my aims and suggested a strategy for achieving them.

His first piece of advice was that I should stop sounding humble – people would be impressed by the idea of the University of London, he said, and my target informants did not go in for diffidence, so I should sound more certain of my credentials and of the importance of my research. His second piece of advice was that I should buy a video camera. The people involved in *mabanga* were show-offs, he pointed out, and would see no point in downsizing themselves to a little Dictaphone. 'Get a video camera and they will fight to be interviewed', he said. Third, he told me that if I wanted to meet musicians and patrons, then I should get to know the arrangers of Congolese music. There were only three main ones in Paris, he said, and all the musicians and patrons passed through them. 'If they let you hang out with them you can meet everybody', he stated. 'Sec Biddens [one of the major arrangers in Paris] is *mon vieux* [my elder]. I will introduce you to him. Can you come now?' We got onto the Metro and went to a studio in Saint-Denis.

Studios for Congolese music are remarkably social spaces and proved to be very good places to conduct participant observation. Patrons came and went, journalists arrived, famous courtesans dropped by, musicians gossiped and, when they left the studio, most of them were generous enough to take me along with them on their various journeys. With the exception of Wenge BCBG, whom I met in London and again in Kinshasa, all of the most popular Congolese *orchestres* passed through Paris-based studios when I was there, and the studios also gave me excellent access to the considerable number of musicians who had at some point in the past defected from one of these large *orchestres* during a tour of Paris. Such renegades and rejects were particularly valuable – they had less of a stake in keeping up appearances, but they still knew a great deal about what went on. That said, like everyone else, they too had their angle and I tried to assess their insights critically. Most of the major Paris-based patrons and producers passed through the various studios I attended. At times they were so crowded with patrons that movement was difficult.

In Paris the major studios where I conducted fieldwork were Studio Harry Son in Pantin and Studio Marcadet in Saint-Denis. Studio Marcadet was particularly popular with Congolese musicians, stayed open all night and had several rehearsal spaces upstairs where people would hang out. The area known as the *pleine* in Saint-Denis also had several Congolese shops and bars nearby, and a number of dope peddlers who were doing a roaring trade. The studios were also spaces where various other transactions took place. Studios in Kinshasa were less crowded with patrons, but these were still useful places to make contacts. I made several visits to Studio N'diaye and the studios of the ICA and spent significant periods hanging out in Studio M'eko.

As I grew to understand my topic better, my conception of what would represent a good sample changed somewhat. I became more sensitive to differences in class and ethnicity and how these affected patronage and musical allegiances more generally. Thus, after about six months, I became aware that informants with origins in the province of Bandundu, and from outlying districts of Kinshasa such as Tshangu, were under-represented in my study given their importance in the history of patronage I was beginning to construct. I also became aware of an absence of female informants and I made a sustained effort to interview more women. Issues of how gender is thought about locally – and how this conception relates to music – are also discussed in depth in Chapter 7.

As my research progressed, I also became increasingly aware of the importance of journalists and of television networks in Kinshasa in the diffusion of music. I therefore conducted several interviews with Congolese media professionals while in Paris. In Kinshasa I gave this considerable attention and took much trouble to establish good contacts with executives, journalists and crew working in television. In several other ways the focus of my research in Kinshasa was somewhat different from my fieldwork in Paris. I was interested in gathering material from various types of Kinois about their attitude to music patrons. Especially interesting to me was to gather their impressions of the 'potlatch returns' to Kinshasa, which seemed to command so much space in the collective imagination.

Another patronage-related topic that offered a sharp contrast to Paris was the preponderance of diamond dealers and political patrons based in Kinshasa. I was able to find several informants who had been in northern Angola in the 1990s and could provide considerable amounts of information about diamond dealing and music patronage. On the subject of politician-patrons, I asked informants quite extensive questions in an informal context and wrote these up in a heavily coded fashion. This may have been rather melodramatic on my part, as several informants spontaneously recounted long and possibly compromising anecdotes to tape about particular politicians, and did not perceive this as a risky thing to do.

Paris

France has the largest population of DRC migrants in Europe, estimated at 90,000 in 2003, of whom approximately half were registered irregularly, if at all (Bazenguissa-Ganga 2005).[3] Anecdotal evidence gathered during my research suggests that considerable numbers of Congolese nationals may have claimed asylum on Angolan documents and that there are also significant numbers of Lingalaphone Angolans present in France. The overwhelming majority of these migrants live in the Île-de-France (the greater Paris region). Perhaps the most important omission in this figure is the very large number of naturalized and second-generation Lingala speakers. The legal prohibition in France on gathering ethnic information through the census makes arriving at figures for this population difficult, but I certainly came across Lingalaphone French nationals very frequently.

Unlike migrations from other parts of Francophone Africa to France, this migration is overwhelmingly from urban areas. Despite Congo's huge Swahili-speaking population and the decade of turbulence in the east, the community in France (and in the rest of Europe) appears to be overwhelmingly Lingalaphone, with proximate origins in Kinshasa. Congolese migrants have high levels of formal education relative to other Sub-Saharan migrants (Bazenguissa-Ganga 2005). Yet the employment profile of this group is predominantly in the low-pay sector. Bazenguissa-Ganga (2005) states that approximately two-thirds of Congolese migrants in the Île-de-France work in low-skill sectors such as security and deliveries, while about a quarter are involved in some form of entrepreneurial activity. Qualitative data (Tipo-Tipo 1995; Bazenguissa-Ganga and MacGaffey 2000; Bazenguissa-Ganga 2005) tend to show that Congolese migrants in Europe also have a fairly high level of involvement in criminal activities, especially in identity fraud, drug dealing and prostitution.

Perhaps the most visible areas of Congolese presence in Paris – in terms of a wider population – are in the north of Paris proper. One such area is Château d'Eau, where several Congolese hairdressers and two shops involved in the production and distribution of Congolese music can be found. Large numbers of Congolese go to the area to hang out and it is popular with musicians, for whom sociability is particularly important. Also prominent is Château Rouge, where a significant number of Congolese and other Africans run shops selling specialist foodstuffs, music, telecommunications or some mix of the three. In addition, there are several shops run by Lebanese that cater to a Congolese market. On Saturday, Château Rouge also contains an illegal street market, which sells large amounts of fake and stolen designer goods. Several *ngandas* – Congolese bars – are to be found in the area. The real heart of Congolese Paris, however, lies elsewhere.

Since the 1990s, most Congolese migrants have settled beyond the *périphérique* (ring road) that divides Paris from the *banlieue*, with the highest concentrations found in the Départment of Seine Saint-Denis, followed by Val-d'Oise and Val-de-Marne. Paris itself is the fourth-largest area, followed by Essonne (Bazenguissa-Ganga and MacGaffey 2000). Parts of Saint-Denis – the *pleine*, for example, or the area around the station – have very high concentrations of Congolese shops, restaurants, churches, nightclubs and other businesses. In summer, several outdoor areas in this zone operate as informal night-clubs and barbecue sites, while dilapidated conference centres and warehouses in Saint-Denis and other northern suburbs act as venues for the majority of pop concerts, large funeral wakes (*matanga*) and other diaspora events. Most of the studios used regularly by Congolese musicians – like Studio Marcadet and Studio Harry Son – are found to the north or northwest of Paris proper. These northern suburbs, above all Saint-Denis, formed the geographical focus of my Paris fieldwork.

London

The Congolese community in the UK is considerably smaller and more recent than that found in France. It is predominantly based in London, and Tottenham and Croydon appear to be the areas with the highest concentrations. Arriving from the 1990s, the community is often said to number thirty thousand to forty thousand. This figure is derived from an International Organization for Migration report (2006) and I strongly suspect it suffers from 'Nigerian census syndrome' in that 'community and religious leaders' were asked to assist in the mapping exercise and may have felt it was in their interests to present the community as more numerous than is really the case.[4] The Home Office estimate is twenty thousand, though it probably has incentives for keeping the figures down, and, again, this figure would exclude the 'cultural' Congolese with EU citizenship, along with the sizeable number of quasi-Angolans. Once again, the community appears to be overwhelmingly Lingalaphone with proximate origins in Kinshasa (International Organization for Migration 2006). The increase in London's Congolese community has clearly coincided with a period of intensifying economic and political insecurity in the DRC. Nevertheless, there is considerable anecdotal evidence (see Chapter 6; Tipo-Tipo 1995) that a large section of the community came to Britain clandestinely from France and Belgium rather than directly from the DRC. While it is only the third-largest Congolese community in Europe, in certain respects the London-based migrants – *bana Londres* – punch above their weight in terms of their impact on the Kinois. Until recently this was because of their reputation as big spenders (and big users of magical devices, *'fétiche'*), but now, increasingly perhaps, it is because of the preponderance of militant anti-Kabila nationalism within the community (see Chapter 5).

Kinshasa

Situated near the navigable limits of the Congo River, the area where Kinshasa now stands has long been a centre of trade and dense human populations (Gondola 1997a). Nevertheless, the city in its present incarnation was a creation of the Belgians. Today thought to house seven to ten million people, it is the third-largest city in Africa.[5] While there are some pockets of affluence, Kinshasa is, in the main, a very poor city. Fifty per cent of Kinois eat only once a day and 25 per cent eat only once every two days (Trefon 2004). Rates of malnutrition in the poorest areas are around 18.3 per cent, with infant malnutrition at 40 per cent. In the poorest parts of the city, average incomes range between thirty and forty US dollars a month and, in areas like eastern Kinshasa, up to 40 per cent of the population's primary occupation is subsistence agriculture (Tollens 2004). The poor data available tend to indicate that there were modest improvements in the indicators of poverty in the years 2000–07, but (despite vigorous gross domestic product (GDP) growth) since then, these indicators may have begun to get worse again from 2007 (Tshimanga Mbuyi 2012). The Kinois have been resilient in the face of economic collapse. Malnutrition, bad as it is, is not as bad as one would expect given the low household income levels, which probably reflects the high degree of social solidarity displayed by ordinary Kinois (Trefon 2004a).

Kinshasa is also a boundlessly theatrical and sensual city (Biaya 1996; De Boeck and Plissart 2004), whose inhabitants define their identity around their ability to have a good time and the sophistication with which they pursue this aim. The Kinois compare their city to Europe – *Kinshasa poto muindo* (Kinshasa, black Europe) – and contrast themselves with the *villageois* or *mbokatier* (country bumpkins from the interior). Along with Brazzaville, the city is the birthplace of the *Rumba Congolaise*, Africa's greatest music.

Theoretical Bearings, Thinking about Popular Music

In my opening statement I described the economic decline and violent social change that characterized the later years of the post-independence state in Congo-Zaire. It is the argument of this book that popular music was important in this transformation. The question of why it was so important will be dealt with in due course, but first we must clear the way by defining the object of study.

Congolese popular music comes from Kinshasa, a big city, and, like popular music elsewhere, relies on sophisticated technologies of reproduction and dissemination. It also serves a mass or popular audience. In this sense it can justifiably be called popular (Fabian 1997). Yet, as Barber (1997a) notes for Africa more generally, there is much about this audience that is likely to be unfamiliar to the outsider. Such audiences have rarely, if ever, been a 'public' in a Habermasian sense – a body whose members are addressed as formally equivalent, devoid of distinctions with regard to status or personal qualities (Habermas 1992). The notion of a popular audience also implies the notion of 'popular culture', and here again we should not assume too much familiarity. Barber (1987, 1997b) makes another insightful contribution when she notes (contra Fabian 1997) that African popular culture should not be opposed to 'elite culture'. This is because in African contexts, social distinction is most often structured around differential access to a common field of ritual, expression and performance, rather than around the differences in taste between social groups. Sometimes this common 'field' is highly contested (Comaroff and Comaroff 1993), but as Mbembe (1992) describes, apparently savage and obscene satire can indicate processes of accommodation or at least mutual nullification between rulers and 'target populations'. Furthermore, as Meintjes (2003) shows in her study of *Mbaqanga* musicians in Johannesburg studios, the attitudes of popular cultural producers to the technologies they use may be starkly unfamiliar.

Linked to this problematic sense of 'the popular' is the idea that modern mediated cultural forms rely on mass consumption as their primary source of finance – in the case of music, the assumption being that this is either directly via purchase of discs and tickets or indirectly via advertising aimed at mass consumers. Again, Africanist anthropology tells a different story. Waterman's pioneering analysis of *Jùjú* music (1990) showed that modern forms of popular music in Nigeria were heavily reliant on patronage and that this was not some throwback to a premodern age, but a set of economic practices very much rooted in the exigencies and inequalities of contemporary

Nigerian life. One could also make parallels with Larkin's (2008) take on the Nigerian film industry or with the approach to radio taken by Fardon and Furniss (2000), where it is made clear that 'liberalized' broadcasting in Africa is very often an endeavour involving extensive clientelistic ties.

Alongside the different structure of the audience/producer relationship in large parts of Africa, there also appears to be a different relationship to the political. It is the case in much of Africa that popular musicians are clearly linked to, or even part of, particular political and economic factions in a way that would be unfamiliar to Western audiences (for example, Ewens 1994; McNeill 2012). Because of this, as Lara Allen (2004) notes in her review of the capacious literature, 'popular music in Africa has become a major site for thinking through politics'.

I cannot do justice to this literature here, but would point to two broad tendencies within its abundance that I draw upon in this book. One is to look at the links between African music and politics using frameworks such as 'identity', 'resistance' or 'hegemony' (for example, Turino 2000; Meintjies 2003; Nyamnjoh and Fokwang 2005). The strength of these works is that they show how popular music relates to broader political frameworks. At the other end of the spectrum are studies concerned with music and dance in Africa, which draw more on literature concerned with 'the body' – with movement, the senses and the emotions. This work has shed light on the subjectivities that have shaped urban life in contemporary Africa (for example, Stoller 1984, 1995; Warnier 2004, 2007; Mbembe 2006; Engelke 2007). I draw on both these tendencies, making use of my personal take on Marxism to integrate such approaches into a broader sense of music as an ideological element within wider political and economic forces. Marx seems to be slightly less *persona non grata* now than when I first started thinking about this book, before the 2007–08 financial crisis, but many readers will still dismiss Marxist arguments *a priori*. Others will tend to associate Marxist theories of culture and music with the kind of arguments made by Adorno and the Frankfurt School, arguments that in fact I reject almost completely. So I think it may be helpful lay out what I do mean.

Marxism

I am not interested in defending Marx the individual writing in the middle of the nineteenth century. By Marxism I mean rather an intellectual tradition, one that connects what men produce and how they think; where thought and production are seen as part of a complex whole. This interrelation is also a process of conflict, as the interests of classes – groups of people with different 'relationships to the means of production' (roughly speaking, different positions in a nexus of ownership relations) – rub up against each other. This is too vague for many true believers, while for others it will be labelled 'economic determinism'. In my discipline – anthropology – numerous objections have come from those who stress forms of cultural relativism and emphasize consumption over production. Such complex arguments cannot be dealt with in detail here, but I would make two points.

First, understanding any group of people, *especially* in terms of meaning and feeling, always involves thinking clearly about their means of subsistence – consider the importance of bread in Christianity or of cows in Hinduism. There is not, as some anthropologists once argued (for example, Harris 1974), a simple relationship between calories and culture, but absence and abundance, hunger and satiation are everywhere phenomenological data of the highest importance. While this may be an obvious point, it is one that well-fed people forget surprisingly often.

This brings me to my second, more controversial point, which is that differences in how life is produced do offer a kind of 'way in' to the meaning of big epochal differences – a starting point for thinking about, say, the differences in societal patterns between Europe in the twentieth and fourteenth centuries or between metropolitan and rural China. In particular, a new kind of marriage between money capital and production comes into existence in Western Europe between the sixteenth and eighteenth centuries (Brenner 1977; Kalb 2013) – this is the capitalist mode of production. Capitalism is a new kind of social imperative, where the market is not just used, but becomes embedded in essential provisioning and where a retreat into self-provisioning, even in times of difficulty, quickly becomes impossible.

This is significant because I believe that for much of the 1980s, 1990s and 2000s, capitalism was *not* dominant in Kinshasa. The way that people behaved and the forms of cultural production that took place cannot be understood without understanding this *epochal* shift, from the kind of rentier capitalism that characterized Congo/Zaire of the 1960s and 1970s to something much less familiar.

Under such conditions of epochal change, prevailing attitudes to all sorts of apparently unrelated things – the conception of the person, the forms of class division, the importance of adornment, the kinds of

ritual thought necessary, how wealth is stored – all change in fundamental ways. Some of these changed attitudes in Congo/Zaire seem,
by the 1990s, to contain many parallels with precolonial social dynamics and conceptions of the world. This makes for a strong temptation to explain unfamiliar practices via recourse to a notion of ancient
and persistent cultural difference.

Certainly there are continuities with the precolonial world, but
looked at closely, we can also see a series of irreparable breaks with
that past. Some of the most unfamiliar forms of social behaviour described in this book were recent phenomena. To take just one example,
artisanal Congolese diamond miners in the 1990s re-created logics of
sharing, dispersal and success that drew on precolonial worldviews.
But, as De Boeck (1998) makes clear, this was not because they nur-
tured some ancient and undying cultural flame from their ancestors.
Rather, it was because in the situation of violence, financial collapse
and fragmented sovereignty in which they found themselves, some
of the imperatives of an earlier epoch *made more sense* than the capitalist ones – banking, wage labour, etc. – that they had grown up with.
Thinking in epochal terms allows us to avoid a slide into notions of
implacable cultural difference or cultural primordialism.

Arguing against the notion of a qualitative epochal difference
between capitalist and noncapitalist modes of production, quite a
few anthropologists have pointed out that money, markets and instrumental behaviour are often ancient (e.g. Bloch and Parry 1989;
Graeber 2011). But this is a refutation of an argument I am not making
and it has little force here. The 'cash nexus' does not control everything and it is probably true that 'the market' still 'floats' on a sea of
solidarity (Graeber 2011), but this does not cancel out the fact that,
under capitalism, without the 'boat' of the market, the people drown.

This kind of Marxism, which links epochal differences to the
'mode of production', is often said to represent a 'bad' Marx – evolu-
tionist, mechanist, positivist and functionalist. This is contrasted unfavourably with the Marx supposedly exemplified by works like *The
Eighteenth Brumaire of Louis Bonaparte* (Marx 1852/1970), which concentrates on contingency and consciousness. Inasmuch as Marxism
retains any acceptability within the academy today, it is generally
this second Marx that is endorsed. But I believe this is a false division
where the frequent, highly misleading appeals to Marxian textual authority made on all sides illustrate the rabbinical nature of the debate:
if the dead guy with the beard said it, it must be right. And the tone of
such arguments has set up a series of pointless and overly rancorous
oppositions. This way of thinking has caused us to utterly abandon

some very interesting thinkers and attribute a monopoly of wisdom to others. Louis Althusser and Gerry Cohen, E.P. Thompson and Ellen Meiksins-Wood all have moments of absurdity, yet all of them have something interesting and important to teach us.

But I cannot simply sit on the fence in this manner. In particular, many have argued that social class is a historically specific phenomenon that is of little use in understanding anything outside Europe or before the eighteenth century. This book is opposed to such a view – I think that social class is vital to understanding the dynamics of society in Kinshasa. In this I draw on the accounts of social class in precolonial Central Africa produced by the anthropologists Pierre-Philippe Rey and Georges Dupré, who argued that in the more stratified parts of precolonial West-Central Africa, above all on the lower Congo, a class of 'elders' was dominant (Rey 1971; Dupré and Rey 1980). This dominance was based in their rights over the labour of others – slaves of both sexes, most women and male 'cadets' – dependants who were held in various states of social immaturity. These elders appeared to have no very strong control of the means of production – land was plentiful and the chief factor of production was the labour of the young. They nevertheless managed to enforce their dominance via their control over 'social reproduction'. This was effected through exchanges in prestige goods. Such exchanges determined the destinies of slaves, women and cadets, and were pivotal in allocating labour between corporate groups. The prestige goods were obtained from European merchants at the coast in return for various commodities – including slaves, ivory and rubber – through chains of exchange monopolized by elders. Thus, via 'articulating' between the 'capitalist mode of production' and their own 'lineage mode', the elders were also able to control the surpluses others produced, extracting tribute or labour from subaltern groups by manipulating an ideology of descent and holding out the promise of social advancement to a select few.

Such works became the subject of a furious polemic (see Trapido 2016 for a detailed discussion), but I would urge the reader to take time and to make up her own mind – these works have been insulted much more often than they have been read. Nor were Dupré and Rey responsible for what others did with their ideas during their brief moment of popularity. Whatever E.P. Thompson (1978) may have said about 'Althusser's progeny', these scholars produced very empirically detailed and historically informed monographs that have been sympathetically received by other regional specialists (for example, Guyer 1993; MacGaffey 2000).

This is not to say that I have uncritically adopted their theoretical matrix. As I argue in more detail below, Dupré and Rey probably overestimated the stability of precolonial forms of social stratification and overstressed the idea of 'the lineage'. This was at the expense of other, much wilder, more unstable exchanges, which were tied to a network of funerary, jural and therapeutic ritual (see the section entitled 'Potlatch' below). And, whatever its previous status, in the contemporary context the lineage is no longer the locus of significant social power. But with the collapse of the centralized state controlled by post-independence ruling classes, a new class – what I term a 'gatekeeper class' – was able to maintain some grip on production via its (very partial) control of certain quite precise forms of exchange.

Ideology and Aesthetics

The origins of the kind of theory I sketched earlier, which stresses the role of production in the creation of value, can be traced back to Adam Smith. Smith held that certain kinds of labour – mining, shipbuilding, carpentry and farming – created a need for more labour, while other kinds of labour – 'men of letters of all kinds; players, buffoons, musicians' – 'perished in the instant of its production' (Smith in Buchan 2007: 106). Buchan points out that Smith, a highly cultivated man, did not regard such forms of labour as useless, but he had little way of accounting for them within his system of ideas. Marx, whose philosophy was heavily indebted to Smith, also held ideas of productive and unproductive labour, but this need not detain us here. More relevant are Marx's ideas of ideology and social reproduction. Men produce 'stuff', but they also produce ideas, practices and ways of feeling. These ideas, practices and ways of feeling combine in systematic ways – known as ideology – to reproduce, or sometimes to change, the existing social arrangements.

A great deal of ideology is simply performed as part of everyday actions – in how we dress, walk about or organize our living spaces, we reproduce a set of understandings of the world (Bourdieu 1977). But I believe that social arrangements cannot rely on such everyday ideology alone. These kinds of everyday performances rely on more specialized and spectacular forms of production. And it is here where there is something implied by Smith's account that is missing, at least in the later writings of Marx'. Ideological productions are a form of *labour* and reproducing the organization of production involves ideological *work*. And it is here that, perhaps, Marx's earlier writings about ideology (Marx and Engels 1846/1998) (where the ruling class produce and reproduce ideology just as they produce other goods) and his later writings on value do not entirely join up. The later Marx argued that under a set of productive relationships, it is possible to calculate the 'socially necessary labour time' it will take to produce a certain good or service. Yet while such socially necessary labour time can be attributed to the building of a ship or growing cassava, does it apply to what we might term 'ideological labour'?

There is plenty of quantifiable labour time involved in training a photographer or a Congolese guitarist, and the production of aesthetic 'goods' clearly requires as much work as anything else. Nevertheless, it is surely the case that two equally well-trained individuals given equal time at a guitar or behind a lens will not produce works of equal (or even similar) value. Marx (1867/1961: 44) suggests a difference between 'simple average labour' and 'skilled labour', but the difference is purely quantitative – skilled labour is just 'simple labour multiplied'. Yet the idea that, say, twenty or even five hundred moderately good photographers produce one Cartier-Bresson, or that one hundred good guitarists are half a Franco Luambo is patently absurd, and even with less brilliant cultural producers, notions of equivalence are problematic in the extreme. It is obvious that the same kinds of thought experiment apply to all artists, and in this book I work with the assumption that it is also true of a much wider group of cultural producers – from newspapermen to sports stars and, of course, musicians.

The formulation that Marx offers in *Capital* relies on a division between use value and exchange value, a divide that he maps onto the divide between precapitalist and capitalist modes of production. Broadly speaking, we can say that use value represents the particular, the qualitative and the sensuous (see Adorno 2002; Swain 2012). Exchange value meanwhile represents the abstract, the quantifiable and the instrumental – value as a 'means to an end'. There are many reasons to be wary of this kind of juxtaposition (for example, Parry 1986 Bloch and Parry 1989), but at this stage I want to draw attention to just one of these, namely the implausibility of Marx's views on exchange value when applied to ideological labour.

The chief ideological effect charted in *Capital* is fetishism. According to Marx, fetishism is created not by conscious efforts by the powerful, but by the abstract nature of productive relations under capitalism – it is this distancing that makes the worker see value as something outside of himself. Writers like Adorno (2002) or Lukacs (1923/1967), who tried to apply Marx's views on fetishism to the sphere of culture, argued that modern consumers are unfeeling drones, who fake sensuous pleasure in culture, while in reality getting some sort of disembodied, distracted and utterly instrumental satisfaction from a fetish of the price that cultural commodities cost.[6] Establishing whether people do or do not really experience emotion is always problematic, and even the mildest empirical strictures are liable to be labelled positivism in this context. But there *is* a wealth of literature showing that distracted and highly instrumental forms of reception were/are common in a variety of early modern and non-Western sources, and, if anything, it is the fixed and disinterested contemplation of Adorno's 'structural listeners' that is a product of industrial modernity (see Freedberg 1989; Muir 1997; Pinney 2001). Certainly, music-saturated ritual was invariably a means to therapeutic or political ends in the Central African tradition (MacGaffey 2000).

I argue that ideological labour defies Marx's division of value in that it is always about the particular and the sensuous, but it is also always instrumental. Making us all treat Nike trainers or shares in Lloyds Bank as valuable independent of the social labour that produced them is not primarily a byproduct of long-distance social relations, but rather the result of energetic and costly ideological work. Some of this work is known as advertising, the news, architecture,[7] etc. Such sensuous labour is necessary to sustaining any and all forms of power in every conceivable set of productive relations. If such particular and qualitative forms of labour underwrite all social arrangements, then another of Marx's projects in *Capital* – the possibility of assigning values to the individual products of labour in terms of their socially necessary labour time – seems remote, even in principle. This is not at all to abandon Marx's basic insight about a necessary link between material production, value and ideology. In any society, those who produce ideological labour will need to obtain food and clothing and a hundred other things, things whose value is connected to the productivity of labour in quite a straightforward way.

What this means is that, more often than not, control over the material circumstances of the ideological *labourer* allows the ruling classes to dominate ideological production, just as they dominate other forms of production. This is not to rule out the role of social distance posited by Marx in *Capital* – it is just to give causal primacy to a rather simpler and more intuitive principle: that he who pays the piper calls the tune. This brings us back to the dialectic – wider relations of production will enable the wealthy to commission ideological productions, which will, all things being equal, play an important role in reproducing the relations of production.

One last point needs to be made about my take on aesthetics. By characterising music as a form of ideological labour, we have argued that art is necessarily caught up in wider politics and history. Many critics will go further still and assess the aesthetic merit of a work of art according to its perceived political character. This is surely a mistake. Scholars who follow this line of thought are left with one of two options. Either they must convince themselves about the politics of the artists they like, arguing that Balzac or Bach, say, were somehow 'progressive', disposing ingeniously of strong evidence to the contrary. Adorno (2002) and Lukacs (1937/1981) present examples of this kind of judgement. Or, like Berger (1975) or Carey (1992), they must bite the bullet and consign vast swathes of cultural patrimony to the fire, an act that surely denies the evidence provided by our senses about the real impact that such works have. Instead of tying ourselves in knots in this manner, why not just admit that all sorts of brilliant art was intended to espouse views that we do not like and that its artistic value has something to do with the emotions it inspires, and not with the political views that those emotions are meant to serve? This is a somewhat disturbing view – one that suggests that there is no necessary relationship between the beautiful and the good – but who arrives at being an adult without learning this? I love Congolese music and believe it to be a great art form, but I do not fool myself that this means it is wholesome.

The Political Economy of Collapse and the Role of Music

The resources that supported the post-independence ruling class in the DRC – above all the industrial exploitation of copper, cobalt and diamonds – all required important 'on-shore' investments in wider industrial infrastructure and, in the context of wider turmoil, these industrial complexes eventually collapsed. The musicians' business model folded with them, since consumer demand and industrial reproduction, on which musicians had relied, also atrophied. As the structures of the bureaucratic state withered, so too did the infrastructure of royalty collection. For most of the period under discussion, the DRC's ruling class had to forgo rents from industrial enclaves (see, for example, Ansoms and Marysse 2011). This makes it a case apart, even within the region. Thus, while much of post-independence Africa, at least until very recently, has been characterized by limited and unsatisfactory forms of development, from the mid 1970s onwards, the DRC became uncoupled from the dynamics of capitalism in a much more fundamental way. For much of the period under discussion, there was no tension between maintaining coercive control of the 'gates' through which production from industrial enclaves passed and encouraging broader productivity because productivity was not an option.

In this context, wage labour has essentially disappeared. Salaries are largely fictions, covering a system of rights in people that much more resembles premodern social arrangements. Consumer demand is essentially nonexistent, there is no banking system, basic infrastructure such as roads between the major cities does not exist, and basic functions of the modern state such as the census have not been carried out for three decades and, indeed, are resisted by local politicians. The story of this book is, in part, about the decline of this 'industrial enclave' type of state into a different and even less productive social formation, where the elaborate long-distance, large-scale handouts of what is often called the 'neo-patrimonial' state were replaced by a much more emaciated patronage economy based on simple personal handouts.

Music led the way, as musical troupes abandoned capitalist strategies and began to cluster around various well-connected 'gatekeepers'. As the industrial enclaves collapsed, much of the rent taken by political elites was thus, as in the early colonial and precolonial past, dependent on exactions from artisanal miners and the peasantry. In place of the pyramid-like enclave state, a collection of larger and smaller social units came to intersect with one another, 'distributed in a chain of parcellized sovereignties throughout the social formation' (Anderson 1974b: 19). In this situation, small, quasi-familial social cells – the diamond-mining crew, the gang, the prayer group, the rent-seeking cell within the decimated bureaucracy or the musical *orchestre* – become the primary economic unit.

Under this set of arrangements, the ruling class's dominance was not, as it had been a generation earlier (and as is generally the case under capitalism), tied to increases in productive power. At the same time, links to the capitalist outside world – above all to Western Europe – remained vital to reproducing social dominance. Nowhere was this more apparent than in the world of music, where travel to Paris became the *sine qua non* of popular success. In this context a class of gatekeepers, with some resemblance to precolonial 'elders' – then as now a kind of class relationship conceptualized in terms of relative seniority – extract surpluses from relatively small social units (Meillasoux 1960), linking with other units in chains of exchange that reach beyond Central Africa. As in the past, power is strongly tied to the ability of this class to connect to an outside world where economic relations are managed in a different way (Dupré and Rey 1980). Gatekeepers achieve this power via a series of rights and obligations in subordinates that do not correspond well with ideas of 'free labour' or the wage contract – as we shall see in the appropriations that the *président d'orchestre* makes on his musicians. As capitalism ceased to be dominant, social forms emerged with strong resonances with precolonial political-economic dynamics.

Potlatch: The Trade Interface between Capitalist and Non-capitalist

Under capitalism, accumulation is stored as money in the market via the banking system. These 'systems of credit and debit which underlie capitalism' (Guyer 1995: 9) have their equivalents in non-capitalist modes of production – but here the primary way in which wealth is conceptualized and stored is in *people* – via notions of rank, via rights in other people and via various kinds of aesthetic sensibility that value the crowds that honour or the adornments that enhance powerful persons. Forms of money are present – indeed, they are often vital – but they are better seen as an element of, or adjunct to, the value of the person. Marx says that, in the capitalist mode of production, capital appears to be 'money that begets money' (1867/1961: 155); in many non-capitalist modes of production, the equivalent of capital might be persons who appear to beget people, drawing them into their social presence on a temporary or more permanent basis.

By the eighteenth century, African social formations were strongly involved with global markets, but they had not become capitalist. Rather, they appear to have become locked into a different dynamic, reinforced by European merchants, where individual prosperity – conceived of as rights in people and theatrical dispersals of wealth over retinue – became dependent on aggregate impoverishment – via exporting, or pushing beyond breaking point, the means of production – be they human, as in the case of the slave trade, or ecological, as in the case of the rubber and ivory trades that were hugely important in the nineteenth century. This exploitation ultimately allowed for a kind of 'extended primitive accumulation' in Europe and America, with pillage in Central Africa allowing colonists to control large areas of territory in the Americas and to provide infusions of capital to Europe during the frequent reversals of the early Industrial Revolution (Blackburn 1997).

In Africa something different happened. As the material base on which power relied became undermined, a paradox emerged. The more retinues came to see that power was weak, the more those who aspired to authority were required to make expensive theatrical gestures stating that it was not so. These gestures served to state that rulers and aspirant rulers were still in control and still connected to the (often sinister) metaphysical sources of abundance. In Central Africa music was particularly crucial to this – music is strongly associated with the dead and praise singing, and trance states acquired via dancing were very strongly implicated in making associations between authority and the legitimating dead (Laman 1953–68; MacGaffey 2000). A ritual nexus with funerals at the centre became the sight of massive expenditure, with gunpowder, huge music ensembles, libations of palm wine and mountains of imported goods becoming a *passage obligé* for aspirant rulers. In sum, the trade interface gave impetus to a particular kind of theatre. In this theatre earlier ideas – which had framed wealth and authority in terms of the accumulation of prestige and of followers – then became yoked to ever more extreme forms of ritual escalation.

In his famous account of exchange, Marcel Mauss used a type ritual common to the Indians of the northwest coast of America, known in some places as the 'potlatch', to represent what he believed to be an entire category of archaic exchange. Many people, including many anthropologists, have come to believe that the term 'potlatch' relates to the destruction of property or 'fighting with property'. But both Mauss and ethnographic sources make it very clear that destruction was just one (rather unusual) possibility and, in a Central African context, the word has been applied, with great insight, to forms of ceremonial distribution found in the region (De Boeck 1998; De Heusch 2002). Mauss, like most of his contemporaries, saw this in evolutionary terms. To study the potlatch was to take a glimpse into our own deep past, the first stirrings of the impulse that would lead eventually to the modern contract (Parry 1986). But more recent works imply that the northwest American potlatch, at least in the form described by Western travellers and anthropologists, cannot be looked at in isolation from the dynamics of European expansion (Wolf 1997: 191–4).

While the central role accorded to concepts of prestige and 'wealth in people' pre-dated contact with Europeans, it seems likely that the fervid pitch and theatrical intensity of potlatching was driven by the dynamics of the trade interface between noncapitalist and capitalist modes of production. As in Africa, this dynamic included an increase in disease and also the inherent instability of meeting the insatiable demand from harvesting wild products (see Ringel 1979; Donald 1997: 232, 280; Wolf 1997; Roth 2002). As in the African case, many of the items of wealth distributed or destroyed during the potlatch – blankets, strips of copper taken from the side of ships and so on – were European trade goods, obtained in return for furs (Donald 1997: 32). As in the classic accounts of Mauss or Veblen, I use the term 'potlatch' to refer to a wider category of wild exchange. Unlike in those accounts, the term does not for me connote an archaic remnant, but rather a particular form of modernity – that is to say, the potlatch was the product of the increased connectedness and turbulence that human societies have undergone since the sixteenth century.

Foucault and Weber in Africa

In recent times the subjectivity of the African 'gatekeeper' figures discussed above has been analysed in a way that could be described as Weberian (e.g. Chabal and Daloz 1999; Warnier 2007) or Foucauldian (Mbembe 1992; Bayart 1993; Bayart and Warnier 2004). Such writing links the dynamics of dispersal to the subjectivity of individual success – shining, eating, the 'politics of the belly', the hilarity and obscenity of the *commandement* and so on. A link is also made between the successful individual and the 'occult' in a modern setting. As in the past, diurnal 'eating' – securing and distributing resources – are imaginatively linked to the nocturnal 'eating' of witchcraft – often conceived in Central Africa as a form of mystical cannibalism, where power is accumulated by absorbing the life force of others (see, for example, Rowlands and Warnier 1988; Geschiere 1997). All this concentration on the person of the *patrimoine* leads Fabian (1990) – and also Benedict Anderson (1990) in a non-African context – to argue that under 'traditional authority', power is seen as a substance, held in large quantities within the person of the powerful. Coming from a different theoretical tradition, works by Jane Guyer and Karin Barber have drawn on the anthropological canon, and in particular Kopytoff's influential discussion of how things and people pass through various value registers, attaining, at the top end, a total 'singularity'. All of these works, which draw out the subjectivity of power in the region, are extremely relevant to an analysis of *présidents d'orchestres* and of music patrons, who display many of these attributes. Guyer's work, which pays particular attention to how valuations of people and things interact, has been particularly important to this study.

But while all the above authors are aware that there is a dark side to all this 'shining', the subjectivity of success is not, I believe, interrogated sufficiently. Many of the works listed above adopt a cynical tone about power, but they lack a framework for relating the conditions of material life to ideological productions. Because of this, all of them reproduce many elements of the local dominant class's own self-representation. The first consequence of this is that the *necessary* relations between the 'shining' of some and the alienation of others are not brought out.

All these works take extravagance and largesse at face value as the essential facts about African economic relations. According to this kind of argument, the African big man embodies a kind of anti-Protestant ethic, where the particular strength of imperatives to dissipate surpluses – as largesse given to extended retinues – explains the failure of accumulation on the continent. This sounds convincing, but in fact it cannot be true. As we will discuss in Chapter 8, the evidence shows that capital flight as a percentage of GDP is higher in Africa than in other parts of the world, and this is part of a deeper historical trajectory where individual success depends on exporting the means of production. Capital flight is crucial because it fatally undermines the story about institutions particularly geared to patrimonial dispersal – money stashed in the British Virgin Islands has, by definition, resisted the clamour of large social networks for redistribution, and African leaders would appear more, not less, effective at resisting these demands than their equivalents in other parts of the world. The relevance of largesse then is not primarily about its real economic effects, but rather its ideological ramifications. The theatre of prestations, where music is a crucial element, is just that – theatre.

Theatre and Alienation

This notion of social success as a dynamic art form and of various retinues as a necessary audience invites the use of theatre as a useful explanatory metaphor, and I use the terms 'theatre' and 'theatrical' throughout this book. The extravagant investment in theatrical dispersal – in musicians, forms of dress and spectacle – is important precisely *because* in reality patronage networks are really emaciated. This is about creating a fetish around the person of the patron, promoting the illusion that the patron is generative – creating the value that he distributes – and hiding the fact that the wealth he distributes over a retinue is but a fraction of the wealth he appropriates; the majority of his wealth being exported in one form or another, in line with the potlatch dynamic we noted above. This takes us into the realm of what Marx called alienation.

For Marx, alienation involved the people coming to see the value of goods as something external to themselves. In other words, part of denying access to value is a denial of the idea that ordinary people were involved in creating value. As Patterson (1982) shows us, in unequal societies, it is not just goods that are divided unequally, but also honour. In this context I want to suggest that honour is generally related to the perceived capacity to produce value – to be dishonoured is to be considered worthless, while 'honour' is strongly linked to the notion of the person as generative of value.

Thus, notions of honour and 'generation' allow the appropriation of goods and the labour that produced them, but they are also themselves the first, and probably the greatest, kind of alienation – an alienation of the sense that one is capable of producing value; a theft not simply of labour, but of *amour propre*. The psychological stresses of such forms of alienation are, I believe, quite staggering – and their effects, above all on young men, are one of the great social forces in history. This is especially relevant to our investigation of the Congolese *mikiliste*, who spend extraordinary sums on clothes and music patronage to try and overcome their status as 'empty men' (see Chapter 6).

It is this matrix of interests that I shall examine in detail through popular music and the forms of patronage and performance linked to it. Apart from being beautiful and fascinating, popular music is a good place to study this for several other reasons. From the way in which the *orchestre* is organized, we can gain an understanding of the various systems of rights in people and forms of alienation that typify the area under consideration. In the emotions inspired by music and dress, we begin to recognize the subjectivities that underpin local forms of accumulation.

In the copyright system we encounter the hall of mirrors that surrounds economic activity in the post-independence state. In the criminal economy of migrants to Europe, an economy closely connected with popular music, we come across young urbanites striving to overcome their status as 'worthless persons'. In understanding music as a form of ideological labour, we see how the gatekeeper 'transforms force into right and obedience into duty' (Rousseau 1762/2006:

9) by appropriating the extraordinary labours of cultural producers and associating them with his person.

Notes

1. Called the Belgian Congo until independence in 1960, the state was known as the Democratic Republic of Congo between 1965 and 1971. It was then renamed Zaire by Mobutu. When Mobutu was overthrown in 1997 it was re-renamed the Democratic Republic of Congo.
2. Kinois Lingala – which abounds in neologisms, mixes vocabulary from French and other languages freely, has a relatively simple grammar and is only moderately tonal – is often said by scholars and by the Kinois themselves to be a bastard form, compared unfavourably to the real 'Lingala ya Makanza', associated with 'bangala' speakers further up the river. This is, it appears, a misconception. The original Lingala was a kind of pigeon Bobangi, Bobangi being a riverine language originating on the Ubangi tributary, with some status as a lingua franca before the arrival of the Belgians. Belgian missionaries, who wrongly assumed it was related to the languages of 'the bangala' – itself an imaginary ethnolinguistic amalgam – considered it a debased form and tried to ennoble it with purifying infusions from various Bantu languages of the middle river. This more complex language was then taught in schools above Kinshasa and took some root in the area of the middle river – roughly in the area between Mbandaka and Kisangani. But the Kinshasa form is probably older and closer to the natural creole language that grew from Bobangi. Kinshasa Lingala is the language of music and it is in this form that the language continues to spread in Central Africa.
3. The community is supplemented by approximately 50,000 legal and illegal migrants from Congo-Brazzaville (Bazenguissa-Ganga 2005).
4. I got this impression from individuals who had participated and from the International Organization for Migration report itself, which includes recommendations for 'outreach activities'.
5. After Cairo and Lagos. There has been no census since 1983, but extrapolation from the register of electors conducted in 2006 indicated that the city was nearer ten million than the six to seven million routinely quoted. The city is projected to overtake Cairo around 2015 and Lagos around 2025 as Africa's largest city with a population of sixteen million (see UN-HABITAT 2008).
6. 'People do not dance or listen "from sensuality" and sensuality is certainly not satisfied, but the gestures of sensuality are imitated' (Adorno 2002: 309) or 'The consumer is really worshipping the money he has paid for the ticket … he has literally "made" the success which he reifies … but he has not made it by liking the concert but by buying the ticket.' (ibid.: 297). This is a line that even Adorno cannot keep up, arguing at other points that culture industry music provides debased but real forms of emotional catharsis to the working man (ibid.: 462).
7. Marble atriums for the bank being rather like gold teeth for the drug dealer.

– Chapter 1 –

BARS, MUSIC, GENDER AND POLITICS

&

In Zaïre music and politics work at the same time. Everything is negotiated in the bars. The stars are an integral part of political life…

—Manu Dibango, *Trois Kilos de café*

Like the coffee house in eighteenth-century Britain (Habermas 1992), bars in Kinshasa were a space where an emerging bourgeoisie met up to socialize. It was from this class that the political leaders who would rule after independence sprang, and the world of music and the bar formed a crucial space where contacts were made and power was negotiated. Those who aspired to social or political dominance took to the world of music and the bar to enjoy themselves, but also to establish or perpetuate the relationships of power.

This chapter is based on a somewhat different set of methods from those used in other parts of the book. First and foremost, this chapter draws on written primary and secondary sources about the period in question. But at the core of this chapter are also several conversations that I held with Congolese people who were witness to the world of bars, music and politics in the 1950s and 1960s. General background information about this time was provided by a range of older people from Kinshasa. Most important were the conversations I held with Lumumba's press secretary, Jean Lema, and with Victorine Njoli, a prominent woman from the time. Both of these conversations were not recorded as interviews and were recorded afterwards as field notes. For the later periods dealt with in this chapter – i.e. from the 1970s onwards – I had access to a much wider set of first-hand reminiscences.

Kinshasa: Music, Money and Madness

Early colonial Leopoldville, the town which became Kinshasa, was essentially a camp for male African labour,[1] with the first significant voluntary in-migrations of Congolese only taking place in the late 1920s. Women in this early urban context were hugely outnumbered, with a ratio of 3.6 men to every woman in 1929 (Gondola 1997a: 87). The overwhelming majority of these women were unregistered migrants without legal means of support. Paying bride prices was beyond the reach of most of the city's male labourers, and for most of these women, prostitution, or other transient and remunerative forms of relationship, was the only career option (Gondola 1997a: 75–6). The sex ratio changed sharply over the 1930s as male Africans, thrown out of work by the Depression, were forcibly returned to the countryside. In the face of ever greater desire by male and, especially, female blacks to migrate to the city, the colony 'faced a dilemma: either reinforce the camp-like aspects of the black city … or redesign African settlements. They opted for the latter' (Gondola 1997b: 67).

One of the first signs of this change in policy occurred in 1932 when a law forbidding Africans to drink beer in public at the weekend was revoked (Gondola 1997a: 257). From then onwards, a series of bars for Africans emerged that would play a crucial role in urban life. From the beginning, the bar supplemented, and afterwards replaced, the funeral wake (Martin 1995: 142) as the main space for music in an urban context. The same period saw many more women migrate to the town, though neither Hunt (1991) nor Gondola (1997a, 1997b) makes it clear whether this marked any particular loosening of colonial policy or simply reflected both the desperate rural situation and the fact that women, unlike most men, stood a chance of making some money in the urban setting. In any case it seems clear that the majority of these women still depended on transient forms of remunerative sexual/affective encounter (Gondola 1997b: 90–91),[2] with 'employment' as a 'ménager' (Biaya 1996) for whites being particularly sought-after. There was a great deal of comment by colonials and *évolués* – the nascent African bourgeoisie – about these forms of urban female sexuality. This was set within the context of a wider anxiety about a 'crisis in marriage' that focused on concerns about sterility, 'racial suicide' and polygamy, both 'customary' and 'disguised' (Hunt 1991). The evolving moral panic led to extensive legislation, initially the taxing of polygamous marriage and then, in the 1950s, the banning of multiple wives and the taxing of 'theoretically single women' in urban areas.

Such efforts, which contained generous doses of both hypocrisy and unintended consequence, can be seen as part of a joint project, reaching its vigorous peak in the 1940s and 1950s, by emergent male African elites and the colonial powers to encourage marriage, recast in an urban context. This emergent ideology of marriage condemned, yet was evidently excited by, transient female sexuality (Hunt 1991; Biaya 1996). Defining marriage in opposition to this public sexuality that congregated around bars, the debate contributed to a division of space between the home and the bar. But this should not simply be mapped onto the division of public and private space of the metropole. Then, as now, the home was overwhelmingly a multioccupied *parcelle*, while the bar was/is the site of intimate connections, a '"private" public space' as De Boeck has put it (De Boeck and Plissart 2004: 33).

There certainly is some kind of conceptual opposition between the home and the bar, but it is better captured by the divide between 'lineage' and 'non-lineage' sites used by Joseph Tonda (2005). This is connected to other divides – the bar and its associate, the street, are also the site of Lingala, the language of music and modernity. It is also a language without ethnic connotations (in Kinshasa), which is often disparaged as rude or undignified. Until the mid 1980s, it seems to have been fairly common to insist on the use of French or an ethnic language at home. The division is also related to the kind of 'hearth or whore' choice women confront in many societies. The bar is the site of the *ndumba*, a prostitute or courtesan, outside the lineage-based economy of bride-wealth, and a woman who exists in opposition to the *mwasi ya libala*, or 'woman of marriage'.[3]

The bar was perceived as a quintessentially modern space by the Congolese themselves (Gondola 1997b; Jewsiewicki 2003). It was of the city, it was dominated by an emerging class of wage labourers, and the activities that took place there were outside of the gerontocratic power structures that were still dominant elsewhere. But at the same time, it was also a site which adapted earlier attitudes. Reconfiguring some of the sensibility of the earlier potlatch economy in a modern setting, the bar became the place where music and socioeconomic 'weight' combined. Dispersals of money and beer, the display of new outfits, the initiation of tributary social relations between power brokers and clients all materialized in this space. Tied to this idea of the bar as a site for music and the exchange of prestige goods is a certain kind of atmosphere. Several terms are used locally to designate this set of emotions, but the most common and all-encompassing is *ambiance*. As Biaya (1996) explains, contained within the emotional complex that is *ambiance* are ideas of romantic love and tender passion, but connotations of crazy joy are also present.

The similarity between this notion of *ambiance* and the kind of culturally validated 'madness' found in precolonial ritual is apparent. Indeed, another word to designate this crazy joy is *kiesse*, a word derived from Kikongo languages that, in an earlier time, designated the happiness/madness brought on by spirit possession (MacGaffey 1991: 7). Nevertheless, compared to precolonial forms of dispersal, the sensibility of the bar in this period was clearly restrained. During the colonial period, an 8 pm curfew put an end to festivities in time to regularize the following workday's early start and, during the 1960s and early 1970s, the socializing seems not to have approached the levels of wild dispersal engaged in by the bana kin's precolonial ancestors or, indeed, by their children.[4]

From Curfews to the Folly of Champagne: Colonial and Postcolonial Hierarchies and the New Ruling Classes

The activities undertaken in the bar are embodied in two archetypes, seen as typical of Kinshasa. For females, it is the courtesan – known rudely as the *ndumba* or by a series of more polite alternatives. For males, it is the *ambienceur* – a good-timing friend of musicians, smart dresser, drinker of beer and romancer of women. Being an *ambienceur* requires a certain level of disposable income and in its early incarnations, the *ambienceur* was overwhelmingly a figure associated with the *evolué*. Belgian colonialism drew on many sources, but in their justifications for racial domination, there is a clear French influence. Like the French, and in conscious contrast to the Anglo-Saxons, the Belgians claimed that their colonial system was not based on race, but rather on levels of 'civilisation' (Young 1966). Crucial to this claim was the creation of a category composed of the upper tier of the African commercial and administrative class who were to be granted special privileges – permission to travel, to live in certain areas, to break curfews, to drink wine (prohibited to Africans in the Belgian colony, this became an important marker of status) – by virtue of their progress towards the noble goal of civilization. Known as the 'evolué' or 'advanced ones', the status of *evolué* was acquired via an exam, which included a special investigation of the habits, possessions, lifestyle, domestic arrangements and organization of the domestic interior of the candidate (Young 1965).

The Belgians took the idea of *evolué* from the French, but they combined it with a form of complacent paternalism that was distinctive.[5] Thus, while at independence the percentage of African wage workers was rather high, reaching 35 per cent of the labour force (Merlier 1966: 166; Prunier 2009: 76) – at the time a figure unmatched on the subcontinent outside of South Africa – the adoption of the system was broad, but not deep. Those with secondary education were a privileged few, a handful held university degrees and almost no Africans had been trained for the upper ranks of the civil service (Young 1966). The colony confident that time was on its side, felt in no hurry to change this situation.

Combine this with the refusal of the Catholic Church to participate in the certification system for *evolués*, and the apparent reluctance of the inspectors to actually pass anyone who did apply – Lumumba was failed initially for 'immaturity' – and one sees why there were in fact very few 'real' *evolués*. Nevertheless the idea of the *evolué* does seem to have contributed enormously to the wider African bourgeoisie's sense of itself (Young 1966). We can note the affinity between colonial race theory and some Central African notions of hierarchy

Illustration 1.1: Mobutu (the tall man in the centre) celebrates his birthday just before the coup of 1965. With Jean Lema, Lumumba's former press attaché, next to Mobutu on the left, and assorted musicians including Franco (on the far right) Joseph Kabasele (on the right, with his arm outstretched) and the singer Mujos (next to Mobutu's on the right). Every effort has been made to trace the original copyright holder.

– specifically in the idea that exhaustive attention to dress or material culture was a crucial factor in rank and social process (see also Friedman 2004).

The photograph inserted here (Illustration 1.1) was given to me by Jean Lema, the small man in a bow tie. Next to him in white in the centre is General Mobutu, later *Marechal*. Jean received a secondary education at one of the Belgian Congo's Catholic boarding schools, a fact which, in the pre-independence period, placed him among a small elite of literate Africans. The school also brought him into contact with Joseph Kabasele (second from Mobutu on our right), who went on to become the leader of the *orchestre* African Jazz.

The band, and Kabasele in particular, would become emblems of urbane sophistication for the aspirant Congolese bourgeoisie. Jean Lema is popularly known as *Jamais Kolonga*, which means 'never defeated'. He acquired the name in the 1950s because, while accompanying African Jazz on a tour of the interior, he had asked a white woman, the wife of a missionary, to dance with him. She had agreed and, for this mighty feat, the title was bestowed. Kabasele's band member Tino Baroza even wrote a famous song about Lema using this title. Kabasele was courted by numerous politicians, but he formed a lasting friendship with the future Prime Minister, Patrice Lumumba, who was then working as a sales representative for Polar Beer. Lumumba organized a sponsorship of the *Orchestre* by the brewery, an early example of the beer endorsements that would become a central source of revenue to musicians. As a sales representative for a brewery, Lumumba had a job that took him from bar to bar, putting him in touch with all the important political and intellectual figures of his day, establishing contacts he could later draw upon and firming up his support base in the capital. One such contact was Jean. It was via Kabasele that Lema also became friends with Lumumba, and Jean remembered well the charm that persuaded influential men and, especially, women into supporting the emerging leader. In Jean's account, fun, music and romance were not incidental to this effort – 'Lumumba says to me, "Quick, grab that woman there, let's dance!"'[6]

This closeness between musicians and the entire political class is attested to by Kabasele's performance at the *table ronde* negotiations, which were held in Brussels to debate the terms of Congo's independence from Belgium. The story goes that talks were not progressing well and, sensing this, two delegates who were also brothers, Thomas and Philip Kanza, put in a request that Kabasele bring a troupe of musicians to Belgium to ease the relationships between the various Congolese parties (Mpisi 2003: 128; Brain 2014). Less often reported is the claim, found in Biaya (1996: 351), that Lumumba circulated photographs of himself in the company of white prostitutes in Brussels. Some informants have expressed scepticism about this claim, but there was certainly no effort made to hide the idea of the political leader as a womanizer. As La Fontaine (1970) notes, an association with a 'string of scandalous beauties'[7] could be an important aspect of political charisma. While the details may be unfamiliar, such associations with celebrity are not uncommon in politicians' attempts to construct a political image. But in the Congolese case, there were also more direct political and economic advantages associated with the world of music, 'scandalous beauty' and the bar.

Accessing these informal circuits of power is difficult, especially half a century later. But there are some indications that, even in this period, it was significant. In 1964 Moise Tshombe – the leader of the Katanga government that had sparked crisis at independence with its bid to secede – was appointed Prime Minister of the Kinshasa government. Already mistrusted by many, both at home and abroad, as the instrument of Western interests, one of Tshombe's first acts was to recruit white mercenaries to put down the rebellions in the east, following the same strategy he had used in Katanga.

Tshombe position was bolstered from an unlikely source. He took as his lover Victorine Njoli. A well-known beauty, style icon and member of several of Kinshasa's most famed female associations, she was immortalized in song as 'La Belle Victorine' by the suave singer Frank Lassan (Tsambu-Bulu 2010). Victorine seems to have gone into battle on his behalf, mobilizing other famous women in her network to intercede for him. During one Organisation of African Unity meeting that Tshombe attended as Prime Minister – where relations with the rest of the delegation seem to have been particularly bad – she claimed to have organized a 'women's strike', citing inspiration from Gandhi.[8]

A more detailed illustration of the links between music, *ambiance* and informal power can be seen in the story accompanying the photograph above (Illustration 1.1). The year is 1965, and Lumumba's murder, planned by the same Western forces that brought Mobutu to power, had taken place nearly five years before, his body dissolved in acid by one of the Belgian policemen involved in the mission (De Witte 2001). On either side of Jean and Mobutu are musicians, most notably Francis ('Franco') Luambo (in white on the far right, later officially known as Luambo Makiadi) and Joseph Kabasele (two down on the same side), leaders of the two most important popular *orchestres* in

Congo. The date is close to 14 October, because that was Mobutu's birthday and, as Jean told the story, the occasion for the gathering. So this, then, is probably within a month of Mobutu formally seizing power in November of that year – though he had, of course, been the power behind the throne since the 'Congo Crisis' period. At some point after the flight of Lumumba from the capital, soldiers had come for both Jean and Kabasele as prominent *Lumumbistes*. It was only the intervention of Daniel Kanza[9] (father of Philippe and Thomas Kanza) that had saved them; others rounded up that day were flown to Kasai and shot.[10]

According to Jean, in the 'folie de Champagne' – some of which we can see in the upraised glasses – Mobutu had turned to him and confided that he would shortly be seizing power, and he had asked Jean to come and work for him. Since Mobutu was deeply implicated in the murder of Lumumba, Jean's close friend, he had replied: 'Never will I go with a military government.' Mobutu had said to him: 'You will regret it for the rest of your life.' Rather to my surprise, Jean remarked to me that he had, indeed, regretted it for the rest of his life. This moment had marked a turning point in the life of a one-time *bon vivant*, a life that had henceforth involved rather less *folie à Champagne* than the old man might have wished.[11] Strict principles meant Jean did not manage to capitalize on such informal networks, but others did, and the story gives some indication of how the bar was central to these networks in the repeated crises of the state.

At independence, the civil service wages bill was already very large, and within two years it was several times the national GDP (Verhaegen 1966: 24). The tax base was much narrower and far more reliant on rent from concessions than in other colonies in Africa, while the degree of labour coercion involved in commercial agriculture was unusual even by colonial standards. The independent state also inherited a higher debt burden than other colonies (Gardener 2013). Lumumba's reputation as a dangerous firebrand was based largely on a perception that, for the state to be viable, it would have to get a better deal from the export of raw materials, a trade that was, above all, related to the complex of Belgian and other foreign-owned interests in the copper and cobalt mines in Katanga. In the decades following the Second World War, copper prices were very high and Western countries were very nervous about the idea that newly independent Congo might try and drive a hard bargain.

As the army rebelled and Katanga seceded, at least two parallel plans to assassinate Lumumba were hatched. One, acting on direct instructions from President Eisenhower, was led by the CIA, while another was led by the Belgians. De Witte (2001) has shown that it was Belgian forces that actually killed Lumumba.[12] 'The West' probably did not intend much of the chaos that followed, much less the collapse in productivity that accompanied the post-independence state. But the bad faith displayed by Western countries, epitomized in Lumumba's murder, clearly articulated the externally circumscribed limits of Congo's autonomy.

These limits were essentially that the state would not have the resources to cover its costs. A small political inner core – as much a court as a class – would be kept on board with appropriated assets and spadefuls of cash derived from import monopolies, rents on mineral resources, and loans. This was accompanied by constant reminders of their precariousness – a spell in prison was as much the mark of the inner circle as a Swiss bank account (see Young and Turner 1985; Nzongola-Ntalaja 2002). The instability generated by such a system meant that most cash and assets were transferred immediately to safe (tax) havens abroad (see Boyce and Ndikumana 2011). The wages of government employees would be paid through printing money, a strategy that, in the absence of adequate economic resources to back it up, had predictable inflationary results. The rest – the vast majority – would have to survive as best they could.

In the years 1966–73 the Mobutu regime was fairly deft, curtailing inflation and controlling the wages bill with a managed devaluation, while high copper prices reduced the deficit to virtually nothing. But this was a temporary respite. From 1974 onwards, as copper prices plummeted and the bribes to the inner circle intensified, the settlement again ate into growth itself and inflation returned with a vengeance, immiserating the salaried sector.

If politicians had entertained close, tributary relations with musicians before, now their monopoly of resources meant that few others were in a position to compete for the association. As Jean La Fontaine (1970) notes, in the years following Lumumba's murder, the two largest *orchestres*, African Jazz and OK Jazz, were associated with two of the most powerful politicians of the time. African Jazz was backed by Cyril Adoula, a one-time *Lumumbiste* and Prime Minister for some of the period, while OK Jazz was backed by Justin Bomboko, who later acted as ambassador to the United States. When Moise Tshombe replaced Adoula as Prime Minister in 1964, OK Jazz leader Franco Luambo also became aligned with him, writing the song 'Moise Tshombe – Tshombe Moise' in his honour and, according to some reports, receiving a full set of instruments for OK Jazz from Tshombe for 'services rendered' (Bazakana 2014).

In 1963 many of the most talented musicians quit African Jazz to form their own group, African Fiesta. As we will see later, these musicians appear to have had well-founded financial grudges against Kabasele, the group leader. But just as important was the fact that the founders of African Fiesta, Tabu Ley and Rogier Izeidi in particular (Banzakana 2014), had connections to the Mbinza group, which was a small band of pro-Western Congolese politicians, all of whom were (like Mobutu) from the north and all of whom lived in the affluent suburb of Mbinza. Kabasele also had such connections, of course, but in the aftermath of Lumumba's murder, he refused to draw on them.

Bomboko is a particularly interesting example in that, after Lumumba, he was probably the most prominent symbol of the *ambianceur* – the adept of *ambiance* – in Kinshasa, dressing in black tie and associating with a string of the aforementioned 'scandalous beauties' (see Biaya 1996). He was also a member of the Mbinza group. The group, which had close links to the Army and to the CIA,[13] was a crucial intermediary between Congolese politicians and American policy during much of the early post-independence period. As Mobutu consolidated his grip on power, he came to see these *éminences grises* as something of a threat and slowly dismantled their network. Another member of the group, Nendaka, head of the security police, who was a lifelong friend of the CIA's Kinshasa bureau chief Larry Devlin (Devlin 2007: 98), was also close to the musician Tabu Ley. In Ley's biography it is suggested that Nendaka was dismissed by Mobutu after an altercation concerning whose birthday party Ley was going to play at (Mpisi 2003: 392)![14]

As the young state plunged into a series of crises and a series of unstable governments proved themselves incapable of mastering the situation, the term 'politician' acquired extremely negative connotations, in popular parlance coming to mean something like 'crook'. This hostility was linked in the popular mind to the wider class of *intellectuels,* a term that referred to the group of literate office workers from whom the politicians had emerged (see Young 1965). Mobutu's *coup d' état* in 1965 justified itself, rather successfully in terms of these popular discourses, by presenting his seizure of power as an everyman's response to the fractious squabbling of the *intellectuel* elite (Young 1965, 1966; Young and Turner 1985). In this context, Mobutu's choice to associate himself with OK Jazz was not accidental, for this was the *orchestre* that was supported by the Kinshasa street. Led by Franco Luambo, a fatherless boy who had had only a few years of schooling, the *orchestre* stated the wisdom of the 'bills' – the young urban unemployed, who liked cowboy films and fought with their hands (De Boeck and Plissart 2004: 36–40). The association between Mobutu and OK Jazz would last until the dictator's fall in the 1990s.

The Changing Political-Economic Situation and the Role of Music

While Mobutu succeeded in stabilizing the economy for a time, the political-economic settlement, mentioned above, was inherently unstable. Zaïrianization, initiated in 1973 and continued on and off in various forms over the next two years, brought out these latent contradictions. This was overtly meant as a transfer of assets from foreigners to a political inner circle, an inner circle that Mobutu seems to have envisaged becoming a kind of benevolent Bantu aristocracy (Young and Turner 1985). Many of the *acquerer* ('acquirers') who received these businesses and farms did not have the skills needed to run the enterprises, but many never tried, liquidating them and transferring the assets abroad immediately.[15] Connections mattered more than ever in this handout, and those close to the political class were those who got the goods. The close tributary relationships that some musicians had already cultivated with politicians took on an even greater significance, as those who were part of the informal networks of power around music and bars had ringside seats for the carve-up.

In the initial aftermath of Zaïrianization, members of the elite pursued the good life with greater resources. A friend remembered his diplomat father leaving the house for a night out with the boot of the car filled with money. He also remembered how his father had bought a house for his mistress opposite the main family home in one of the most expensive parts of Kinshasa. The female savings associations, mentioned earlier, were key in the way in which elites took advantage of the new environment. Dominated by sex-symbol female courtesans, these associations were invariably linked to launching new fashions and to popular *orchestres* (Gondola 1997a, 1997b; De Boeck and Plissart 2004: 240). Contact with the glamorous women in these associations was inviting to political leaders for reasons that were both personal and political. For the women also, alongside the aphrodisiac of power, such relations represented a clear route to accumulation. The money being thrown around by elite men was often used by these women to start businesses. Particularly important were various kinds of import-export trades and bars, which now proliferated as regulations were circumvented.

One of the most important female associations concerned was the Moziki 100 Kilos. Its members were well known as supporters of OK Jazz and they held their monthly reunions – where the members' contributions were paid over – at Franco's nightclub the *Un Deux Trois*. The presence of these women and their lovers, who included some of the best-connected men of the regime, reinforced the link between OK Jazz and the Mobutu regime. Several of the women of the Moziki 100 Kilos were pioneers of the trade in wax cloths, which developed in the 1970s. In this trade businesswomen would travel to Lomé in Togo, where the cloths – and other consumer items – could be obtained more cheaply for resale in Kinshasa. Pavillon 8 – a prestigious area near the centre of Kinshasa's Zando or Great Market – was dominated by the women of the Moziki 100 Kilos, who used their stalls to sell the latest and most expensive Dutch and English wax cloths.[16]

As inflation became entrenched in the 1980s, the practice of changing between the Zaïre, the CFA franc (used in neighbouring Brazzaville) and the dollar became another profession strongly associated with these women from the *Moziki*. Such women relied on powerful political connections in the first place for protection – in theory the trade was illegal and unpaid soldiers roamed the streets. But they were also reliant on major sources of hard currency for their business, and it seems this was chiefly gained from the smuggling of primary commodities, a trade dominated by powerful members of the regime (Schoepf and Engundu 1991; De Herdt and Marysse 1996).

Musicians also benefited from Zaïrianization. This took place directly, in that they were allocated ownership of property formerly held by foreign nationals, and indirectly, in that they were sometimes able to take advantage of changing economic structures. Franco, whose fortunes over the 1970s and 1980s I trace below, is a good example of this. Yet Franco's trajectory also illustrates something else. The precipitous economic decline that began in the 1970s was not a process over which elites had any real control, and in some ways it presented a challenge to their dominance.

Congolese musicians are divided into five generations that also map onto the generations of Kinois, who have lived in the city since the 're-urbanization' of the area by Africans in the early twentieth century (see Gondola 1997b; White 2008). The first generation corresponds with the first generation of permanent urban residents in the 1930s and 1940s. It is with the second, *deuxième génération* that the music reaches a stylistic maturity. This generation was also the same age as the political class that took power at independence. From its outset, the music business – studios, record labels, pressing plants – had been in the hands of Europeans (mostly Greeks) who had inserted themselves into the spaces between African and European worlds in the Belgian colony (Stewart 2001; White 2002). At Zaïrianization, all their holdings were transferred to nationals.

The key beneficiaries of this musical redistribution were Franco Luambo, Tabu Ley and Verkys Kiamuangana, all of whom bene-fited from this event to such an extent that they became part of the *Mobutiste* elite themselves. All these figures became central to the production of music in Zaïre of the 1970s. Among them, Franco was clearly the closest to Mobutu. During Zaïrianization, he was given ownership of the main record pressing plant, known from this time as MAZADIS. Within months he had experienced severe difficulties in the running of the plant and had re-engaged Pelerims, its former owners, in a 60–40 per cent ownership deal (Ewens 1994).

The progressive failure of the formal economy and rapid inflation meant that the supply of raw materials was inconsistent and spare parts became ever more expensive. MAZADIS was unable to re-equip and did not convert to tapes even though, by the late 1980s, these had come to dominate the Zaïrian market. Throughout the 1980s the difficulties of MAZADIS, which was the only factory to press discs, surely acted as a break on the entire Zaïrian recording industry (see Tsambu-Bulu 2005). Ewens (1994) reports that Franco, in a manoeu-vre entirely typical of the Zaïrian 'big man', used undercapacity to increase his own power – making sure that his discs and those on his label were pressed first.

In 1980 Franco transferred his record business to Brussels, a move whose immediate motivation was the collapse of Fonior, the Belgian group that had handled the distribution of Zaïrian music in the rest of the world up to that point (Ewens 1994). In addition, however, we can discern an array of other motives for Franco's move that reflect or even anticipate wider trends among the *Mobutiste* inner circle at this period. First, his relocation was part of a general move by the Zaïrian elite and, like the majority of such figures, he moved his family to Brussels. The ubiquity of such a residence change among the elite points to it as a central form of social capital at the period. In Franco's case it also reflected physical insecurity. He had a longstanding feud with Kengo Wa Dondo, one of the Mobutu regime's canniest and most durable operators,[17] and it was long suspected that Franco's absences were not unconnected to Kengo's periods of favour at the *Mobutiste* court. As we have seen, such instability was not uncom-mon in the inner circle. Another attraction for Franco was almost cer-tainly the trade in drugs. It was very widely rumoured that Franco was trafficking marijuana into Belgium – a thing he explicitly denied, both in interviews and in the song 'Kinshasa Mboka Makambo', a title that rages prolix against the accusations of wagging tongues in Kinshasa. Yet I was told by several credible sources who were connected to the matter that these allegations were true. Certainly drug trafficking was not uncommon among musicians of the period.[18]

The role that smuggling played in paths to accumulation was multifaceted. In the 1970s, a youth *orchestre*, Orchestre Sosoliso, was hugely popular both in Kinshasa and next door in the Central African Republic, where President and later Emperor Bokassa was a particular fan. Bokassa is said to have paid Sosoliso in diamonds, which they smuggled back to Zaïre and sold on the thriving black market. Franco got wind of this and used his political connections to have the *orchestre* busted, with their musicians' licence revoked for a year. This caused Sosoliso to break up and Franco took the musicians he wanted.

Verkys Kiamuangana, who was less well-connected politically (to begin with at least), also illustrates aspects of this trajectory. Widely rumoured to have accumulated capital through the smuggling of mercury-based skin-lightening creams, Kiamuangana established Studio Veve in Kinshasa. In the late 1970s and 1980s, it was in his studio and on his record label that many of the biggest *orchestres* of the next (*troisième*) generation recorded. It was in part to escape Kiamuangana's machinations – such as stealing musicians and withholding instruments and recording time from unfavoured groups within his stable – that many of the younger generation began to look for alternatives to recording in Zaïre.

Music, Politics and the Evolving Forms of Patronage

The pillage of *Zaïrianization* was accompanied by the cultural policy of *Authenticité*. As in China, whose Cultural Revolution may have inspired Mobutu, new citizens were to be fashioned in new forms of dress and in new forms of sonic and kinetic mobilization. *Authenticité* is discussed elsewhere (Young and Turner 1985; Sang'Amin 1989; White 2008). For the purposes of this discussion, we need only say that the central idea was to produce a Central African modernity that valued and drew on a (somewhat ersatz) version of the past. Music was at the heart of this. The popular *orchestres* had always drawn on traditional music, known as *folklore*, and they responded to *Authenticité* with enthusiasm, foregrounding and making explicit these indigenous elements, and incorporating traditional instruments into their lineups. At the same time, well-funded *troupes d'animation politique* were created. Drawing more heavily on a neo-traditional repertoire, these would perform at various public events, connected to the compulsory single party, the *Mouvement Populaire de la Révolution* (MPR).

The revival of various praise-singing forms, praising party cadres or, above all, Mobutu himself became a model for the evolving Zaïrian take on the cult of personality (see White 2008).[19] The troupes included many female singers and dancers, and the idea of these as part of the gratifications of high office seems to have been important – almost all sources mentioned to me that female dancers made considerable fortunes by acting as sexual offerings to high party officials (see also the discussion in White 2008). In similar vein, it is during the state ceremonials of this period that the handing out of envelopes containing money to performers and public seems to have taken off. One informant remembered both receiving an envelope and wetting her knickers as her school processed past Mobutu during his visit to the town of Mbandaka in the late 1970s.

The performances of the state troupes also served as a kind of model for more ordinary performances, which were introduced as a daily ritual in all workplaces and schools. Known as 'saluting the flag', this included a compulsory quarter-hour of singing, chanting and dancing in praise of the regime every morning, with stern penalties for those deemed not to be participating sufficiently. Such forms of *animation* became generalized and fused with other forms of music making – including funerary ritual, popular petitioning of local big men and the performances of popular *orchestres* (Sang'Amin 1989; Vangu-Ngimbi 1997; White 2008: 73–77). As the industrial enclaves that had financed the state began to decline, forms of patronage dependent on modern infrastructure also fell away, and authority came to be more diffuse and reliant on open clientelism. These evolving forms of performance, which generally clustered around a 'big man' as a source of largesse, provided a medium for this political-economic transition.

This increasing tendency towards highly personalized patronage performance fed into another, pre-existing trend embodied by the popular *orchestres*. Since the earliest times, Congolese popular music has included songs about real, named individuals. Such namings – *dédicaces* as they are known – had always involved some form of exchange between the named person and the musician, though it was not the precise transaction it later became. Tabu Ley, one of the most gifted composers, provides some examples of how these early exchanges worked. His song 'Silikani', now a classic, was dedicated to the eponymous Monsieur Silikani from the Lemba district of Kinshasa. The two were really friends, but Silikani was also the head of what was then the city's largest printing press, which Ley used extensively. According to Silikani's son, Papy Silikani, this was at well below market rates. A similar story is told of a furniture business in the Ngaba district, a business where Ley had obtained furniture on credit. Ley was so slow to pay his bill that the owner opened legal proceedings. Ley then wrote a song about the man and the matter was dropped. This kind of exchange, grounded in a wider repertoire of gifts and relationships, seems to have gradually fused with other forms of patronage that emerged towards the end of the 1970s.

Conclusion

This chapter has illustrated that a nexus centred around music and the bar was politically central in the post-independence period. While the space of the bar was valued as a site of romance and crazy joy, this was not held separate from political and economic considerations, for the bar was a space that allowed the rich to negotiate and renegotiate both the political connections and the aesthetics of social dominance in a period of violent social change. For musicians themselves, it offered opportunities to become wealthy, though these were open only to a limited group and, for most, the locus of opportunity narrowed considerably as the years wore on. One of the reasons why the bar was so central was that it was a site for a particular kind of exchange with clear links to the nexus of the precolonial potlatch explored in the Introduction. In the 1980s and 1990s, such exchanges became even more extreme as economic growth fell away and precolonial dynamics around gatekeeping and dispersal came to the fore. We follow the unfolding process in Chapter 2.

Notes

1. The Pool Malebo – the site of modern Kinshasa and Brazzaville – had been an important and populous commercial centre, especially in the seventeenth, eighteenth and nineteenth centuries, though estimates vary quite widely. See Gondola (1997a: 33) for a summary of the debate.

2. The point, which I pursue below, is that there was a field of relationships that elude descriptions such as mistress, courtesan, prostitute, etc. Other authors get around this via seemingly robust terms such as transactional sex, but this is wrong for two reasons: first, because, except in some extreme cases, it is not just sex that is being transacted; and, second, because all relationships, including the most successful and loving marriages, are highly 'transactional'. See Cole (2009).

3. This hearth/whore division can be seen reproduced in contemporary slang where a good girl is known as a *Palestinien* – from *mwasi ya palais*, 'a woman of the house' (the French *palais* – palace – is Lingala slang for the home), while a girl of dubious sexual reputation is known as a *Libanais* – Lebanese – a word play derived from the Lingala *mwasi ya libanda*, 'a woman of outside'. For boys, the divide between the house and outside has more of a class connotation – a *mwana palais*, 'child of the home', tends to mean a rich kid who is not involved in economic activity outside the home.

4. Fieldnotes, Jean Lema, 14 November 2007.

5. In 1957, less than three years before independence, Belgian colonials reacted furiously to an article by Van Bilsen suggesting that the Congo should have a plan for independence in thirty years' time (see, for example, Young 1966: 53).

6. Fieldnotes, Jean Lema, 14 November 2007.

7. Biaya also lists a series of 'challenges' that the true *ambienceur* was supposed to have accomplished, including sleeping with a white woman, a dwarf and an albino.

8. Fieldnotes, Victorine Njoli, 15 November 2007. Struggling to follow, I did not follow up on what was meant by a woman's strike, I have since assumed something similar to Lysistrata's oath, but that may be quite wrong.

9. Daniel Kanza was Governor of Kinshasa and a prominent member of ABAKO, the party of then-President Joseph Kasavubu.

10. Fieldnotes, Jean Lema, 14 November 2007.

11. Fieldnotes, Jean Lema, 14 November 2007.

12. Larry Devlin, who was then CIA bureau chief for Congo (Devlin 1997: 260) has used De Witte's work to claim personal and national innocence in Lumumba's death. This is causistry – Lumumba was recaptured because of CIA intelligence and, more widely, the CIA was hugely implicated in the downfall of an elected leader and the rise of a military government.

13. Links to the CIA remained important to the story of Zaire. In the first decade of his rule, Mobutu is estimated to have received $150,000,000 from the bureau (Boyce and Ndikumana 1998: 208). The roots of the close friendship between George Bush Senior and Mobutu lay in the fact that both had spent so many years working for the agency.

14. For what it's worth, I think there is probably something in the story; that said, in the same biography, Ley makes some rather extraordinary claims (Mpisi 2003: 86). In case this sounds disrespectful, I should say that I consider Ley one of the great artists of the twentieth century, if also something of a fantasist.

15. Earlier appropriations had left multinational and Western capital well alone, but eventually Mobutu's improvisations led him to attempts to appropriate some Belgian-owned companies. The led to the withdrawal of credit lines by parent companies and, very quickly, to a much wider withdrawal of credit.

16. This draws on notes made from several conversations I had on the subject of the *Moziki* 100 Kilos while in Kinshasa in 2007, and one conversation with the offspring of a member of the Moziki in Belgium in 2006.

17. Now Leon Kengo, President of the Senate.

18. Likinga, a frontline singer with Zaiko Langa Langa, for example, was imprisoned in Portugal for several years in the 1980s on drug-trafficking charges. During my time in Paris, I also came across musicians involved in the drug trade.

19. By the early 1980s, this role of music and dance in the performance of deference had become so naturalized that it is mentioned in a famous letter signed by those who would henceforth become opponents of Mobutu: 'What have we not done for you? We have sung we have danced we have animated.'

– Chapter 2 –

EXCHANGE, MUSIC, PATRONAGE

 ℰ ∽

> He had tied a bit of white worsted round his neck – Why? Where did he get
> it? Was it a badge – an ornament – a charm – a propitiatory act? Was there any
> idea at all connected with it? It looked startling round his black neck, this bit
> of white thread from beyond the seas.
>
> —Joseph Conrad, *Heart of Darkness*

This chapter takes as its theme the theatrical forms of patronage in
Congolese music that have developed since the late 1970s, and it considers the close relationship that patronage has had with migration.
Specifically, we look at how and why a well-recognized social type –
the *mikiliste* – along with various tangible and intangible goods, most
particularly designer clothes and sponsored name-checks on records,
emerged together at the end of the 1970s as key forms of value. It
is clear that such practices are also related in some way to precolonial economies, where wealth, fertility and the exchange of things
and people were closely linked (Douglas 1968; Dupré and Rey 1980;
Guyer 1993). This was not a simple revival of 'deep tradition'; rather,
it came about in a situation of violent social and economic change in
which certain precolonial forms of rationality made more sense.

Mabanga, Mikiliste

In 2005, Wenge BCBG gave a concert in Dublin. The concert attests
to the growth of the Congolese community in Ireland, but many
patrons of the *orchestre* had also come from the United Kingdom. As
is the custom at such concerts, many fans came on stage and pressed
banknotes on the musicians, giving, above all, to J.B. Mpiana, the
président d'orchestre. The previous year, Wenge BCBG had released

the album *Anti-Terro,* on which the song 'Nungu Nungu' had been dedicated to (that is, bought by) a patron called Kazadi. During the concert, the band started to play 'Nungu Nungu' and, in response to this, Kazadi strode on stage and began pressing fifty pound notes on J.B. Mpiana. This act of prestation continued for a quite breathtaking length of time, until the sum amounted to several thousand pounds. Eventually J.B. himself declared, 'Ekoki!' ('Enough!') – a comment that has contributed to the mythology of the event for, as *président d'orchestre* and a Luba (an ethnic group associated with a particularly voracious financial 'appetite'), J.B. is seen as being all but insatiable in his desire for money.

The word *mabanga* – literally meaning 'stone' – has come to refer to a set of patrimonial practices, all of which involve some form of music-related prestation. The main connection with *mabanga's* literal meaning appears to be with the idea of 'throwing' a stone. A musician who cites a patron is said to 'throw' – *kobuaka* – him (see White 2002), but certain informants also linked *mabanga* to the idea of 'breaking rocks' – *kobeta libanga* – a phrase that has come to denote the activity of hustling and is used, in a wider sense, to refer to an ideology of amoral resourcefulness that, as the state has fallen away around its citizens, has been elevated to a kind of credo by the Congolese (see Bilakila 2004). The origins of this phrase may be linked to the earlier use of an identical phrase in Kikongo, where *bula matadi* – 'breaker of rocks' –follows a fascinating historical trajectory.

In nineteenth-century Vangu, on the lower Congo, *bula matadi* referred to an individual 'whose head was so hard he could break rocks with it'. It was 'the praise name of a chief whose accession to the title was opposed by his fellow chiefs but who overcame them by his wealth and aggressiveness' (MacGaffey 1986: 35). It was subsequently applied to the explorer Henry Morton Stanley and, by the twentieth century, had become an indigenous term for the colonial state – a term that the colonizers themselves then enthusiastically embraced. For the Belgian rulers, it came to encapsulate their deluded self-image as stern-but-benevolent rulers of the Congolese.

Thus, if the term has a common origin, then its semantic progression – from violent leader in a fractured precolonial landscape, to the violence of a colonial leviathan, to its denoting an individual in the act of aggressively pursuing a living in the postcolonial metropolis – it provides a nice encapsulation of the kind of trajectory we are tracing in this book. And, whatever the etymological accuracy, keeping this kind of trajectory in our heads will help us to grasp certain kinds of large-scale social changes – changes that I am calling epochal.

Mabanga is typical of a number of patrimonial practices in Congo that emerged, or were transformed, at the collapse of the state as inherited at independence. At this point, a set of political arrangements emerged that, though still unequal and violent, were much more diffuse and unstable, and were also based far more on localized forms of clientalism.

Since its emergence in the early 1980s, *mabanga* has developed into a reasonably formalized system of conventions.[1] As I shall discuss in the pages that follow, *mabanga* has come to represent the mainstay of a musician's income. In subsequent chapters we shall see that this incredibly dynamic system is, once again, in the process of transformation, but for most of the past thirty years, monies from the diaspora have represented the most significant source of *mabanga*. A short 'name-check' on a record (also simply called *mabanga*) with a top *orchestre* like Wenge BCBG will cost a patron between five and six hundred dollars. A *dédicace* – where the patron is inserted as the named object of desire in a song's narrative of love – costs around five thousand dollars, though more is often given. *Mabanga* during a concert is more discretionary, though to give an insufficient amount, or without the required panache, can be a humiliating experience for the patron. I remember witnessing an occasion during a concert in Brixton, London, where Koffi Olomide ostentatiously threw away an offering he considered too small.

Kazadi is an example of the *mikiliste*, a *bon vivant* who lives in or travels frequently to Europe, wears designer clothes and associates with musicians. Since explaining the social significance of the *mikiliste* will occupy much space in subsequent chapters, a few introductory remarks will suffice here. First, it should be noted that several other terms – *sapeur*, *parisien*, *miguel* – are also used by the Kinois to refer to aspects of this cultural icon. The term *mikiliste* has been selected both because it encompasses the meanings of the other terms and because it stresses the aspect of travel, along with access to a highly mythologized West – things that are central to this mode of success. Etymologically the word *mikiliste* is derived from the word *mikili*. *Mikili* may be related to the word *mokili*, which means 'world'. That said, *mikili* is a term that is used to denote not the entire world, but rather the collection of 'vrai mboka' – 'real countries' – (see Chapter 3) that constitute the rich and, to the Kinois, desirable part of the world.

In 2007, Kazadi paid for another song from J.B. Mpiana, which appeared on a more recent Wenge BCBG album. I met up with the *orchestre* while they were recording this album at one of RTNC[2] studios in Kinshasa where, excited about the song for Kazadi, they were especially impressed that he had managed to pay for his song despite having been in prison for over a year, serving a sentence for his participation in a U.K.-based syndicate involved in identity fraud. Kazadi was released from prison in 2008 and returned to Kinshasa with a Mercedes Jeep, to shower cash on musicians and admirers. The song, and the largesse, made Kazadi one of the biggest stars in Kinshasa. One story tells that, after a previous prison sentence, Kazadi went to collect his car from the police pound where he paid the parking charges accrued … using a stolen credit card. Many have said that Kazadi, who was expelled from the United Kingdom at the end of his most recent sentence, has returned there on new papers and is now involved with a group of Cameroonian *feymen* who produce counterfeit money. Certainly he was present in Brussels in mid 2008, again giving huge amounts of money to J.B. Mpiana. Kazadi's acts earned him a nickname from J.B.: *Zadio*[3] *arretez le temps* – 'Stop time Zadio' – because his acts of prestation went on for so long. Another fraudster, Tony Kabongo, currently in prison for fraud in South Africa, followed Kazadi onto the stage and gave even more money than Zadio, prompting J.B. to dub him *Tony rachetez le temps* – 'Buy back time Tony'.

As the rivalry with Tony Kabongo indicates, while Kazadi was a particularly famous fraudster in the Congolese community, his activities are fairly typical of the *mikiliste*, for whom fame, rank and competitive prestation are linked. In many forms of exchange, as Mauss argued, fame and the circulation of goods, people and things become interwoven. This chapter will show that *mabanga*, as a form of exchange, and the *mikiliste*, as a cultural icon, are associated in this way. The chapter will therefore look at the two phenomena together. Kazadi used dollars, and money is frequently deployed in these exchanges, but this is only one of the value forms in circulation. Cars, clothes, praise names and a range of other types of wealth are used.

Accumulation, Wealth in People, Mediums of Exchange

Edmund Leach wrote of the peoples of highland Burma that they 'do not look upon moveable property as capital to be invested, they regard it rather as an adornment to the person' (1954: 143). Expanding upon this, David Graeber (2001: 93–96, see also 2011: 127–210) notes how often noncapitalist societies hold wealth in objects that adorn or are otherwise stored about the body. Social currencies in the precolonial Congo often bear this out: brass wire made into necklaces, camwood which was ground into a red paste and applied to the body (known as [*n*]*kula* in kiKongo and related languages), amulets and cloth currencies made from local raffia or imported cloth (see Douglas 1968; Martin 1986). Indeed, the imported cloth currency of the lower Congo, known as *libongo*, gives us the contemporary Lingala word for money – *mbongo*.

Reflecting on this kind of material, Graeber makes a series of theoretical leaps that tie Leach's observations of the Kachin to Mauss' ideas about the category of the person in archaic societies and on to Foucault's ideas on the material body of the king in feudal Europe. In Foucault's conception, 'power is what was seen', in endless, highly visual rituals (Foucault 1999. 'The powerful were "individualised", made "material" and "particular"', while the powerless remained 'faceless spectators' (Graeber 2001: 95). This has a series of resonances with material on precolonial West and Central Africa, where at the bottom of the social scale people were 'empty', 'vain' or 'insignificant' (*mutu pamba*), while the big men (*mutu munene*) at the top attained a total 'singularity', their bodies fetishized via ritual and wealth (Guyer 1993: 256–57; MacGaffey 2000: 13–14, Barber 2007a). In a similar vein, the aboriginals of the American northwest divided people into 'name holders' or 'real' people, who performed expansive potlatches, while the rest were divided into 'other', 'unhealed' and 'slave'.

Foucault (1998) argued that in modern systems, this is reversed – with technologies of surveillance anonymizing the powerful and scrutinizing and singularizing the bodies of the masses. Graeber (drawing on the historian of dress J.C. Flugel) connects this process to 'the great renunciation' whereby Europe's seventeenth- and eighteenth-century male elite progressively abandoned the ornamental costumes, jewellery, makeup and swagger that had characterized their renaissance forbears. Fascinatingly, something like the reverse of this process can be seen in Kinshasa. As the productive base of the society shrivelled, the capacity, but also the desire, of the ruling elite to acquire the kinds of large-scale utilitarian/disciplinary forms of knowledge Foucault mentions also atrophied the census – surely the tool of the 'bio-power' state par excellence – was carried out for the last time in 1984. At around the same time, there was a dramatic rejuvenation in the rituals that, in Foucault's terms, 'materialise' the powerful body, alongside a dramatic expansion in the repertoire of male adornment.

This did not emerge from nothing: 'specific sets of body centred interests and the ludic sense of fashion, music and dance' had long been an important part of the city's repertoire (De Boeck in De Boeck and Plissart 2004: 238–41). But it does seem to go into a different gear precisely at the time when the capitalist mode of production ceased to be dominant. The cult of the· *beau gars* ('pretty boy') – male use of skin-bleaching creams, hugely expensive currency-like circuits of designer clothes (often referred to as *kula*, possibly in reference to the camwood paste used in ritual male adornment in precolonial times)[4] – took off, while potlatch-type rituals intensified

This is key to the arguments made in this book. In places where capitalism is not (or has only intermittently been) dominant, longer-term cycles of accumulation are invested in the person. In these circumstances goods are secondary – essential but nevertheless an adjunct – to performances that establish the rank and value of the person (see Guyer 1993, 2004). One of the signs of this adjunct status is, as Leach and Graeber both note, the degree to which valued goods are, in these societies, concerned with personal adornment.

Rank and personal value are clearly related to a general performance of abundance that includes juxtaposition and multiplicity of people and things as an essential characteristic (see Guyer 2004; Barber 2007a). The *mikiliste*, as a contemporary variant on the big man, both draws towards himself and gives off a diversity of good things – cars, women, designer clothes, clients, names, influential friends, bottles of beer, noise, dollars and the rest. This primacy of wealth in people in this context is, I believe, a vital first step towards understanding the diversity of wealth forms to be found.

But before we proceed further down this line, we need to examine some important facts of the recent monetary history in Congo. Inflation took off during the 'Congo crisis' just years after independence and, though it was brought under control in the late 1960s, it began to escalate again from 1974 onwards as revenue plunged and the state tried to monetize deficits. Inflation in Zaïre reached 80 per cent per year in 1978 and averaged 57.5 per cent a year throughout the 1980s. In 1991 it reached 2,154.4 per cent and peaked in 1994 at 23,760.5 per cent (Sumata 2001: 15).

In this context, standard economic theory offers its own explanations. Just as falling prices will drive people to hoard cash, very rapidly rising prices – such as those experienced by Zaïre in the 1980s and 1990s – will drive them away from money and towards a portfolio of goods, which can act as a hedge against instability.

But while inflation is important as a driver of wealth diversification, it was not the initial cause of currency multiplicity in Kinshasa. The diversity of goods demanded, for example, in bride-wealth payments, where alongside a sum of money a selection of goods is always required – oil lamps, wax cloths, bags of rice, goats, crates of beer, precolonial iron valuables, cooking pots – tends to indicate that this kind of multiplicity is connected to much deeper historical forces.[5] Many of these goods, such as beer or wax cloth, carry over into the world of the bar – where, again, they were well established as mediums of social exchange well before modern inflations became important.

Potlatch and Instability

Thus, the instability of inflation is important, but to understand what is going on, we need to think about instability more broadly and in a more historically informed way. Fundamental aspects of instability are related to the dynamic of potlatch. As we discussed in the Introduction, extreme forms of status competition, along with unsustainable forms of exploitation, were generated in the interface between capitalist and human modes of production. As the forces of production were undermined and authority became more fragile, a greater emphasis on competitive rank emerged as *nouveaux* aspirants tried to break into the unstable social order. Those who found a niche in a particular economy – such as a special trading relationship or special access to a resource – tried to create and institutionalize this status. They set up a 'gate' and installed themselves as 'gatekeeper' via some form of exchange ritual, often involving a new medium of exchange that could be validated in ritual performance.

Mediums of exchange allowed certain actors to extract rents by restricting exchanges to currencies where they had built up surpluses or where trade connections meant that they could access this item more easily than other people could.

This gatekeeping was just one element of a social dynamic that would have pushed towards still greater multiplicity in wealth forms. Other elements could be monetary: with increasing diversity, there were increasing possibilities for processes like seigniorage (the profit made by the producer of a currency) and arbitrage (the profit made on trading between currencies). Another crucial dimension was aesthetic – the kinds of ritual escalation that we noted in the Introduction required ever more dramatic displays of abundance emanating from the person of the powerful, and abundance required giving off a diversity of material and immaterial goods. As Barber notes, it is precisely in those places that were within the Atlantic slave trading zone – that is to say, where human modes of production were drawn most intensely into the dynamic of the potlatch – that an aesthetic of personal abundance, which 'foregrounded disjunction and contrast' (Barber 2007a: 117), seems to have been most exaggerated.

Thus, in place of the stable set of 'spheres of exchange' proposed by earlier authors, each stacking neatly on top of the other as part of a tidy social order, we have a bewildering delta of partly overlapping economic and social claims, with currencies, claims to authority and the ritual performances that established them emerging and perishing regularly. Jane Guyer writes that there were:

> a multiplicity of control and access mechanisms [yet] ... all control, however apparently effective, was partial, provisional and ephemeral. People could move in and out of the value register in new ways: insert new products, convert old ones ... The interval gaps had to be maintained against the brilliant manoeuvre ... The conversion of intervals into the qualitative thresholds ... was a major political achievement. (Guyer 1993: 252)

This brings us back to the significance of inflation. The dramatic inflations of the post-independence period were just part of a more general economic collapse. GDP shrank in most years from 1974 to 2000, remaining in 2010 just over two hundred dollars (2005 PPP dollars US), less than 20 per cent of its 1974 zenith of over 11,000 dollars (Exenberger and Hartman 2013: 31); in the 1990s, the banking system (Jewsiewicki 1992; De Herdt 2002), remaining enclaves of industrial production (Jewsiewicki 2003) and, indeed, anything resembling Western economic institutions disappeared.

Under these extreme conditions, what I am calling 'epochal' changes occurred. During the late colonial and early independence period, logics of wealth in people and subjectivities of competitive ritual dispersal had existed, but were subordinate to capitalist forms of authority and accumulation. From the second half of the 1970s, these logics began to overspill their containers, moving from the margins to the centre. This is not to say that the population simply responded to economic events – to paraphrase Marx (1852/1970), men made history, but they did not do so under circumstances of their own choosing.

Niarcos and *les voyous*

Most notable among the early *mikiliste* was the Teke gangster Adrien Mombele, also known as Stervos Niarcos, and it is around him that much of the oral testimony I collected was clustered. Born Adrien

Mombele, he became Mombele Ngantshie in around 1973, when Zaïreans were pressured into adopting 'authentic' Zaïreian names, under the strictures of Mobutu's programme. By the late 1970s, he had already taken the name Stervos Niarcos,[6] adapting it from that of the Greek shipping magnate Stavros Niarchos. The Congolese Niarcos and his admirers often retained the 'Ngantshie' and he is frequently hailed on record as 'Stervos Niarcos Ngantshie'.

The significance of this is that Niarcos's father, Pierre Mombele, really was the *Ngantshie*, which is to say a member of the area's pre-colonial Teke aristocracy. His father was also a minister in several of Mobutu's governments. In this way Niarchos was clearly a privileged individual.

Many of the trajectories that underlie Niarcos's rise appear grounded in the Central African *longue durée*; the growth of the informal economy and the consequent power this gave to the amoral 'social pivot' find echoes in the precolonial eighteenth and nineteenth centuries, where 'chiefs' emerged at nodes in the commercial networks, in unstable and violent interactions with the world system. Yet for actors in the midst of the situation, this turn came as a shock, amplified by a demographic explosion as the *troisième génération* came of age. After two generations of economic growth, Niarcos's contemporaries found their prospects worse than those of their parents, a turnaround that must have been especially galling to aspirations stoked by a massive expansion in higher education (Young and Turner 1985).

In part, Niarcos's strong associations with Brazzaville can be ascribed to his ethnic origins. As a Teke, he would have had significant kin networks there, but he was not the only one spending long periods of time in Brazzaville. With the growth in the informal economy, new pathways were carved out, old trading routes were revived and cross-border smuggling with Brazzaville expanded dramatically in this period (see Bazenguissa-Ganga and MacGaffey 2000). It appears that Stervos Niarcos and many of his associates were involved in this trade and made connections with underworld figures in Brazzaville. They also picked up the cult of designer clothing that had developed in the 1970s among the youth there (see Gandoulou 1989a, 1989b). While in Kinshasa, the main hangout for Niarcos and friends was the Village Molokai.

The Village Molokai

Situated in Matongé, then Kinshasa's principal entertainment district, the Village Molokai was, and is, a plot belonging to Papa Wemba, who had named it after Molokai in Hawaii (see Luttman 1998). A venue for *les voyous* – dandies and gangsters from Kinshasa and Brazzaville – it was clearly a place that generated a great many social ties, both between various supporters of Wemba's Orchestre Viva La Musica and between these supporters and the musicians. It was here, from this mass of social ties, that *mabanga* emerged.

Even as a teenager, Niarcos seems to have exhibited delinquent tendencies. Friends remembered him smoking and selling marijuana close to where the Stade des Martyrs now stands. At some point things became more serious. According to an informant who had been his close friend, Niarcos was involved in a series of robberies on banks and cash deposit boxes in Brazzaville, and several of his accomplices were fellow regulars from the Village Molokai. Soon after this, in 1979 Niarcos came to Europe. According to the same informant, he was fleeing Kinshasa because things had become too hot for him. But, in addition, he was undertaking a kind of pilgrimage.

From the early 1970s, youngsters in Brazzaville had developed a kind of youth movement called *Le Sape*, based around designer clothing and a voyage to Paris, where one would acquire a resplendent wardrobe and return in glory to Brazzaville (Gandoulou 1989a; Friedman 2004). This mythology went on to influence Zaïrian youth, with the Village Molokai as an important conduit. There were two influences in particular that the Village Molokai introduced to the Kinois. The first of these was that Paris was drawn to the foreground in the Kinois imagination – though this had already been captured by a somewhat mythological view of Europe.[7] The second was the central role played by designer clothing in social life. Youths who associated at the Village Molokai would collaborate to make up their outfits, borrowing a watch here, a pair of trousers there. Those who had a good selection of designer clothes – those with a connection to Europe or at least to Brazzaville – were at an advantage. That said, the Village Molokai was a stylish but relatively peripheral institution. Yet the social need for *griffe* (labels) took Kinshasa by storm in a way that very quickly transcended the subculture of the Village Molokai and, as we will see, designer clothes became a central medium of exchange.

An Exchange Institution Emerges

How did this transformation come about? The regulars at the Village Molokai made prestations of clothes to musicians and, in return, the musicians would sometimes sing the donors' names. In this way the musicians of Viva La Musica gained splendid wardrobes and certain individual benefactors became known. These prestations were not yet formalized and seem to have been an extension of the fictive kin relationships that the Village Molokai generated. The popularity of Viva La Musica, who were frequently on Tele-Zaïre, drew many people to the cult of fashion, as most of the early *sapeurs* in Kinshasa were also supporters of Viva La Musica. Above all, Viva's musicians would sing the names of those who were currently abroad, the effect being to publicize the glamorous status of the individual and also to increase the likelihood that, on his return, this individual would make prestations of clothes to the musician.

As we have seen, the notable musicians of the independence era *deuxième génération* (though not rank-and-file musicians) held considerable social and political capital. But this was not true of the *troisième génération* of musicians. Record sales were relatively high during this period, but this did not necessarily translate into money for composers or performers – an outcome I will investigate in Chapter 4. Musicians were trapped in a situation where accessing artists' rights payments depended on political support. Bereft of direct political patronage, younger musicians were forced into patron–client relations with the well-connected musicians of the *deuxième génération*, men such as Franco and Tabu Ley. There was a sense in which, despite their popularity, the musicians of the *troisième génération* were seen as 'little people' – *mutu pamba*. Thus, while one might pay for an *orchestre* such as the *troisième génération* Zaiko Langa Langa to perform at a function, entering into an extensive social relationship with such musicians would have been anathema to the children of the elite. This meant that while several musicians of the *troisième génération* travelled to Europe as individuals in the 1970s,[8] they did not have the patrons to put up capital for a tour with their *orchestres* or for recording sessions in European studios.

Papa Wemba's journeys to Europe in 1980 with Viva La Musica and again in 1981 on his own stand out because of the extent to which he was able to establish a network of Europe-based patrons. A necessary condition for this broadening of his social network was an increase in Congolese immigration to Europe in the 1980s. In 1981 the Mitterand government relaxed the visa requirements for

Zaïrians (Bazenguissa-Ganga and MacGaffey 2000) and this liber-alization, combined with the cult of Paris among the youth, meant that Paris overtook Brussels as the principal centre for Zaïrian migra-tion. A large number of these migrants were not from the elite and most were contemporaries of the *troisième génération*. These youths had come of age in a Zaïre that was suddenly unable to provide for them and the experience may have taught them that the state was a temporary resource, to be strip-mined before it ran out. Papa Wemba was able to develop a new kind of patron–client interaction. Based on new artistic forms and a new sensibility, it also contained the germ of a new political economy. This did not emerge from a clear blue sky, however. It drew on older cultural logics, along with recent narrative and melodic conventions in popular music.

The principal form in Congolese music since the 1940s has been the love song, sung from the point of view of a fictional first-person narrator (see Chapter 7). It has also been common for this narrator to be female, even though musicians singing these songs have almost always been male. From the early 1980s releases of Papa Wemba, this device was married to another narrative conceit: the status of the love object/patron as a resident of Europe was consistently stressed. Often this took the form of a declaration of love for a beau in Europe from a lover in Kinshasa, as the following example of 'Beau Gosse ya Paris' – originally released in 1985 – illustrates. In the song, the 'Beau Gosse' – pretty boy – called Juliene is in Paris, while the fictional female nar-rator is pining for him in Kinshasa: 'ngai awa na kin eh, yo kuna mosika ozali' – 'I here in Kin [Kinshasa], you there are far away'. In this state Papa Wemba and Luciana Demingongo's voices inter-twine plangently, personifying the female lover desperately awaiting a return visit by the suave *Parisien* 'Mokolo nini Nzambe nakofete ya ngai eyenga tango okoya?' – 'On which day, God, will I celebrate Sunday [with you] when you come?' (Wemba 1985/2000).

The format did several notable things. The model of success it promoted – the *mikiliste* – was clearly a version of the *ambianceur*, the good-timing romancer of women (see Chapter 1). The figure of the *ambianceur* was associated with a certain kind of rather fetishized 'European' modernity and thus with an African bourgeoisie oriented to, and even seeking to imitate, the world of the whites (see Biaya 1996). But the *mikiliste* took this orientation much further, wedding the idea of the *bon vivant* with a direct and physical access to Europe.

At the same time, the format also stressed the idea of a retinue in Kinshasa. Unlike other states in Africa, where the weakness of the central state seems to have made the adulation of the natal village or region of origin of primary importance, the obsession in contemporary Congolese models of success is associated with having a retinue back in Kinshasa. Despite a disastrous fall in standards of living, Kinshasa continues to be construed as the premier site of pleasure, the *mboka elengi* (pleasure town) that is the fount of *Kin kiesse* (Kinshasa joy). Indeed, in some respects this is *because* of the collapse in incomes. Income disparity makes Kinshasa all the more pleasurable for those with money: a place for sex, music and the joyous giving-off of imported goods. Those who earn money elsewhere – the *Bana Lunda* (diamond miners) and other successful migrants – will return to Kinshasa to engage in prestige consumption and receive the adulation of retinue (see Chapter 6). Like music, clothing plays an essential role in this adulation.

Titi Le Vallois,[9] a famous patron from the early 1980s, claimed only ever to have paid for *mabanga* in clothing, and all informants confirmed that until the mid 1980s, designer clothing was the major medium of payment for *mabanga*. The close relationship between *mikiliste*, designer clothing and popular music acted in several ways to imbue music, people and things with a mutually reinforcing aura of value.

A striking example of this is in the song 'Matebu', written by Stervos Niarcos and passed on to Wemba during the latter's visit to Paris in 1983. The song is sung from the point of view of Niarcos himself, who is at the top of the Eiffel Tower. Niarcos transmits a plea to his lover, Marie Therese Butu (hence Matebu), that she come from her home in Brussels to Paris where they will resolve their differences and get married.

For the sake of their love and for their daughter (Gianni Versace), Niarcos asks that they 'finish the wedding',[10] and he is very specific as to the nature of the festivities, where the labels will be 'Voya Torrente', 'Giorgio Armani' and 'Daniel Hechter'. And the shoes – 'Pona ba Sapato eh J.M. Weston' – 'For the shoes, J.M. Weston' (Wemba 1982/2004).

More often, this nexus of music, the value of persons and the value of clothes occurs in more implicit ways; the status of the individual *mikiliste*, so assiduously created through *mabanga*, was transferred to the clothes he wore and, as the subtleties of *griffe* were picked up with alacrity by the Congolese, the clothes were a necessary part of the valuation of individuals. Music was, and is, essential in creating the right emotional tone for these highly performative tournaments of value.

Several of the dances popularized by Viva La Musica, and subsequently by others, were explicitly designed to allow the dancer to show his *griffe*, as in the *Griffe Dindon*, when dancers open their jackets to show the labels and slide forward their feet to show their shoes. Clubs and concerts (and, more recently, Pentecostal churches, which are also musical spaces) are the primary locations for the display of designer clothing. Central to the theatre of such locations are idiosyncratic demonstrations of dress. One can observe a man dancing with a shoe on his head or another holding aloft a *Hermès* umbrella – all the better to draw attention to it. Towards the end of the concert, members of the audience remove their designer tops, joyously slapping, throwing and shaking them.

Oratory, Hilarity and Exchange

Another aspect of these performances began to take place via a burgeoning genre of boasting and ritual insult called *polémique*, broadcast on Tele-Zaïre.[11] These insults very often concerned a comparison of the dress of rival musicians. Some of the most intense jousts took place between Wemba and Kester,[12] a musician in Viva La Musica who left to form his own *orchestre*, Victoria Eleison, taking the majority of Viva's designer-obsessed musicians and fashion-conscious supporters with him. One occasion, remembered by many informants, concerned a performance on the hugely popular Saturday music programme *Zaïre Numero 1*. On this particular Saturday, in the early 1980s, Kester and Wemba were to play face-to-face (*fara-fara* in Lingala). Both performers were carefully dressed for the occasion and Wemba came on proudly displaying his pair of J.M. Weston shoes. Kester, also wearing Weston shoes, announced: 'Na lekisa ye na trois points…' – 'I beat him on three counts. My shoes are crocodile skin, they are triplestitched [a special and more expensive type of Weston shoe] and they are boots.' At this point he lifted his trouser leg to reveal, lo, ankle-length boots. Sensation, clamour – match Kester! During a much later television appearance, Kester claimed that his pair of black crocodile-skin Westons had taken nine months to make, including 'three months to catch the crocodile in the Amazon; then three months for them to cure the leather; and they take three months to deliver it' (Emeneya 2007).[13]

This same mix of music, hilarity and real valuations of persons and things is widespread in contemporary Congolese life, where performances are required to establish a new label as a fit object of exchange.

In 2004, Herculio, a Congolese resident in London, claimed to have 'discovered' a new Japanese label by the name of Kasamoto. The exclusivity of the label was further enhanced by the fact that it had only one distributing outlet outside Japan, in Brussels. Herculio paid for television appearances where he announced to those in Kinshasa, and those in Europe watching via DVD, that 'soki Kasamoto eza te vie eza te' – 'if there is no Kasamoto, there is no life'. It should be noted the verb to live – *kovivre* – is commonly used in colloquial Lingala to denote a kind of flourishing connected to potlatch-like consumption of prestige goods (see De Boeck 1998).

Whether or not such television appearances were influential, it is certain that a path was beaten to the shop in Brussels by eager patrons. Kasamoto was worn by all the major singers during concerts and by all the most famous *mikiliste*. Within weeks of the craze starting, samples had been carried by Congolese entrepreneurs to workshops in south China and fakes began to appear. By 2005, fake Kasamoto was on sale everywhere in Kinshasa. Higher-quality fakes were also troubling the upscale Congolese buyers in Europe and Congo. This was commemorated in a shout, and an accompanying dance, by Gentamicine, the *atalaku*[14] of Wenge BCBG:

> *Bawuti mikili bamemeli biso ba Kasamoto ya Ngwanzu*
> They went to Europe. They brought us fake[15] Kasamoto
> *Eh Ngwanzu eh! Eh Ngwanzu eh!*
> That is Fake! That is Fake!
>
> (Gentamicine 2006)

The social clamour for a garment only available from one shop in Brussels is somewhat reminiscent of Georges Dupré's (1995) article about the *Zong* – a strange anchor-shaped piece of iron available only from a French rubber trader on the coast – which was in high demand among Africans as a medium of exchange in the late nineteenth and early twentieth centuries in the French Congo. But its relationship with performance and music also recalls the highly theatrical exchanges recounted by many ethnographers of the region (among them Balandier 1961; Fernandez 1982; Janzen 1982).

As we will investigate further in the next chapter, the apparent similarity with the precolonial and early colonial Central African exchange practices is not really due to 'cultural survival', though clearly there was some continuity in the symbolic order that was drawn upon. It was more a case of coming up with similar solutions to similar problems. The forms of fragmentation in sovereignty and of economic collapse that took place in the 1980s and 1990s created a series of imperatives that, in some respects at least, resembled those of the noncapitalist precolonial and early colonial social worlds. But where these precolonial and early colonial exchanges were made with reference to a symbolic order that was overwhelmingly local, the lexicon of postcolonial exchange has been constructed in response to a far deeper engagement between local moral matrixes and European symbols.

One way in which this is apparent is in the ideological inter-connections made between the ranking of goods, 'races' and their respective regions of origin, and individuals. Since at least the early twentieth century, the biggest of big men in Congo are clearly the *mindele* (singular *mundele*), the whites. In the wealth of symbolism attached to the *mindele*, there is a kind of ambivalent glorification, which is similar to the ways in which local powerful men are re-garded. For *mundele* is a category constructed more with refer-ence to the consumption of material culture and status than skin colour or facial morphology. 'Real whites' come from *mikili* – rich countries in Northern Europe and America.[16] Thus, *mundele madesu* – 'beans white', a reference to the rice and beans eaten by blacks and Portuguese alike – remains as a term for a white person of no account.

Yet this term has largely disappeared from the local vocabulary, to be replaced by 'mundele ya Ngwanzu'. Generally this term is used to refer to the host of 'lesser whites', above all Pakistanis[17] and Lebanese, who dominate the commercial sectors of Kinshasa's economy (although this writer was also popularly known as *Ngwanzu* for using public transport and for general shabbiness). The term *Ngwanzu* – which is often now used in Lingala simply to refer to China – is derived from Guangzhou (Canton), the man-ufacturing city in south China. In recent years, huge numbers of African traders have travelled to this city to buy cheap consumer goods, such as clothes and mobile phones, for resale in Kinshasa. The items bought are often imitations and are always of the very lowest quality, causing *ya Ngwanzu* to become an adjective denot-ing fake or low quality across all domains (see also Guyer (2003: 87) for a Nigerian example of such interlinking of goods, persons and 'overseas'). One may speak of 'mapa [bread] ya Ngwanzu', or 'politician ya Ngwanzu'. By association, China itself is often seen as something of a second-class country.

An example of this ideology can be seen from a discussion I had with two schoolgirls. Like many Kinois, the girls were obsessed with the idea of visiting Europe and pestered me for letters of invitation. Given that they were twelve years old, I did not have to take this request too seriously and suggested they might like to visit *Ngwanzu* instead. 'Te! *Ngwanzu* eza faux mboka!' – 'No! *Ngwanzu* is a false country!' – they screamed. As Pype (2007) notes, the *vrai/faux* (true/false) split is an important axis of meaning in Kinshasa. 'True' and 'false' are used in a way that more resembles the English use of good and bad, encompassing both moral and aesthetic qualities. A *vrai cherie* is an attractive woman, while a *faux vieux* is an elder who is considered not to have fulfilled his responsibilities. What is important to this discussion is that *vrai/faux*, *mikili/ngwanzu* and *mutu munene/mutu pamba* all map onto each other in the local cosmology.

The scorn lavished on China is interesting. To be sure, it is frustrating when one's Chinese-made sandals break or one's mobile phone gives out, but it is the capacity of the Chinese to produce large amounts of cheap, low-quality goods that has allowed most Kinois to own such goods in the first place, as they well know. Nor is the scorn for China (or the *mundele ya Ngwanzu*) based on simple racism regarding skin colour or facial morphology. Congolese perceptions of race are rather different from our own. The Chinese are generally said to be *mundele* – albeit fake ones. The prestige of Japan, meanwhile, is extremely high among the Kinois, who love Japanese designers – so much so that *un Japonais* is, in Kinshasa, a synonym for *sapeur*, a well-dressed, designer-clad person. Pop stars boast of visits to Japan and innumerable *mikiliste* have named themselves after Japanese designers like Kikush or Miyake. There is a guitarist called Japonais and a pop group called Station Japan.

Rather, it would appear that countries are judged by the same logic that governs people Once again, consumer items and narratives about respective rank intertwine, and thus the rush of cheap material culture from China has had a detrimental effect on its status.[18] The connection between Chinese material culture and rank can be taken further. One woman commented to me that 'Bachinois babebisi mokili' – the Chinese have 'deteriorated' the world. Again, this comment was made in relation to Chinese goods, but I believe this must be interpreted to mean that an influx of cheap Chinese goods represented a threat to the meaning and value of prestige items and the social orders tied to them. This kind of threat can be related back to the sense of hilarity discussed above.

In 2007 I was at the wedding party of someone's cousin in Asnier, a suburb in northern Paris, and wrote the occasion up in my notes afterwards:

Two *sapeurs* started competing, slapping their clothes and pulling at labels. Brown pulled out 20 Euros and slapped it on the older of the two *sapeurs'* heads. After that several people took out notes and slapped them on the same guy. This is kind of a sign that he had 'won'. In fact the younger guy was more expensively dressed, but the older one had more presence and a kind of cheek that people liked. The younger guy got annoyed and, to general hilarity, pulled down his trousers to show that his underwear was Versace. J.B.'s 'Kipe ya Yo' song was playing and at the exact moment that he pulled down his trousers the bit where they shout 'eh Ngwanzu eh!' came over the stereo ['That is from Guangzhuo, eh!' – from China, a fake. The cry was part of a popular song in 2007] and so it was a total disaster for the younger guy, even though I don't think anyone really thought his clothes were fake at all, but we all just hurt ourselves laughing at him. (Notes, Paris, 2 June 2007)

The instability inherent in this kind of performance seems obvious and prompts a few remarks about the interaction between personal subjectivities and political economic forms.

Boasting and Power

Such informal performances are indicative of a cultural tendency towards boastfulness, which regards successfully carrying off an assertion, however ridiculous it appears at first, as a source of prestige in itself. While conducting fieldwork, I was frequently identified in improbable ways by friends trying to garner prestige by association. I was variously a *grand producteur* and even 'Le producteur de Peter Gabriel', a 'millionaire' or, on one memorable occasion, 'Leki ya Michael Jackson' – Michael Jackson's younger brother.[19] Sometimes people would recount stories about themselves that seemed like such transparent untruths that they had to be veiling an important sphere of meaning.

Tabu Ley, an immensely powerful politician in the Kabila era and one of the greatest musicians during Mobutu's time, told me that he had played to 'a million' spectators in Madison Square Gardens, New York. In Ley's biography he claims to have acted as voice coach to the Beatles after meeting them in Hamburg, where he set them on the path to fame with his 'humble' advice (Mpisi 2003: 165). This tendency can be seen in televised interviews with musicians. Though these are often known as *polémique* and are frequently seen as being largely about 'dissing' your rivals, the slights are frequently far more subtle than the boasts, which revel in excess.

The most important aspect of boasting is the appropriation of power at a more fundamental level. This can be seen in the naming practices – exchanges that constitute another source of value within the multiplicity of this potlatch economy. Very often the praise names and honorific titles adopted by prominent figures in Kinshasa today are self-awarded, but just as often they are invented by a member of the name holder's retinue.[20] *Shege* – street children – are considered particularly adept at inventing titles and it is not uncommon to see them following the 4x4 of a *mikiliste* shouting praises.

A good name may garner an extra reward for the retinue; it may also be adopted by the patron. A snappy name that sticks in a listener's head is a valuable commodity in an economy of prestige. The ability to come up with appropriate names and honorifics is a valued skill and, like *shege*, musicians are considered to be particularly good at this. Often these names reference powerful forces. As the extraverted political economy of Congo would lead one to expect, very often these are global rather than local forces. Here naming and consumption seem to meet as part of a general outward-oriented trend. Indeed, names will often reference imported prestige goods. A famous courtesan based in Brussels has the title *Mama la Kompressor*,[21] a reference to a car, the Mercedes Kompressor. The names of designers are very commonly appropriated – Weston, Yamamoto, Gianni Versace (as in the daughter of Niarcos) and Adolfe Dominguez.[22]

All this may seem to accord well with the various theories of imitation in colonial situations, which have stressed that mimesis is a strategy to appropriate the power of the colonial 'other' (see, for example, Taussig 1993; Stoller 1995). Yet, as Mbembe (1992) notes, Central Africans are just as likely to imitate local forms of power. What is important is that the thing should be powerful, not necessarily that it be 'other'. A good example of this is the titles adopted by popular musicians. *Présidents d'orchestres* will adopt a large number of praise names and these will often reference a mix of local and global forces, combined with a smattering of zeitgeist-redolent nonsense, in a way that seems to prize the kinds of multiplicity and disjuncture discussed by Barber (2007a).

Werrason, one of the most popular musicians in the DRC, has titles that include Afula Atala Te – he does not watch (that is, he gives out freely) his breath – a reference to beliefs about breath as life force and munificence (see Chapter 8), and Igwe, the name of a producer of Nigerian films popular in Kinshasa. Werrason's arch-rival, J.B. Mpiana, includes among his praise names Sultani, Lui-qui-a-mis-l'eau-dans-le-Coco (He-who-put-the-water-in-the-coconut) and Le Maréchal – a clear reference to Mobutu, whose own self-bestowed military promotions can be seen as a related phenomenon. *Président d'orchestre* Koffi Olomide[23] has been variously known as Le Grand Mopao (Mopao is a meaningless name, except that it now means a pushy big shot of the sort embodied by Koffi Olomide for the Congolese), Mopao Mokonzi (Mokonzi means chief), Milkshake, Benoit XIV (after the ex-pope), Sarkozy, Rambo, Tcha-Tcho, Ganga Film (the star of the film) and Petit frère ya Yesu (Jesus's little brother).

There are examples of name use that are subversive, but such subversion is far from the most common form of humour and in any case relies on the presence of another kind of logic to be subverted. For this reason I would concur with Mbembe in arguing that such mimetic practices are not well understood as the kind of carnivalesque inversion proposed by Bakhtin (1965/1993). But nor does James Ferguson's (2002) notion of mimesis as a 'plea for inclusion' really fit the bill. For one thing, many of the appropriators – diamond dealers, politicians or *présidents d'orchestres* – are powerful themselves. One might cite Claudia Sassou (daughter of Sassou Nguesso, President of Congo Brazzaville), who is often sung on record as Ikea,[24] or Mobutu's own son Kongulu – an archetype of uncontrolled power who raped and murdered more or less unchecked – who called himself Saddam.

To call yourself Bill Clinton, Saddam or Kashoggi is to claim the power of these individuals. But it is more than just a claim – it is also a kind of demonstration of such power. Calling yourself Bill Clinton indicates a degree of panache and bravery, in short a capacity for bullshit.[25] Philosopher Harry Frankfurt (2005) has argued that bullshit is a style of deceit designed to convey a false impression about the speaker rather than about what he says. This is a constant factor in Kinois social relations, as this fairly trivial incident I experienced in Kinshasa illustrates:

> We were trying to get an express to the airport [i.e. a taxi in the Western sense; normal taxis in Kinshasa are more like buses, with a set route for a set fee]. Someone jumped in the taxi at the same time as us and said he was also going to the airport. Papy wanted him to make a contribution and he refused. I would have let it drop, but Papy was insistent and the other guy started puffing himself up and saying 'Do you know who I am? Do you know?'– making out like he was the son of the President and he would have us all thrown in jail. I was suitably scared but Papy called his bluff and he puffed up even further and said, 'Well I will show you!' and pulled his wallet out and flashed a card at us, which turned out to be a card indicating membership of the Red Cross. We laughed at him and got another taxi. (Field notes, Kinshasa, 2008)

While Frankfurt's is a philosophical treatment, he also implies that there is an important sociological phenomenon to be investigated, with an important growth in bullshit in Western countries. While this is clearly beyond the scope of this study, we might note in passing that the rise in Western bullshit relates to particular interests within a different kind of social structure – perhaps the managerial class fraction within the core capitalist states? While some of this management discourse has, delightfully, been incorporated into Congolese speech – J.B. talks of one of his patrons as *le valuer ajoutée de la RDC* (the added value) – the dynamics of bullshit in Congo are in fact very different. Here bullshit reflects a social structure inflected by the potlatch and forms of gatekeeping generated by low productivity.

In local terms, being a fearless bullshitter is an outward sign of an inner strength – just the kind of fearless, joyous inner strength that the original Bill Clinton or Kashoggi must themselves possess, but at the same time there is the perception that all power is extremely unstable. Nor is this a recent phenomenon: both Karin Barber (2007a) and Jane Guyer (2004) stress the possibilities of social mobility in nineteenth-century Atlantic Africa, and while this is true, they do not bring out fully the fact that the most dramatic instances of this social mobility were *downward*, as resources collapsed, factors of production were disrupted, entire polities were enslaved or the route to the coast was monopolized by another group.

Here this boastfulness and, in general, the frantic fluidity, inventiveness and creativity of Congolese cultural forms reflect desperate attempts by actors to control or remain attached to networks of patronage that are themselves constantly in the process of being violently disrupted. And in this desperation lies another element of the humour – the irony that exists in the disjunction between the wild assertions being made and the precariousness of the performer. Wild ritual and extravagant claims are interpreted by the audience within an aesthetic keenly attuned to the knife edge that exists between authority and the ridiculous, but this is a humour that reinforces rather than subverts the dynamic of potlatch. The general perception that power teeters on the edge of risible failure also drives those who aspire to power into ever more emphatic-sounding claims and ever more desperate demonstrations that they do in fact possess the real attributes of power.

In this sense, the humour is most often not directed at the powerful or the external, but at themselves as Africans. Indeed, there is a kind of general mockery of themselves as global pariahs. As the vocalist/band leader Bill Clinton Kalonji[26] himself said to me: 'You whites, you aren't like us. You, the whites, make things like planes! We blacks, we watch…' Or, as he put it in the song 'Ma Personnalité', 'the whites', 'Ethiopians' (viewed as distinct from black Africans) and 'Chinese' all eat choice parts of the turkey, while 'we', i.e. the black Congolese, eat the bum 'libabe' ('Ma Personnalité': Werrason and Kalonji 2002). As De Boeck (De Boeck and Plissart 2004: 44) notes when he quotes this lyric, the last line plays on the fact that *libabe*, while referring to cheap bits of imported turkey bum fat eaten by the Kinois, also means misfortune.

Conclusion

This chapter has argued that the productive collapse of the economy from the mid 1970s onwards has led to a series of epochal changes. Conceptions of wealth and value that focused on the person and on ritual demonstrations of personal worth ceased to be secondary forms and moved to the centre of social life. Drawing on the rich tradition of anthropological works on exchange in West and Central Africa, I have argued that one of the main ways in which actors have attempted to institutionalize socioeconomic advantage – a particular connection to the coast or a connection to a resource base – has been by creating a 'threshold' around a particular object of exchange. This chapter has concentrated on the way in which *mikiliste* created a threshold around designer clothing, which allowed them to hold on to certain kinds of social advantage. Given the long-term instability of the region, sustaining a threshold relied on a series of spectacular performances. This chapter argues that, via a series of spectacles, the *mikiliste* succeeded in creating one such 'threshold' – between ordinary dress and designer clothing. Imbuing themselves and their exchange objects with aesthetic qualities also, for a time, helped to sustain their sphere of value. In Chapter 6 we will explore more closely the relationship between *mikiliste* exchanges and wider political concerns. But first we will concentrate in more detail on the musicians who are so crucial to these exchanges.

Notes

1. *Mabanga* is the general name for a complex of musical prestations, but it also refers specifically to a short 'name-check'. While 'mabanga' is technically a plural form, it is this form that is most often used when referring to patronage in general, whether singular or plural. 'Libanga' is used to refer to a very specific, individual patronage 'shout'.

2. Radio Television National Congolaise.

3. This being a common short form of Kazadi.

4. My thanks to Filip De Boeck for suggesting this possibility.

5. This is not to argue that bride-wealth payments represent some sort of unaltered continuity with an ancient tradition. Both MacGaffey (1983: 179) and Hunt (1991) show extensive evidence that during the latter part of the colonial period, bride-wealth demands probably increased – either as a kind of tax on the salaried sector by rural elders (MacGaffey) or as part of a concentration of power and wealth in the hands of Belgian-appointed customary chiefs, which led to their buying up all the women in the district (Hunt). More recently, De Boeck (2004) and Faveri (2013) show that dynamism in the forms of marriage payment are still important. Nevertheless, whatever the vagaries of such exchange, a fondness for a diversity of payment media does seem to be a constant.

6. Naturally enough, his name accommodates many variant spellings; this appears to be the most common one.

7. Furthermore, as we have seen, in the Belgian Congo/Zaïre there was already a considerable metaphysical load attached to the idea of whites and of Europe. Nor did Zaïrian youth adapt wholesale the strictures of Brazzavillois *sapeurs*, for whom the business of acquiring a wardrobe and travelling to Europe is a process full of formalities, fixed ritual stages and prescribed purchases. As Gondola (1999) and White (2008) have both observed, Zaïrian *sapeurs* are much more informal and individualistic, wearing a much greater range of styles and designer fashions, and eschewing formal competition or a formalized hierarchy.

8. For example, Bozi Boziana, Lita Bembo or Papa Wemba. Gina Efonge went to Europe, but gave up music to pursue his studies. The acclaim such figures received from their peers back in Kinshasa underlines how rare such trips were. Lita Bembo adopted the honorific *awuti poto* – been to Europe – just for having achieved this feat.

9. Named after a (rather dull) suburb of Paris, Le Vallois. It was a name he adopted in Kinshasa, long before reaching Paris, and in the event he only spent a year there before moving to Switzerland (see Chapter 5 for discussion of names and nomenclature).

10. To 'finish the wedding' – *silisa libala* – the groom's family make the prestations of bride-wealth that solemnize marriage in Congo.

11. Such ritualized insults were not confined to musicians. From the earliest days, *mikiliste* were involved in performances that aggrandized the self and insulted others, but it is only relatively recently that these have made it into the media.

12. Emeneya Mubiala, *née* Joseph, often known as Kester Emeneya – Kester was a German detective in a popular series shown on Tele-Zaïre in the late 1970s.

13. Some helpful soul has posted a reprise of this interview at http://uk.youtube.com/wa tch?v=SSyKqyjle2w&feature=related. The whole interview is a thing of wonder and delight.

14. *Atalaku*: a kind of ludic singer who shouts over the *sebene* or 'instrumental' section of the music; see White (1999).

15. *Ngwanzu* (from Ghuangzhou or Canton) has in popular Lingala come to denote China and is an adjective meaning fake or no good. See below and also in the next chapter.

16. Generally speaking, Japan is not thought to be *mikili*, but nevertheless its status is extremely high, and the question of whether *Japon eleka mikili* – if Japan surpasses *mikili* – it is a fairly standard point of debate in Kinshasa.
17. *Mundele* can include Chinese and often designates non-African identity rather than whiteness.
18. This has now been supplemented by a widespread suspicion of the Chinese due to their financial support of the Kabila regime, but this very intense hostility for more conventional political motives is linked above all to the signing of the Sicomines agreement between 2007 and 2009, and thus postdates the emergence of discourse about *Ngwanzu*.
19. Though to declare oneself a younger sibling can be to show allegiance in a number of ways. In this case I think he was indicating I was a man of a similar, supreme calibre.
20. One can cite many traditions and cultural proclivities that have fed this phenomenon, most notably praise singing (Mufuta 1969; Swa-Kabamba 1997; MacGaffey 2000; Barber 2007a).
21. The song 'Liputa' on the album *Droit Chemin* by Fally Ipupa is dedicated to her.
22. Adolfo Dominguez, a Spanish fashion brand, is, in this slightly adapted form, the assumed name of one of Wenge's singers.
23. 'Olomide' itself is said to be derived from *l'homme-aux-idées*, the man with ideas, a one-time praise name for Koffi.
24. Thus appropriating the mighty power of Swedish furniture?
25. Given the nature of the political class, it is not hard to see how a capacity to bullshit might come to occupy a central place in local theories of power.
26. Who, like so many Congolese, has used large amounts of lightening cream on his skin.

– Chapter 3 –

POTLATCH MIGRANTS
Travelling to Europe, Arriving in Kinshasa

ℰ⁀

This chapter confronts a central paradox of Congolese music during the 1980s and 1990s: Congolese musicians travelled to Europe ever more extensively, but this increased travel coincided with a *retreat* of Congolese music from international markets. Looking in particular at two key spaces for musicians in Europe – studios and concert halls – I argue that the need to access these spaces was not, as the musicians and spectators often asserted, about the superior technical qualities of European studios or as a way of participating in some kind of circuit of global stardom. Rather, it was connected to a more local kind of fame – the related logics of potlatch and 'wealth in people' that increasingly structured Congolese society. As I will show, musicians went abroad to garner resources; resources that flowed there from the form of music patronage known as *mabanga*, within an economy where ideas of prestige and competitive rank were central. Far from opposing French society, or 'Western Hegemony', as some (e.g. Bazenguissa-Ganga and MacGaffey 2000) suggest, these narratives glorify *mikili* – as the rich north is known – and seek to harness its 'power'. Note well, however, that the average Western reader would find popular Congolese ideas of French (and Northern European) society pretty unfamiliar. White people and *mikili* figure prominently in Congolese narratives, but these narratives are related to notions of wealth and rank in Central African society.

This is in line with much recent(ish) anthropology, which has focused on the interplay of the global and the local (as in Miller 1992, 1995; Barber and Waterman 1995; or Meyer and Geschiere 1999). The general tenor of these arguments has been that 'appropriation' integrates the 'external' into 'internal' cultural projects. This is an important insight. Nevertheless, drawing on earlier critiques (Fardon 1995; Cooper 2001), I note a somewhat 'culturalist' inclination in this literature and show that, in the Congolese case, the social efficacy of the external can only be understood in relation to a wider appreciation of historical, political and economic factors. Here in Congo it was not increasing trade flows, but intensifying scarcity and political-economic closure that structured the appropriation of the external.

One last thing before we cast away. This chapter is based on field-work, most of which was conducted between 2006 and 2008. It de-scribes a social institution as it was during this period and I have found it less cumbersome to use the present tense to describe much of what happened. As the previous chapter has shown, this institu-tion was not particularly old and, as it turned out, was just about to fall apart. My use of tenses should not indicate an ahistorical ap-proach to this phenomenon – subsequent chapters discuss its unrav-elling and the vexed question of *for whom* this institution did (and did not) work.

Europe and Legitimacy

Europe is a source of legitimacy because you can return to Kinshasa with the prestige goods that will shore up your reputation as the 'tree that is planted by the rivers of water that bringeth forth his fruit' (Psalm 1:4). This applies to musicians and to their patrons, and indeed to anyone who aspires to status in Kinshasa. The imperative to *voyage* in order to return laden with consumer durables is well summarized (and satirized) by the comic miniseries *Maisha*, which was screened on TV in Kinshasa and watched on DVD by the diaspora. One of the actresses, playing the role of a dancer in an unsuccessful *orchestre* (Victoria Eleison), comments:

> *Misusu bakende putu bazonga na ba voitures. Biso tokende Kikwit tozonga na ba sacs ya fufu.*

> (Other groups go to Europe and they come back with cars. We go to Kikwit [a town in Bandundu, the province adjoining Kinshasa] and we come back with sacks of cassava flour). (*Maisha*, Vol. 1, 2006)

In one sense it is clear that at the very bottom of the heap in this con-ceptual scheme are *bato moyindo* (black people), while the DRC itself is likewise seen as the lowest of the low in the global family of nations – its only products, like cassava, belong firmly in what Bohannan

(1959) called the 'subsistence sphere'. Yet at the same time, it is crucial to note that the value of prestige items from elsewhere and the value of the persons who display and disperse them are only truly to be realized in Kinshasa. While sites of potlatch exchange are various and include important sites in Europe, these are in a sense directed back to Kinshasa. Part of the appeal of music patronage to migrants was precisely its effectiveness in creating a name 'back home' and, partly for this reason, artists not popular in Kinshasa were ignored by the diaspora.

This importance of Kinshasa is clearly also related to an aesthetic of crowds and clamour – only Kinshasa can supply the satisfying hubbub of spectators needed to validate the drama of potlatch exchange. It is also tied to the amorous success that the returning migrant is expected to enjoy. But enmeshed in this rather sensory aspect, the ideology of travel between Europe and Kinshasa is linked to a series of rather fantastical narratives, which tie rank to the idea of returning laden with goods from a mythologized 'elsewhere'. This is well illustrated in Papa Wemba's song 'Proclamation' (1984/2001), addressed to one who, in place of studying, is 'breaking rocks' (i.e. hustling), buying clothes so that on his return to Kinshasa, women will call out to him – 'tala Parisien! Wana omoni a success!'.

Europe and Kinshasa as Recording Centres

One of the complications of studying musical spaces in Europe is that people will propose superficially plausible explanations for why they need to travel. It is claimed that musicians need to come to Europe to take advantage of superior recording facilities or that performance in Europe places Congolese musicians within a world of international show business, but, on closer inspection, neither of these claims is true. As I will show in detail, the technical differences between studios in Kinshasa and Paris cannot explain the imperative to reach Europe, and familiarity with the Congolese music industry in Paris likewise dispels any idea of 'international show business' as the focus of performance.

One apparently practical reason why *orchestres* come to Europe is to record albums. During the period when I did fieldwork, the majority of recordings by the top *orchestres* were made in Europe. And it was often insisted upon by musicians, producers and fans that issues about sound quality lay behind this tendency of Congolese musicians to work in the Paris studios. The finest *orchestres* from Kinshasa had to work in European recording studios because, so the story went, by working in these studios, stars partake of their greater *professionnal-isme*. The well-known producer KTC, for example, decided to make the album *Le Tenant du Titre*, by the artist Madilu System, in Paris because he said that if the album had been recorded in Kinshasa, the resulting quality would not have been high enough to satisfy the public. While this sounds convincing, and at some level the Congolese do believe this, the evidence shows that it is not in fact the case.

History of the Kinshasa Studios

The idea that studios in Kinshasa are greatly inferior to those of Paris was true once upon a time, but this perception was long out of date by the time I started my fieldwork. The 1980s was a time of decline for music studios in Kinshasa. In the 1970s the city had lots of studios, but by the following decade, only two, Studio Veve and Studio Bobongo, were still in a state to undertake commercial work. Both these studios were using old technology and lacked skilled technicians (see also Tsambu-Bulu 2005). Artists themselves were hungry to use more advanced facilities and, in addition, the Kinshasa studios were unable to cope with the demand for studio time.

But by the mid 1990s, the decline in studio capacity had begun to reverse. Studio M'eko was started in 1992 as an outgrowth of a Methodist project, now owned by the Texas-based businessman Luis Onema. There is Studio N'diaye, which is owned by the Kinshasa-based Senegalese record producer M. N'diaye, who moved to Kinshasa from Brazzaville in the late 1990s, fleeing the war there. When I did the main fieldwork for this project, the Institut Congolais de l'Audiovisuel (ICA) was a studio and filming complex in the grounds of the state broadcasters, the Radio Television National Congolaise (RTNC). Extensively renovated after the fall of Mobutu, initially with money from the French state, the ICA has mushroomed into a warren of different studios and production companies producing sound for advertisements, music productions and other commissions. All of these studios are rather well equipped and also embody large amounts of technical knowhow.

When I conducted fieldwork, N'diaye and M'eko contained improvised elements – M'eko was less than perfectly soundproofed and neither studio contained the absolute top-of-the-range mixing equipment. The qualifications of the studio engineers here and elsewhere are somewhat improvised too. But they nonetheless produce a sound that is perfectly compatible (and comparable) with European studios.

Many of the studios in the grounds of the RTNC, meanwhile, come close to matching the technical quality of European professional studios. Technological changes that allow home recordings of a reasonable quality have also led to a huge expansion in the number of 'home studios'; these are in constant use by Kinshasa's gospel music artists and ever more of these studios approach professional quality.

Recording in Kinshasa

One may also ask how much the small differences that now separate the quality of a European studio from a Kinshasa studio matter to the public when set against other considerations. For the products of gospel artists, which are mainly recorded in 'home' studios, the Kinois appear ready to accept recordings of a much lower technical quality than those offered by N'diaye, M'eko or the ICA. The recent move towards very poor-quality MP3 formats by most of the listening public again begs the question of who is it that is so interested in sound quality? While there appears to be a certain residual difference in standards between European and Kinois studios, other considerations strongly support the proposition that this preference is not about sound quality. As a studio engineer in Kinshasa said to me, if it were really about the technical quality of the sound, then perhaps artists would do some of the post-production work – the mastering[1] – in Europe, but the majority of the studio work could be done in Kinshasa without any ill effect. An examination of what actually happens during recordings backs up this point.

The proof is that from time to time, the big *orchestres* have made records in Kinshasa and no one noticed the difference. In recent years it has become the habit of the big *orchestres* to release a shorter album of four or five songs (which is called a maxi-single). Most of these recordings have been made in Kinshasa, while *orchestres* will go to Europe to record their longer albums. Thus, in 2006, Koffi Olomide released a maxi-single called *Swi* which was recorded almost entirely at Studio M'eko. Werrason and Wenge Maison Mère recorded the maxi-single *Sous-sol* at Studio N'diaye and mastered it at Studio Marcadet in Paris, while J.B. Mpiana and Wenge BCBG recorded their maxi-single *Quelle est ton problème?* at the studios of the ICA and N'diaye. All of these albums were popular with the public and there was no comment at all about sound quality.

At the same time, there are huge costs associated with recording in Europe. The cost of studio time in Kinshasa was appreciably cheaper than it was in Paris – in 2007 a day at ICA studios cost US$200, compared to approximately $292 a day at Harry Son, a studio popular with Congolese in Paris. And studio time itself is the least of it: plane tickets, visas for musicians and living expenses in Europe add up to a huge sum (see Table 5.2 for a breakdown of such costs). So, on the one hand, the notion of technical quality does not stand up as a motive for travel. On the other hand, the costs associated with recording in Europe were so large that there must have been good reasons for going there. As I will show, this choice of Europe by musicians and producers had more to do with a certain kind of economy of prestige, strongly linked to *mabanga*, than it did to the ostensibly reasonable sounding motivations that were often produced in superficial conversation.

Tonton René, *Mabanga* and the Demi-monde

'Tonton' René lives in north London, where he shares a four-room flat with his partner Aurélie. René and Aurelie are the children of Zaïrian diplomats and came to Europe in the 1980s. Both are associated with the world of *ambiance* – Aurelie's previous lover was the subject of a hit song by Wenge Musica in the 1990s. René and Aurelie are both HIV-positive and for this reason they receive a disability allowance. Using the identity of a dead French woman, Aurelie also goes out to work for the local authority, though she often looks quite unwell. Tonton stays at home, where there is a constant passage of visitors through the flat. Generally these people want something. René studied graphic design at university and offers IT help to the Congolese community. Specifically he helps them by producing fraudulent documents like bank statements. In 2005–6, a frequent visitor to the flat was one of the singers with J.B. Mpiana's *orchestre*, Wenge BCBG. Tonton is also an aspiring music patron eager to get his name on record.

Probably the second most popular *orchestre* in Kinshasa during the period when I did fieldwork, Wenge BCBG was one of the offshoots to emerge from the split of Wenge Musica BCBG 4X4 in the late 1990s. Following a disastrous tour of Paris in 2001, where half of his entourage claimed asylum, J.B. Mpiana was unable to obtain visas to the Schengen Area European countries for most of the first half of the 2000s. He recorded the album *Anti-Terro* in Johannesburg, but this was apparently not to his liking. Then in 2004 he received a set of visas for himself and his *orchestre* to record in London. After this, between 2005 and 2006, J.B. and his *orchestre* spent more than six months in the UK. Their great rivals, Wenge Maison Mère, spent almost as long in Paris in 2007, while other top *orchestres* spent equally extended periods in Europe. There were many reasons for these long stays, but a major reason was patronage.

According to musicians I talked to, most of their income came from *mabanga* rather than from recordings or ticket sales and about 60 per cent of *mabanga* was, as of 2006, being sourced in Europe. While readers who are knowledgeable about the Congolese scene will not find this surprising, for other Western readers – especially those with some knowledge of 'world music' – it is worth insisting on this point. Other sources of money were peripheral to the business model, and the occasional release of albums on Western record labels or performances to European audiences were particularly unimportant, at least in financial terms. Indeed, the artists who have been most successful in getting an international profile – Koffi Olomide, Papa Wemba and more recently Fally Ipupa – have all also been particularly adept at managing the rather closed *mabanga* system. The amount of money Koffi and Wemba have made from their 'world music' efforts – either in concert or on record – is miniscule compared to the resources they have garnered from the Congolese audience. Indeed, after an initial burst of enthusiasm, both Wemba and Koffi essentially gave up on these much less financially important productions. Fally, whose crossover success is based in his links to Nigerian 'Afrobeats' stars, also makes the vast bulk of his income from *mabanga* derived from Congolese and Central African patrons.

Until the collapse of a certain kind of criminal economy in the late 2000s (see Chapter 6), people like Tonton René in Europe were the main source of patronage to musicians. While there are significant complications, most of the patronage from Europe came from this economy, while most of what was garnered in Kinshasa came from the political class. This is not to say that all of the monies musicians sourced in Europe came from the Congolese *demi-monde* of which René was part. Paris in particular was also useful as a place for interacting with Francophone politicians from other countries in Central Africa, whom musicians were more likely to encounter in Paris than in Kinshasa.

In this way the singer Ferre Gola received money to produce his album from General Dabira, an army man and television station owner from Congo Brazzaville. Vincent Gomez, a politically well-connected lawyer, also from Brazzaville, used his frequent visits to Paris to commission songs from numerous Congolese artists, including Koffi Olomide, Fally Ipupa, and Werrason. Other songs that grew out of contacts made in Paris were Koffi's 'Ikea', dedicated to Gabon resident Claudia 'Ikea' Sassou (the aforementioned daughter of Congo-Brazzaville President Sassou Nguesso) and Werrason's song 'Na Touche' (Werrason 2004), dedicated to Omar Bongo, the now-deceased President of Gabon.

High-flying *orchestres* derive appropriate plumage from these widely sourced celebrity commissions, but most of their money comes from the *demi-monde* of Congolese migrants, where *mabanga* is most often perceived as a kin-like social tie. Patrons will refer to musicians whom they patronize in the language of gerontocratic quasi-kinship, while ties of ethnicity and/or former co-residence in an area of Kinshasa – *mwana quartier* – are also invariably deployed. Related to this is the fact that the *orchestre* itself has features that resemble a kind of quasi-familial corporate body, with patrons, lovers and hangers-on as a part of this 'family'. In this way, being a member of a large *orchestre* can key you into an extensive set of pre-existing patronage networks. This can be a valuable asset, and musicians will try to hold on to these patronage networks if and when they split from an *orchestre* and try to go it alone. This can be seen in the case of Fally Ipupa, now one of the most popular young artists in Congo. Fally was a singer with Koffi Olomide's *orchestre* Quartier Latin. In 2004 he decided to record a solo album. Everywhere on the album, Fally drew on Koffi's peerless patronage network, a colourful example being the hit song 'Liputa', which is dedicated to Tabu Fatu, a courtesan living in Brussels. (We met her earlier as Mama la Kompressor, after the Mercedes Kompressor she drives). At one time rumoured to be romantically linked to Koffi Olomide, she also has numerous *mabanga* shouts on Quartier Latin songs, notably the hit song 'Ko Ko Ko'.

A musician who was very much in demand could simply wait for patrons to come to him unsolicited, but this is unusual. *Présidents d'orchestres* often receive so much patronage that dealing with it individually would be impossible, but even here they rely on these familial logics. A *petit ya confiance* who lives in Europe will be delegated to collect patronage for the *président*, at least from the less important patrons. If he does not take too much for himself, the *petit* will be rewarded with *mabanga* on the album. An example of this would be Apo, *petit ya confiance* for Koffi Olomide, who receives several shouts on Koffi's albums. The assumption is that if a musician wants money from a patron, they will share some kind of quasi-filial or fraternal bond. Prior connections – via ethnicity, the pre-existing network of the *orchestre* or notions of *mwana quartier*, are all useful for creating this bond – but a lot of hanging about and deferring to the patron may be necessary too.

This brings us back to the spirit guide of this section, Tonton René, and the Wenge BCBG singer who was his frequent visitor. Tonton had already spent one stint in prison, where he had lost a lot of weight. He became reluctant to undertake any of the more profitable scams that might have landed him back in jail. This restricted his income and inclined him not to give money away lightly. Worse still, he was not really a supporter of Wenge BCBG; his real passion was for an *orchestre* of the generation before, Zaiko Langa Langa. But he had spent part of his youth in Bandal, the district of Kinshasa where the original Wenge Musica – the *orchestre* that launched a thousand splinter groups, of which Wenge BCBG is one – started out, so he felt some kind of connection. In addition, the young musician spent a long time listening respectfully to Tonton hold forth on various subjects – about what car to buy, about what to do with his money if he ever had any, about how to avoid the mistakes that most Congolese made and so on. In the end, Tonton René paid for a *mabanga* shout, the musician got his money, and Tonton is there on the album.

The difficulty of this process of attaching oneself to a patron can be seen in the case of the song 'Chaud Lapin', which was written by the musician Eboa Lotin[2] and features on the Wenge Maison Mère album *Temps Presents*. Eboa brought the song to Europe partially written and developed it further when in Paris. As he did so, he entered into negotiations with several potential patrons. Initially a patron emerged – Coco – who held an office job in a company that organized home deliveries of groceries in the Île-de-France. People working for Coco also allege that he despatched workers to make deliveries of other, mysterious, goods between France and Belgium. The initial sketch of the song was made with his name inserted as the love object:

> *Eza yo kaka yo epai na tshaka yangai miso Eza yo kaka yo* **Coco Ndombe**
> It is you, only you, where I cast my eyes, it is you, only you, Coco Ndombe

Coco happily bestowed a certain amount of his time on sitting around the studio being patronizing as 'his' song was worked upon. His position of authority among Congolese in and around Paris was confirmed, and he took to referring to Eboa as *petit*.

As time wore on, Coco appeared unable or unwilling to pay. But as the song took shape, several others, who had also been listening in the studio, expressed interest. In the end, the song was given to Adrien Mukiadi, who, along with his brother Papi, was producing the album and had also observed the song's progression. The two brothers run a security guard business. In the event, the chorus was recorded as:

*Eza yo Kaka yo epai na tshaka yangai miso eza yo Kaka yo **Adrien Mukiadi***
(Eboa Lotin, 'Chaud Lapin', 2008)

In Europe, unlike in Kinshasa, there are no spaces for public rehearsals by the *orchestres,* and musicians' lodgings are cramped and spread throughout the city. In this context, studios represent a good place for patrons to build relationships with musicians. More important still, the musical performances involved in recording are important in persuading the potential patron to 'invest', because the decision to spend money on patronage is largely based on emotional criteria – the virtuosity, the communication of intense feeling effected by the musician, the pleasure of participation in a creative event and the pleasure of asserting a relationship with such a figure.

And it is notable that studios operate an open-door policy with regard to spectators.

Indeed, there is an incredible tolerance for multitudes of sundry people hanging around while a recording takes place. These spectators will talk, offer ignorant and ill-mannered advice, and on important occasions they can be so numerous as to render movement in the studio difficult. More than once I have seen fights break out between the spectators, and even musicians are sometimes attacked. Many musicians claimed to dislike the presence of such crowds, yet the only people I ever saw making spectators leave were the European studio engineers. My sense was that the musicians were in fact ambivalent about such hordes – they did get frustrated by the practical inconvenience, but at the same time following crowds have a positive connotation in Congo, and they were gratified by this mark of success. But, even if they wanted to, clearing the studio was not an attractive option – for the musicians, it was not possible to offend potential patrons in this way.

Western studio engineers, on the other hand, did from time to time try to clear the studio of all patrons and hangers-on, and often seemed on the verge of a nervous breakdown. Ambrose, a black Frenchman of Caribbean origin, made no secret of how much he disliked recording Congolese artists. During one session, he stood up and, large brandy in hand, announced: 'I am diabetic, I do not drink – but you people you have driven me to it!' Jean-Marc, a remarkably calm and tolerant French engineer who is the favourite of the Congolese, told me that he only did so many Congolese sessions because he could not break into the closed circuits of the French rock scene. Indeed, the chaos of spectators associated with such recordings means that many studio engineers refuse to work with Congolese musicians.

This consideration of how Congolese artists and patrons actually behave in the Paris studios does seem to be connected to an elaborate mythology about the rich north, but it is totally different from the kind of disempowering 'technological fetish' that Meintjes (2003) discusses. In Meintjes' work, black South African artists felt intimidated by high-tech studio spaces in Johannesburg. In the Congolese case, however, the effect on those in the studio was felt as empowering. Most of the time, musicians, hangers-on or patrons were exuberant in the studio space – noise, an 'always room for one more' attitude to spectators, elaborate greetings, extravagant dress and clouds of Indian hemp were the watchword. At the same time, the imaginative elaboration of the myth of *mikili* left their interactions with 'real' Europeans shrouded in mutual incomprehension and, unlike the situation that Meintjes describes, here it was generally the European professionals who felt out of place.

Another reason why physical presence is demanded by patrons is because there is such a lack of trust between patron and musician – an instance of a much wider trend relating to cash transactions.[3] This is one of the reasons why there are so many people hanging around the studio in the latter stages of a recording. *Mabanga* tends to be inserted towards the end of the process and many patrons will only feel secure if they can actually watch their name being inserted onto a track. In addition, physical presence can allow a patron to make sure he gets value for money. For the $600 price of a name check, a patron should have his name uttered at several places on the album, and some patrons will have their names sung as part of a vocal line, which is more prestigious than simply having it spoken on a separate *piste*. However, there is no formal agreement about either of these procedures and, all things being equal, those not present in the studio at the time of recording will get fewer mentions and be cited only on the spoken, overdubbed track.

As we can see, occupying the space of a Paris studio is an important strategic consideration for Congolese *orchestres*, but this appears to have more to do with the dynamics of *mabanga* and a wider potlatch economy than anything inherent in the quality of the studio. Thus, the search for *mabanga* among the numerous Europe-based patrons is more important than real or imagined technological factors in motivating travel. But this is not to make the argument that this complex institution is to be explained by simple 'bottom line' rationality. *Mabanga* itself is embedded in a complex ideological structure, where notions of wealth and success are not at all reducible to Western economic categories.

Serge, the Patron and the Sunglasses

It is a winter's day in 2006. I and a musician friend, Serge, leave the recording studio in Saint-Denis, walk to the metro station just inside the *périphérique* that divides Paris from the suburbs, and travel to the Gare du Nord. When we arrive, we enter and climb to the top floor of the Quick (the French-owned version of McDonald's) opposite the station. Waiting to keep our rendezvous, it becomes clear that this site represents something of a market for stolen goods. Congolese come and go, holding up designer clothes and bottles of perfume, moving from table to table. Eventually the person we are waiting for arrives and he and my friend fall into a discussion about *mabanga*. The discussion concerns the *dédicace* for one of the songs on Serge's forthcoming album. The patron is offering eight mobile phones in exchange for the *dédicace*. He produces one of these extraordinary devices – slim, black and stylish with all the latest additional features. In the shops, we are told, these sell for €400. Serge seems happy to accept mobile phones, but there is a problem. The phones have not 'become available' yet. They will arrive, the patron assures us, but Serge wants a 'deposit' from him. Recording will soon begin and there are many others who wish to pay for the song, says Serge, fooling no one. 'This is my manager', Serge says, turning to me. By now he is grasping at straws. The patron is unimpressed and declines to hand over even the one mobile he has shown us – perhaps it is bait to be used again on other fish. Eventually, after extended negotiations, the patron agrees to hand over the pair of Coco Chanel sunglasses, which have up to now obscured his eyes. The deal done, we quit the Quick and catch the train to Saint-Denis, Serge's eyes now shielded against the fading light of the November afternoon. As the train pulls out, Serge rather surprises me by expressing himself well satisfied with the transaction.

Serge came to Europe in the late 1990s with the *orchestre* of Wenge el Paris. He is a talented vocalist, being able to produce a strong *tenor* (in Western terminology a male falsetto or countertenor voice). The *tenor* voice is prized by the Congolese and is also hard to produce. There is no doubt that, in technical terms, Serge's voice is excellent and he is regularly asked to provide backing vocals on the albums of Congolese stars. And yet the closest Serge came to being paid for *mabanga* for his own work was a pair of sunglasses. 'The race is not to the swift, nor the battle to the strong…': life is unfair and the vagaries of popular preference are very perplexing – but there are some very clear reasons why Serge's solo career was, from the outset, very unlikely to succeed. Above all, there is the fact that he is based in Paris.

Being perceived as *na Kin*, from or of Kinshasa, is central to Congolese representations of musical success, and patrons will only invest in musicians who are a success. Musicians who spend prolonged periods in Europe will go to great lengths to preserve their aura as being *na Kin*, paying *bashege* (street children) to carry banners about them through the streets and hiring cheerleaders in the Kinois media. But Serge, a longtime resident of Paris making a solo album, cannot conceal the fact that he is, in every sense, a musician *na poto* – of Europe – and among the Congolese this is considered incompatible with musical success. Like everyone else in Congo, musicians harbour dreams of an easier life in the rich north and very frequently stay behind after a tour of Europe. But in so doing, they are abandoning any realistic hope of becoming musical stars – it is a very popular saying that 'Europe is the graveyard of our musicians'. This reflects the fact that prolonged residence in Europe tends to mean career suicide for Congolese musicians, but the image of the graveyard is also significant at a symbolic level. Europe is perceived as a centre of lifeless technical proficiency, while Kinshasa is the site of emotion and musical creativity.

Once again, the notion that Europe makes no creative input to Congolese music is transparently untrue. The studio was, during the 1990s and 2000s, the space where an *orchestre* would innovate. And over the last twenty years, the majority of studio work by the large *orchestres* was undertaken in Paris. No one had more creative input into this collective *oeuvre* than various Congolese arrangers – like Rigo Star, Suzy Kaseya or Maika Munan, all of whom were based in Paris. So what was really going on? This equating of Kinshasa with emotion and creativity, and Europe with an arid technical prowess, is related to colonial modernization theories. Nineteenth-century romanticism saw 'reason' as opposed to 'sentiment', equating 'art' with 'sentiment' and 'science' with 'reason' (Barbalet 1998). Numerous colonial ideologies mapped this opposition onto the north–south axis: at the equator, man was ruled by the passions, while in the north, reason held sway.

But this internalized ideology is underlaid with local logics related to the potlatch, in which to live – *kovivre*[4] – and flourish, but also to create, or author, are associated with highly emotional forms of consumption and the dispersal of largesse. The idea of Europe and

Kinshasa as polar opposites does capture an important aspect of social reality, in that musical success (and perhaps wider forms of social and political legitimacy) seems to be linked to negotiating access to both Europe and Kinshasa. All the successful Congolese *orchestres* travel to Europe regularly, but are essentially based in Kinshasa.[5]

Concerts: Narratives of Performance in Europe

Musicians also come to Europe to play in concerts, and here again we see a similar confrontation of claims, deeper ideological systems and resource flows. In Congolese discourse, travel to and performance in Europe projects the musician into an imagined world of global stars. But looking at the kinds of stories that accompany their performances, we get the sense that while 'the international' is frequently referenced, the meaning of the places and events mentioned has undergone a sea change. This is particularly evident in the rich and strange stories Congolese tell about large venues in Paris. In the 1970s the main setting for this imaginary construct was the Paris Olympia, where, in 1969, Tabu Ley became the first Congolese artist to perform in a major European venue. In recent years the vast Paris stadiums of the Zenith, and above all Bercy, accommodating forty thousand spectators, have staged 'the great globe itself'. Congolese stars who have played there are explicitly compared to Western stars popular in Congo, like Céline Dion or Johnny Hallyday. The symbolic pull of Bercy can be seen in the way that it has entered colloquial Lingala, where it is used as a word for 'full', with further connotations of success and popularity. A church or bar full of people will elicit the comment 'Basimbi nkisi cuna. Eza Bercy!' – they have got a magic device/gris-gris there. It is Bercy! [full of people]!.

The first Congolese artist to play Bercy was Koffi Olomide in 1999, followed by Werrason a year later. After this, J.B. Mpiana booked himself to play, announcing in an interview that he was going to 'correct' the previous artists who had played Bercy 'with a red bic'. But J.B. had the misfortune to play Bercy a month after 9/11. The success of the concert was blighted, since thousands of Congolese people were deterred from travelling to it. Under normal circumstances, a huge contingent of Congolese from Belgium, Germany, and the United Kingdom would have descended on Paris for the concert. Many of them would have been either without papers or, in the case of the U.K.-based Congolese, with papers that did not allow them to travel to the Schengen Area. Many did not dare travel for fear of the heightened security they would face. Such bad luck – itself the sign of an absence of *lupemba* (as in 'luck' or 'blessing'; see Chapter 6) – was greatly savoured, of course, by J.B.'s rivals. Koffi Olomide, in particular, began to incorporate references to Al-Qaeda into his act, using the initials OBL (Osama bin Laden) as one of his honorific titles and sporting a variety of Ali-Baba outfits in the video that launched his album *Monde Arabe* (Olomide 2004).

The fantastical nature of all this hardly needs to be underlined. J.B. may have fared worst, but in reality all the Congolese artists who have played Bercy have struggled to make the venue appear even remotely full, with the most successful artist, Werrason, perhaps half-filling the stadium and resorting to such expedients as advancing the podium to make the contact zone smaller.

This points to a wider phenomenon – live performance in Europe was cast as *the* mark of global stardom, and stars are frequently said to have 'convinced' or 'won over' Paris or London. But, in fact, concerts in Europe take place before entirely Lingalaphone audiences. And it is not hard to see why. Simply attending the concert involves understanding a number of conventions that are completely opaque to non-Congolese. Shortly after my arrival in Paris, Papa Wemba and his *orchestre* performed a concert in the Elysée Montmartre. This was widely advertised by a series of posters around Paris that announced the event as starting at 11 pm. Outside the DRC, Papa Wemba is probably the best known of all Congolese artists and at 11 pm, there were twenty to thirty people in the hall, all of whom were non-Congolese. By the time the music started to play, at 1 am, all these people had left, having paid €20 to stand around for over an hour doing nothing. Papa Wemba, dressed in a feathered hat and sky-blue poncho made by the Japanese designer Kassamoto, came on stage at 2 am and the concert ended at around 5 am.

This habit of announcing a starting time at least two hours before anything really started was, in my experience, universal and acted as a kind of filter – always understood by a Lingalaphone audience, it was always missed by everyone else. Even if this hurdle was cleared, there were several more. It was common for concerts that had been advertised not to take place, and attending one depended on a great deal of phoning around to ask those with an inside track whether it was really going to happen. While Wemba's concert took place in a relatively salubrious part of inner Paris, this was not always the case. Quite often concerts were staged in warehouses in dilapidated indus-trial zones dispersed in the distant reaches of the Paris suburbs. One learnt to press on past the insistence of locals that no such address existed, scanning passers-by, latching on to anyone who might know where a venue could be: 'Ask him, he must be Congolese; look at his shoes.' On into the dark, into remote business parks in the small hours, following distant sounds. More than once I found nothing at all, out past machinery, ship containers, drums with chemicals, out to where ploughed fields were visible beyond the tower blocks, a solitary blackbird singing as fingers of light began to appear in the sky.

If the concert was on, fights were invariably part of the entertainment. If one waited until near the end, one could almost guarantee a fight between women dating the same man or a flare-up among the *zoulous* – as the young, second-generation Congolese teenagers brought up in the Paris suburbs are known. At the concert/funeral wake for the singer Cele le Roi, bottles flew as various rival female associations tried to monopolize the event.

This rather closed Lingalaphone environment in which concerts took place has a corollary in contemporary Congolese musical taste. While the musicians of the 1960s and 1970s carried 'Congo music' all over Africa while remaining popular at home, in recent decades the Congolese have shunned artists who have obtained an international audience – like the Kanda Bongo Man, Nyboma or Awilo Longomba, who play a speeded-up version of Congolese popular music known as *soukous*. These artists enjoyed a brief vogue in the West and have been enduringly popular in many parts of Africa, but not at home and not among their own communities abroad. Papa Wemba, who did manage to attract both audiences, nevertheless performed a completely different style of music for Western music fans – a kind of synthpop that abjured the rhythmic and melodic complexity of his 'Congolese' music – and gave up on this style after a reasonably short time.

Among the Kinois and the Congolese diaspora, such 'soukous' music is despised. The very word *soukous* is emphatically rejected by Congolese artists themselves; indeed, it is used as a term of abuse. In one sense this is right – compare the work of *soukous* artist Kanda Bongo Man to Kinshasa favourites like Zaiko Langa Langa and it is easy to see that *soukous* is a lesser art form. It strips out the progression of melodic and rhythmic cycles, the complex polyphony, the poetry and pathos of the lyrics, the variety of dance styles. But at the same time, *soukous* is a term that people around the world might have heard of – and it would be the obvious marketing term for various related styles of Congolese music on a world stage. Just as confusing to the non-Congolese is the practice of naming a group in such a way as to indicate a genealogical link to earlier musical formations, a practice that results in a profusion of groups, all apparently called by a generic name[6] – Wenge el Paris, Wenge Kumbela, Wenge Musica BCBG 4X4, Wenge BCBG, Wenge Tonya Tonya, Wenge Maison Mère and Les Marquis de Maison Mère. This seems to me to indicate how local ideas about seniority and segmentation (see Kopytoff 1987; White 2008: 213–16) overwhelm any imaginative sympathy that might be directed towards a non-Congolese audience.

If, then, stars did not come to Europe to participate in a world of global show business, why then did they come? As with occupying European studios, money is clearly a big part of the story. While the big concerts at the Zenith and Bercy were dubious commercial endeavours – filling Bercy would require attendance by almost a quarter of the entire Congolese migrant population in France – other concerts generally made money[7] (see Chapter 4). Above all, an important concert could generate very serious amounts of *mabanga*.

Fifi Motema and Other Scenes from the Concert Potlatch

It is late December 2006 and Werrason and Wenge Maison Mère are performing in the Elysée Montmartre. Fifi Motema, a very large woman in her forties, is on stage giving cash to Werrason. She keeps on giving and giving – 'Fifi Motema! Fifi Motema! Fifi Motema!' – until euros bulge from his pockets, fill his fists and fall on the floor. Werrason does not deign to pick up these notes (which are snaffled by other performers), but offloads handfuls towards nearby musicians. Fifi is a famed 'scandalous beauty' who lives in Paris. She used to be romantically linked to Brigade, at one time *atalaku* with the *orchestre* Quartier Latin. At the time of the concert, Brigade had recently switched to Wenge Maison Mère, the *orchestre* of Werrasson, but his new position was far from secure and many Maison Mère fans thought he was not really committed to their cause. Her *mabanga* to Werrasson was probably meant to be interpreted as a gesture in support of her beau. If, on the face of it, this was an ingratiating gesture to the boss of her lover, it took place, and took effect, within a wider context where such prestations were not unusual.

During the later stages of any concert, there will be a continuous stream of patrons who stride onto the stage and press notes on the musicians, above all on the *président*. Those who have given money will then wait in the wings, where, during a successful concert, they will begin to outnumber and crowd out the musicians. In this winners' enclosure they will greet each other with exaggerated handshakes or simply stand, arms folded, showing off their designer clothes with (they hope) mesmerizing effect on the hoi polloi down below in the normal audience. *Mabanga* during a concert does not follow the set pattern of *mabanga* on record. The patron gives as much or as little as he likes, though (as noted earlier) giving an insufficient amount can be a humiliating experience for the patron. I once saw Koffi Olomide simply throw away a donation he considered too small.

For *sapeurs* from Congo Kinshasa, the concert in Europe represents probably the major venue for wearing and displaying of clothes – the notion that one must *kotelema* or 'stand up' in an effective outfit is repeated in numerous songs. And other displays of expensive adornment and style are common. Very large amounts of expensive cologne are worn and Cuban cigars and bottles of Scotch whisky are also very common accoutrements. The *président d'orchestre* will generally come on stage wearing a new outfit. This outfit is bought for the *président* by a particular patron whose name is circulated. In general the outfit will be a hugely expensive item – I know, for example, that the Paris-based nightclub owner José Kongolo gave Papa Wemba a Yohji Yamamoto suit worth €10,000 before one of his concerts.

Although largesse on this scale awaited some musicians who travelled to Europe, simply identifying a financial motive, as we noted earlier, does not explain the structures within which wealth was understood or desired. Stars came to Europe because it was profitable, but this profit should be seen as part of a series of ritual accomplishments embedded in a set of narratives demonstrating the criterion of relative social 'weight'. In this sense, the vocabulary of international venues and global stars was not insincere, despite the apparent lack of consideration given to non-Congolese audiences. Places like Bercy and stars like Michael Jackson or Céline Dion were markers of rank within larger conceptual schemes related to the potlatch. And concerts are, indeed, important as sites of potlatch.

Conclusion

Congolese music is highly absorptive of external influences, but these are set within what appear to be fiercely local projects. Noting such selective appropriations and local/global interactions has formed an important part of anthropological research in the last two decades (Miller 1995; Hannerz 1997; Geschiere and Meyer 1999). Particularly relevant here is an article by Barber and Waterman (1995), which shows how Nigerian Fuji music pulls together diffuse fragments referencing a huge range of different cultural signifiers. But they argue that while the cosmopolitan references are indicative of diverse cultural flows, they are not evidence of a new or 'postmodern' sensibility. Instead, they point to how the fragmentary nature of the Fuji performance relates to the disjointed and aphoristic structure of *Oriki*, an earlier poetic form in Yoruba.

In an earlier work, Waterman suggests that forms taken by the contemporary *àríyás* (parties in Ibadan, where Jújù music is played and forms of theatrical dispersal take place) 'provide evidence for the tenacity … of deep Yoruba images of the social order' (1990: 178). In a similar fashion Friedman (2004) argues that the practices of *sapeurs* from Brazzaville should be understood as the expression of an older Kongo cosmology, where the flow of prestige goods from the outside was theorized by locals as a way to capture the flow of 'life force' within a hierarchical political tradition.

Yet, important as Waterman's insights (1990) have been in formulating my approach, there is something problematic about this notion of a 'deep tradition' as a constant current below the surface effusion of events. For one thing, it causes the authors to ignore the discontinuities that they themselves record. Waterman notes that the greater importance and ostentation of *àríyás* is a product of the Nigerian oil boom, something that, to me, suggests that the deployment of 'Yoruba images of the social order' is not 'deep' or even 'tenacious', but fairly contingent – a mode of action that assumes greater or lesser importance in dialectical relationship to political and economic events.

The point is brought out nicely when studying the historical researches of Congolese anthropologist Justin Gandoulou on *sapeurs*. Gandoulou relates how the *sapeurs* grew out of an earlier youth movement of the 1950s called the *existos*, who spent their time dressing like Sartre and hanging around Brazzaville smoking, posing and trying to pick up girls. In Gandoulou's account, the passage from *existos* to *sapeurs* reveals a mental chasm between the generations. In bemused comments by former *existos*, the *sapeurs* appear to be almost as exotic to them as they are to us, suggesting that ancient cultural difference might not be the main issue:

> One can follow fashion, but not blindly … today the youth like to dress expensively and there is too much that is fantastical … and they live beyond their means. They exchange and lend clothes – that is not done! We worked to acquire them [clothes], we didn't steal them. (Former *existo*, quoted in Gandoulou 1989a: 39, my translation)

As Gandoulou notes (1989a: 38–41), these 'elders' express this in entirely moral and cultural terms, ignoring the different socioeconomic conjuncture that confronts the young. The *existos* used plenty of 'local appropriation' of global flows, but the appropriation took place in a context where, at least for what was a relatively privileged sector of the urban population, certain assumptions about wage labour, economic growth, price stability and other economic 'facts of life' could be made. In this context, the *existos'* behaviour, while colourful, was undergirded by an understanding of the meaning of wealth and consumption that is commensurate with our own. For an increasing section of young people in Congo-Brazzaville and even more dramatically still in Congo-Zaïre, beset with vertiginous economic decline, the previous generations' understandings of wealth and investment ceased to make any sense at all – it underwent an epochal change. In this context, Congolese youth created forms that drew on earlier 'moral matrices' (De Boeck 1998) and modes of action that had not been entirely forgotten – the hunt, the division of spoils, notions of blessing and luck, the potlatch (De Boeck 1998; Bazenguissa-Ganga 1999).

But the discontinuity with the past is also clear. The forms of 'wealth in people' so created often drew on the mixed, 'colonial lexicon' discussed by Hunt (1999) and avoided the rituals of an earlier lineage economy, such as initiation (traditionally understood), childbirth, funeral wakes or bride-wealth negotiations. And, in any case, as De Boeck's (1998) essay shows, pointing to an affinity to an ancient political tradition cannot tell us why these modes of action suddenly became central, having been marginal before. To understand this, we must look at dialectical relations of ideas and material realities. As production declined, a nexus of economic and ideological factors bound musicians and public ever more tightly to a series of rituals and transactions connected to the potlatch, rituals that were ever more intense and ever more impenetrable to outsiders, and that were ultimately obsessed with the reaction of the Kinois to their exploits.

This forced Congolese in Europe into a rather strong 'either/or' set of choices – whether to throw in their lot with an economy of potlatch, fixated on Kinshasa, or with the wider societies in which they found themselves in Europe. In Chapter 5 of their classic study *Congo-Paris*, Bazenguissa-Ganga and MacGaffey argue that the behaviour of the more potlatch-minded Congolese migrants expressed their active, oppositional encounter with French society (2000: 157).[8] Loath as I am to part company with such a great work of ethnographic writing, my chapter has shown that this was not the case; these practices were formed in relation to Central African society and contained little that was consciously oppositional to the West. Indeed, the rather solipsistic set of rituals they were engaged in demanded a determined lack of engagement with the reality of their surroundings in Europe, to which they preferred a highly fantastical and largely glorificatory set of stories about *mikili*, precisely because of the cachet these narratives granted them 'back home'.

As I will show in more detail in subsequent chapters, participating in the potlatch demanded not only a suspension of disbelief in the more improbable aspects of their ideology, but also the stamina to stay up all night in bars and concerts, dispensing wealth in a way that was appalling to anyone engaged in wage labour. Conversely, those involved in wage labour quite often eschewed Congolese identity altogether – keen music fans would avoid concerts, even going as far as pretending not to speak Lingala to avoid unwanted embroilments. Again, I must reluctantly disagree with the thesis of Bazenguissa-Ganga and MacGaffey's classic study. Those who saw themselves in relation to the actually existing European society were precisely those who *did not* participate in the transnational rituals of potlatch.

This prompts a brief reflection on some wider discussions in sociology about 'globalization' and modernity. Arjun Appadurai (1996) has argued that 'flux' and 'disjuncture' are the keys to understanding contemporary social realities. Sociologist John Urry (2000), in a similar vein, has propounded that we should do 'sociology without society', as all fixed relations melt into the air of constant movement. This chapter suggests the opposite. The forms of transnational link followed a relatively restricted set of connections, and this was a tale of *decreasing* flows of information and trade. As Rey (1971) argued, the social efficacy of the external is a product of its rarity – it is the low productivity from within this social formation, and the scarcity of connections from without, that make the few points of articulation that do exist so important in social reproduction.

Notes

1. Mastering includes various post-production processes such as hiss reduction and correction of minor errors.
2. As many readers will know, Eboa Lotin was a Cameroonian singer songwriter of the 1970s – one of the rare musicians from another African country to become popular

with the Congolese. Werrason gave Eboa this name because he said that Eboa (Mark 2) had a similar vocal tone.

3. This may appear to contradict the argument made about 'familial' connections between patron and musician, but this is not the case – such a combination of financial obligation and perceptions of theft are quite typical of Congolese families.

4. Both Filip De Boeck (1998) and Remy Bazenguissa-Ganga (1999) have noted the use of the concept of *kovivre* to denote the kinds of ostentatious consumption and largesse in the cultures of Kinshasa and Brazzaville respectively.

5. The analysis in this chapter is essentially synchronic. For ease of understanding and following convention, I express myself here primarily in the 'ethnographic present', describing the system as it 'worked' between the mid 1990s and the mid 2000s. As the analysis presented in other chapters shows, the 'system' described here fell apart, and musicians and politicians found it increasingly difficult to negotiate access to Kinshasa and Europe.

6. Or Zaiko Langa Langa, Langa Langa Stars, Zaiko Langa Langa Nkolo Mboka, Zaiko Langa Langa Familia Dei or Grand Zaiko Wa Wa.

7. And even when they lost money, it was not the musicians who bore the loss.

8. My discussion of Bazenguissa-Ganga and MacGaffey's work here relates specifically to the argument made in Chapter 6 of their book. At many other points in *Congo-Paris*, it appears that they are speaking about 'resistance' directed elsewhere – either to the regimes in the two Congos or to a more general resistance to global power structures. This is a more complex issue and will be discussed in Chapter 6.

– Chapter 4 –

RIGHTS, PIRACY AND PRODUCERS

$\mathcal{C}$

This chapter concentrates on artists' rights payments, piracy and the decline in professional producers that has been apparent in the Congolese music scene over the last thirty years. Earlier accounts of the Congolese recording industry (see Ewens 1994; Stewart 2001; Tsambu-Bulu 2005; White 2008) conclude that piracy and economic decline must be important factors in explaining the fall in record sales, and this book does not disagree with this. In this period record sales have collapsed, both in Congo and in the wider African markets. This collapse corresponds with a period in which purchasing power fell and a series of technologies made unlicensed reproduction of music easier. But beyond these very general truths, locating how and why these factors were important, and whom they were important to, is not so straightforward. Rather than assuming familiarity, we need to set piracy in the context of political and economic life in the DRC.

The Thing and its Double

It is very common to examine the way in which social life 'works' in Kinshasa through the prism of failure. And nowhere is this temptation stronger than in state institutions, including those that administer copyright, or indeed 'fail' to do so. In one sense this is correct. In many areas of life, the Congolese aspire to state institutions that work in the way that is designated, and it is both patronizing and politically dubious to claim that the current state of affairs is not a failure for the citizen in some very fundamental sense. But as a way to understand how society actually proceeds, this prism of failure is actively misleading:

Faced with words and interactions that no longer correspond to the social interweave as we tend to conceptualise and experience it, one becomes aware that it is futile to explain some of the processes currently taking place in Congolese society by means of the standard vocabularies. (De Boeck and Plissart 2004: 34)

Piracy, Artists' Rights and Paternalistic Practice

Bob White's discussion (2008: 82–96) provides a useful starting point for looking at the DRC's music industry. Drawing on original re-search and on the work of Stewart (2001), White puts in place some essential parts of the story. He recounts how music sold heavily in the first half of the 1970s and how those sales were undermined progressively from the second half of that decade onwards. He cor-rectly states that easily pirated tape technology was just one of many factors causing that decline. His account is important for linking a general move towards the 'informal' to events in the music industry. He sketches in some important areas, such as piracy and economic decline, and handles the poor quantitative data available judiciously.

But good and useful as the works of both Stewart and White are, I think they rely too heavily on 'common sense' and on the ways that actors represent themselves. A closer inspection of the Congolese cultural industries, especially in the light of what has happened in the intervening years, presents a scene where common sense is con-founded, and the protagonists do not always perceive full disclosure to be in their interests. In this way the changes in the recording indus-try draw our attention to wider problems in assessing the nature of African bureaucratic forms.

Interpreting what may really be going on is complicated by the fact that cultural industry professionals, if specifically asked, will tend to concur with narratives of decline. I, like White, found many music professionals expressing frustration about piracy and, just as frequently, about the absence of 'serious' or 'professional' producers (see White 2008: 93) who could help to finance and organize musical performances and recordings. These stories are undoubtedly based in something real – piracy and a falling away of professional producers have indeed been immensely significant. But the way that such nar-ratives tend to work is to present the impact of these changes so as to make them appear as 'shocks': external events that befell musicians, rather like a rise in the price of petrol or a natural disaster. This char-acterization is deeply misleading. In reality, the role that musicians have played in processes such as piracy or the decline of professional producers is much more intimate and complicit, and much more of a piece with wider political economic processes in Zaïre/Congo. In this story musicians were victims, but also agents and beneficiaries. In understanding it, we need to unpick a series of complex and sometimes perverse jural and political economic imperatives.

The relevance of all this for Congolese music is that piracy ceases to be a clear point around which to base analysis and becomes itself a puzzle. We cannot assume that what piracy 'means' is simply the obverse of Western intellectual property. Such an assumption universalizes structures of law and administration that should be understood as historically contingent. In the case of Congo, artists never received 'rights' payments – if by this we mean a predictable percentage of official sales paid as an entitlement – even when record sales were very high.

Until the mid 1970s, local sales appear to have grown in most years. White (2008: 83) quotes a record executive estimating sales of five million units a year in Kinshasa alone in the first half of the decade. Talks I had with various record executives in Kinshasa painted a similarly rosy picture of the industry around this time. One informant recounted to me how, within the middle-class Kinois milieu in which he grew up, having your own copy of a record by an *orchestre* that you supported was considered a central aspect of being a fan. As he recounted, this could mean that siblings within a household would buy separate copies of the same record. Record sales to the rest of Africa were also dominated by Congolese releases and, in Africa generally, music sales were very significant during this period – Stewart quotes a Philips record company executive saying that: 'In the 1970s Africa made up 40 per cent of our sales' (2001: 321). While the good times declined in Zaïre somewhat earlier, sales in the rest of Africa seem to have held up into the 1980s.

Yet during this period, payments were routinely kept from authors and performers by politically powerful people. People involved in the rights body Soneca, the president of the musicians' union, producers, promoters, heads of the record labels, and the leaders of *orchestres* themselves were all very widely alleged to have made important deductions from what 'should' have been artists' income. This retention of income had generational aspects. Powerful musicians who were of the same age cohort as the politicians who took power at independence – like Verkys, Tabu Ley and Franco – had a store of political capital that facilitated their appropriations at the expense of the next generation of musicians. This is not to say that artists did not benefit from successful compositions – money (filtered through several hands) was paid to them and they would quite often get expensive presents or additional envelopes of money from pleased superiors. But payment was always cast by superiors as a generous and somewhat arbitrary *ex gratia* donation rather than an entitlement.

The purchase of cars for musicians was a recurrent theme in conversations about this time. Both Stewart (2001: 272) and White (2008: 83) also recount stories about this, and in the difference in emphasis between them, we can see the moral ambiguities of such relationships. In White's story, a producer recounts the purchase of cars for musicians as a sign of his generosity in the good old days, while, in Stewart's story, the musician (Pamelo Mounk'a) gets a sympathetic car dealer to charge a car purchase to a nonpaying producer's account.

A set of conflicts over the moral order underlay the appropriation. Joseph Kabasele, a man of high principle who refused to compose a song for Mobutu, was nevertheless particularly notorious for appropriating monies from artists beneath him. When, inevitably, this led to the departure of his talented underlings, he saw this as a betrayal (see Mpisi 2003: 157–63). One of his close friends expressed to me the view that the artists who had left him had not appreciated the amount that he had spent on them in terms of transport, outfits and other outgoings. Setting aside the fact that this assessment of expenses is almost certainly generous to Kabasele (see Dibango 1995; Mpisi 2003), the fact that he felt a right to decide how he spent money derived from their compositions merely underscores the fact that income was distributed according to paternalistic rather than liberal/ possessive individual logic.

A second, even more effective way in which a *président* may appropriate the works of underlings is by registering a composition in his name. It is clear that this has gone on for generations. Stories are rife, but again Kabasele provides a good example because others have openly accused him in print (Dibango 1995: 62–65). Tabu Ley's song 'Pesa le tout' ('Give Everything') was listed as a joint composition, for which Kabasele would receive half the money and half the glory. In this case it was particularly ironic, as the song contained a veiled dig at the fact that Kabasele was always away from the capital on business and that during these absences, the other members of the *orchestre* could not work or make any money (see Mpisi 2003: 158–59).

In Kabasele's day the main advantage to be derived from appropriation, apart from garnering prestige as the composer of a beautiful song, would have been the possibility of collecting rights payments.

For those in authority, this form of appropriation was preferable. Where a song was not registered in the appropriator's name, appropriation was possible – indeed, it was the norm – but clearly there was pressure to give the composer at least a part of the money. This way of doing things not only granted prestige to the appropriator, but also denied the subordinate artist any kind of moral purchase. This kind of appropriation continues up to the present day – though nowadays the financial stake is in being able to claim the *dedicace*, not the royalty. Then, as now, it was almost always presented as some kind of tribute due to the *président*, in return for a certain, often rather metaphysical, 'munificence'.

Such arrangements are typical of societies where patronage is an important principle; they are part of the dynamics of the wider society. De Boeck (1996), for example, recounts how Mobutu was able to create a sense of debt among professors at the University of Kinshasa by buying each of them a car, converting wealth that was rooted in theft into a sense of obligation. While wider elements of this ideology are explored in subsequent chapters, it is important at this point to note that, even during a time of plenty, issues of authorship and power were treated in a way that would be unfamiliar to Western cultural producers.

Nevertheless, it seems that in the 1970s and for some of the 1980s, Soneca continued to bear some relation to a Western rights body, in that it paid out some money – albeit to the 'wrong' people – and administered reciprocal arrangements with other rights bodies around the world. At some point in the 1980s or early 1990s, this seems to have broken down altogether. Monies paid into Soneca by local record producers or by other federations simply remained within the organization. This was a breakdown typical of the period, as Soneca employees, like all other public officials, would have seen their incomes eroded to well below the poverty line by inflation and the nonpayment of salaries. Elvis Nkunku, who played guitar for the *orchestré* Empire Bakuba, one of the most popular groups in Africa in the late 1980s, remembers the moment when this became apparent to him:

> I remember Pepe Kalle [*président d'orchestre* of Empire Bakuba] went to Soneca and they said they had nothing for us – at the time we had had some big hits in West Africa – Pepe [who was a large man] picked up the table and threw it at the wall.

Other copyright federations around the world seem to have reached a similar realization a little later. As Soneca ceased to pass on rights payments for the sales or diffusion of foreign artists in Zaïre/Congo, it was cast out of the global federation of rights bodies. This meant that sister organizations ceased to send in payments for the sales of Congolese artists abroad. This process affected everyone, including the big fish, and through the 1980s and 1990s, all the prominent artists cut their losses with Soneca and registered for copyright in France or Belgium, where at least their non-Zaïrian royalties would be paid.

Among the rank-and-file musicians that I spoke to in the second half of the 2000s, none was registered with any rights body. What was surprising was that even those who had travelled to Europe several times had not registered. This was in part because very few songs would be registered in their names – as we will explore in Chapter 8, the *président d'orchestre* will often insist that compositions by others be registered in his name. But I think it also indicates how little attention was paid to royalty income by musicians in the 2000s and how little experience younger Congolese had in dealing with Western-style officialdom. As for Soneca, it has not handed anyone a royalty payment for the best part of two decades, but continues to deduct 'rights' from producers as a percentage of sales. This lead to the very widespread allegation, made to me by well-connected insiders, that production outlets underdeclare their sales in order to pay less to Soneca.

To anyone familiar with the Congolese scene, this story of institutional collapse and subsequent undead existence will not be a surprise; indeed, the story of Soneca is that of the state writ small. In the 1970s Soneca drew on the apparatus of the modern state to distribute monies, albeit according to principles that were more 'paternalistic' than 'legal-rational'. By the middle of the 1980s, however, the severity of the economic contraction had meant that state institutions were being used in ways that bore no relation at all to the activities of ostensibly equivalent institutions in other countries:

> Why is a building called a national bank, university, state department, hospital, or school when the activities which take place in it cannot be given the standard meanings and realities covered by those words? (De Boeck in De Boeck and Plissart 2004: 34)

More Piracy – Intimacies of Theft

Just as the copyright body in Kinshasa is an important agent in the appropriation of copyright fees, so it is widely alleged that artists commonly pirate their own works. *Présidents d'orchestres* are said to have obtained master copies of their own recordings prior to release and to have used these to distribute pirate copies onto the market. This accusation came from a wide range of insiders in the music industry – experienced producers, several of the top arrangers of Congolese music, and Congolese musicians themselves. A sound engineer in Paris told me how nowadays he would only ever give a copy of the master to the producer, as he had had so many problems in the past with officially unreleased albums that were suddenly available all over Africa. As a contact at the French copyright body Sacem said to me, apropos this piracy: 'The question almost always arises of who owns the master.'

An understanding of the financial accords between the producer and *président* can shed some light on this. In the case of a major artist, the producer will pay the *président* an upfront fee, *le cachet d'artiste*. This is the case for a live production and for a recording. For a recording, this will be paid in three *tranches*: the first when the deal is signed, the second when he enters the studio and the third when the work is delivered. Under a Western system, the artists would receive both authorial royalties and performing rights on any works sold. As we have seen, the payment of copyright has always been problematic in Congo and it is apparent that since the 1990s, such fees have entirely failed to reach authors and performers.

Thus, the *président* had no direct financial stake in sales or in public broadcasts of his music in the DRC as, aside from his *cachet d'artiste*, he would receive no further payments on the work. Paradoxically, therefore, on sales in the DRC, it was only by pirating his own works that he would receive any direct income from music sales. In the wider African market, where rights bodies still maintain reciprocal arrangements, sales of legal copies were so low that the *président* was unlikely to see much in the way of authorial rights payments anyway. Thus, a *président* will benefit from pirating his own disc in other parts of Africa in much the same way that all pirates benefit – he does not pay production costs and can price his editions more cheaply than his producer. Nevertheless, explanations premised on such 'bottom line' rationality feel a little bit strained. Surely the dislocating effect of such behaviour must have outweighed the gains?

The state of the industry has undoubtedly caused a retreat of professional actors from the cultural industries. This retreat can be seen over several stages: into the 1990s, global distribution for major groups like Wenge Musica BCBG, Viva la Musica or Quartier Latin was undertaken by major French-based record labels, above all Sonodisk. Like most Western labels, they retreated from the

African market as they saw sales shrink. The behaviour of *présidents d'orchestres* may have contributed to this. I was told that an executive of French West African origin, working for a major label, struck a deal with one *président d'orchestre* to release 'real fakes' – discs made in the same factory but kept off the books – and divide the profits between them. I have no way of proving such allegations, but they were made by a credible source. Certainly similar things do seem to have happened – Gary Stewart's book (2001) contains an allegation from the head of a French record label who discovered that a factory in Gabon, contracted to reproduce works by Congolese artists, was producing copies of the discs for both the official and the pirate markets.

After major labels withdrew from the African market, the big artists were handled outside Congo by a series of small operations mostly based in Paris, such as Jamil of Sonima Music or Mr Simon of Simon Music. Gradually more and more of these figures have got out. Low sales were the backdrop to these decisions, but often one senses that working with musicians as unstable business partners also played a role. Producers routinely lost eye-watering sums as musicians stole money or pulled out of commitments without warning. I met the Johannesburg-based producer 'Ntemba' Kayembe the day after he had lost $100,000 when a prominent musician had pulled out of a concert at the very last minute. Kayembe was not about to withdraw from the business, but nevertheless I had the sense of a man winded by the affair.

There does seem to have been some kind of retreat by 'professional' producers, but it is my belief that we should be wary of interpreting this as a symptom of a wider decline in the Congolese cultural industries, as is argued by various authors (like Tchebwa 1996; Stewart 2001; and White 2008: 94). Growth or decline, in what was an industry characterized by informal flows, can of course be hard to assess, but there are several indicators that this may be an incorrect reading. As we saw in the last chapter, Kinshasa had no functioning studios in the late 1980s, but by the mid 2000s there were three professional studios and innumerable home studios operating in the city. In a similar fashion, the number of television channels grew from one at the start of the 1990s to nearly fifty by the mid 2000s. This growth of television stations is relevant to our study, first because during the period in which I did fieldwork, it was via television (or in the diaspora via DVDs) that most people consumed music and second because it attests to a general growth in the cultural industries. And while some people in the music business appear to be losing money and dropping out, others – notably the *présidents d'orchestres* – appear to have grown very rich indeed (see the next chapter for details).

I doubt that all the bad faith shown within the music industry was truly rational, and some of the behaviour I saw seemed gratuitous, as if something more important than mere calculation was involved. But what is clear is that the changes in the cultural industries have followed a pattern consistent with wider shifts in the mode of production. Those who sought to make money from the sale of physical units to a mass market became progressively less important. This was not really a shift from 'the market' to 'rent-seeking' because, as we have seen, monopolies secured by political connections were crucial even during the period where mass sales were the major source of gain. But there was a qualitative change: from capitalist forms of rent, based on the assumption of productive growth, to noncapitalist forms of rent, which were based in low and stable rates of production (see Brenner 1977). Capitalist rentiers face the twin imperatives of encouraging production and monopolizing what is produced. In noncapitalist systems, increases in production are not an option and the imperatives all point towards monopoly. In the next two chapters we will add flesh to this story of political-economic change, but the rest of this chapter will simply spell out in greater detail the conflict between senior musicians and their producers.

Producers, *Présidents*, Pinball Tables and Prudent Ways of Behaving

It is noon and I am at Studio Marcadet in Paris. The studio is full of musicians from Wenge Maison Mère, then the most popular *orchestre* in Congo. Adrien Mukiadi, one of the two producers on the album, has just punched through the plate-glass top of a pinball table with his bare fist. Why there is a pinball table in the studio I have no idea, but the reasons why Adrien wants to punch something are easier to discern. Adrien and his brother Papi Mukiadi run a security business in Paris. Longtime patrons of Wenge Maison Mère, they have decided to go into music production, calling themselves Le Duo d'Enfer. For their sins, many of the travails of the contemporary producer in the area of Congolese music have been inflicted upon them. The brothers have booked the studio in a block for the next month, from 10 am to 6 pm, seven days a week. The studio rental is €400 per day and the studio engineer charges €80 per day. Yet the musicians will rarely arrive before noon. Or rather, as Jean Marc, the studio engineer observes: 'Often someone will arrive at ten but it is never the person who is actually recording that day.' And the wasting of time that happens as the day unwinds is quite phenomenal. Hangers-on of the *orchestre*, known in Lingala as *staff*,[1] come and chew the fat, laugh and distract everyone.

No one appears to be in charge, either to ensure a reasonable work rate or to coordinate the production. Wenge Maison Mère had hired an arranger, Sec Biddens, and conceivably it was within his remit to direct the artistic arrangements of the album. He did give it considerable time at the earlier stages of recording, constructing reasonably polished *maquettes* – musical sketches – in his own less high-tech studio. But, having passed these *maquettes* on to the studio engineer, he seems to have lost interest in the production. He is re-cording several other albums late into the night and never arrives in the studio before 1 pm. The *chef d'orchestre*,[2] Flamme Kapaya, is a little more hands-on, but often he appears more like 'one of the boys' in this group of young men and he lacks the authority to make the musicians set to work in earnest. Besides, he has problems of his own. He is trying to sort out residence papers in France and is secretly con-templating leaving the *orchestre*. He often arrives later than the other musicians. The presence of the *président d'orchestre*, Werrason, in the studio makes a very appreciable difference to the work rate. He sends a frisson through the assembled company and everyone sets about the task with vigour when he is there, but he is very rarely there. He is working on a solo album, financed by another producer. Adrien and Papi have repeatedly asked that Werrason be present, but to no avail. So Adrien has plenty of reasons to feel angry.

The blow that shatters the pinball table is triggered when Adrien learns that Wenge Maison Mère has entered into contracts with other producers for a large number of live performances in France, Belgium and Switzerland. These performances will mean that at least one and probably two days of prebooked studio time will pass completely unused each week. The incident illustrates the kind of conflict of in-terest that arises between the producers, the *président d'orchestre* and the musicians. Such conflicts occur in almost all aspects of music pro-duction. Indeed, live performances are even more prone to disputes between producer and *président*.

The magazine *H+M* is produced in Paris and is read both by the diaspora and by sections of the elite in Kinshasa. The March 2007 edition contains a story entitled 'Koffi Olomide: le kleptomane de la RDC?', in which the producer and patron Buya Mayola directly accuses Koffi Olomide of stealing the proceeds from a concert he produced in Belgium.

> BM: I organised his concert in Brussels. He stole the takings after the concert and he escaped with the money from the concert. This inhuman act has pushed me to speak the truth. Koffi Olomide IS A THIEF [capitals in original].

> H+M: He has dedicated a beautiful song to you. You should know his way of behaving. You have spent a long time together. Why did you lack prudence with him?

> BM: I did not forget his behaviour. I know his habits and I was prudent. I didn't think he would run away from me in less than five minutes. He was asleep and he was in his pyjamas ... he had been snoring for a little less than five minutes. ('Koffi Olomide, le Kleptomane de la RDC?', H+M *Magazine*, March 2007: 34–35, my translation)

As the questions put to Koffi imply, such an act is not unprecedented. Indeed, the interviewer seems chiefly offended by the idea that someone would leave Koffi alone with money. And most aspects of the case are not uncommon. Accusations of financial irregularities in dealings between the *président d'orchestre* and the producer are legion. Many things are striking about the article, not least the fact that it appeared at all, which underlines how recourse to the law – either by Buya for theft or by Koffi for defamation – was clearly out of the question for both parties.

Congolese music production would seem to abound in alleged offences – breaches of contract, theft and defamation, to name but a few. Yet I know of no case where parties to a contract have successfully brought a prosecution. There are several causes for this, but all of them are linked to the jural informalism in which social actors in this milieu operate. In Kinshasa the important *présidents d'orchestres* have considerable powers to stretch the law so long as they remain attached to powerful patrons. For example, one of the big *présidents d'orchestres* is well known to have sprung a musician from Makala prison where he was being held on a manslaughter charge, after a young man in his entourage died of a drugs overdose. Another *président* who was subject to an arrest warrant for a charge of raping a minor in France (admittedly the charges were linked to an asylum claim and were subsequently dropped) was able to avoid extradition by remaining in the DRC.

In Europe all the actors are often too involved in illegal activities themselves to risk involving the police. But even when a producer appears keen to pursue a musician through the courts, the mutual legal obligations have been so weakly established to begin with that a subsequent prosecution appears impossible. Contracts are signed, but these documents appear almost entirely ceremonial. Take the example of the Paris-based Cameroonian producer Mr Simon, who in the period 2006–7 opened legal proceedings against Claris Musique, a company linked to J.B. Mpiana, and also claimed to be about to initiate proceedings against Ferre Gola, Bill Clinton Kalonji and Jus d'Eté Molopwe for breaches of contract, and against Koffi Olomide for contracting Ferre Gola when, Mr Simon argued, Ferre was already under contract to him. All of these proceedings were abandoned by Mr Simon before they reached trial. Ferre subsequently left Koffi Olomide, who, having paid Ferre a large 'signing on' fee (reputedly $10,000), seemed minded to use the law to enforce his contract. But few were surprised when this action also folded; the contract that broke Mr Simon's contract, it seems, was equally worthless. According to an informant involved in the case, Ferre's contract was shown to a French lawyer, who burst out laughing as he read the document.

Conclusion

Commentators and musicians point to the impact of pirates on Congolese music. They are correct to identify this as a major issue – piracy had a great impact on the recording industry. But such discourse cannot be taken at face value. Rank-and-file musicians probably never received 'rights' payments as such even before piracy became an issue, while *présidents d'orchestres* are positively implicated in piracy and the destruction of the copyright system. Likewise, the absence of professional producers was not a force of nature that visited itself upon the cultural industries, but a consequence of processes in which the more powerful musicians were active participants.

At the start of this chapter we cautioned against using the prism of 'failure' to understand what happened to the music industry. This was in part a restatement of an old anthropological principle – searching for the internal rules by which a society 'works' rather than judging it a failure according to an external standard. In this way we have penetrated the logic of state bodies and musical organizations. In some broader sense we could connect this to more general theories of African politics that point to a 'shadow state' that exists behind a legal rational façade (Bayart 1993; Reno 1998) and that 'works', albeit according to a different and disturbing logic (Chabal and Daloz

1999). Yet, as we will explore in the following chapter, this imputes a unity of purpose to a social processes that were, in reality, utterly fragmented.

Alongside their insipient functionalism, another problem with the kind of 'Africa works' interpretations given above is that they can read like an endorsement of a social situation, when in fact most locals find that situation hateful. One of the ways to avoid such glibness is to pay attention to winners and losers – those for whom the system did and did not 'work'. The social processes described in this chapter led to outcomes that no one entirely intended, but some people, above all the leaders of some popular *orchestres*, were more powerful than others in the interventions they were able to make, and the current shape of the industry reflects their interests at the expense of others. Such power differences form the central focus of the next chapter.

Notes

1. This is separate from the word 'staffeur', which for my informants meant free spender, or the related Lingala verb *Kostaffer*, to spend freely, as in *tostaffer danger!* – we spent loads! Pype (2006) also lists *staffeur* as a word for a middle-class kid in Kinshasa. Staff as a noun means entourage, as in *staff ango*. Interestingly, the term *manager* is used in a similar way to refer to all kinds of sundry loafers. I am unclear as to whether this is because hanging around is seen as a kind of profession or if the words have simply passed into general use with little regard to their English meanings.
2. Also the lead guitarist.

– Chapter 5 –

THE *PRÉSIDENT* AS GATEKEEPER
Patronage as a Class Relationship

❧

This chapter looks at the unequal relationship between the *président d'orchestre* and his musicians. This set of unequal social relations is interesting in its own right, but it is also indicative of much wider social trends. In particular, it tells us something about the characteristic forms of class inequality that exist in this society. The kinds of class division we will look at here are not those that are familiar under industrial capitalism, where monopolizing capital and controlling the increasing productivity of an industrial society are the major imperatives. Here activities I term 'gatekeeping' and 'control of social reproduction' are crucial.

As the Zaïrian economy shrank, the activity of gatekeeping – obtaining fees through acting as the point of entry for resources or opportunities – became ever more important in the exercise of social power. Such gatekeeping was interwoven with the control of social reproduction. Social reproduction here, as was the case in precolonial Central Africa, concerns the progression to a socially recognized adulthood or, conversely being held back in the status of an 'empty man' (*mutu pamba*), who is eternally destined to have his labour and his creative potential denied. As we have seen in previous chapters, social reproduction in contemporary Kinshasa revolves around being able to produce and distribute various Western consumer goods during certain rather theatrical ritual encounters. Thus, control of access to the outside became a powerful mechanism of social control.

Présidents d'orchestres were a good example of this trend. Using a wide repertoire of techniques, from simple contacts with patrons to people-smuggling and withholding passports, the *président* did his best to turn increasing scarcity and the ever-stronger role of migration in social reproduction to his advantage. But he did not have everything his own way – this was a highly contested process and this chapter will also detail how *présidents* struggled to maintain their position, against the resistance of subordinates.

Class in Africa and in the DRC

It has often been argued that class can only really exist in industrial societies, where the bourgeoisie and the proletariat are dominant. In Africa, and above all in Congo/Zaïre, where these classes were never in the majority, class is generally thought to be unimportant, outside of a few select settings (for example, Cooper 2002; see also Freund 2013 for a summary of arguments). Inasmuch as such a point of view is argued for (as opposed to simply assumed), this is put in terms of the supposed incompatibility between patronage-dispensing intermediaries and social class. 'Vertical' factions, so it is said, exclude the 'horizontal' solidarities of class (for example, Scott 1969). Such a position has also been bolstered by a very careless and inaccurate reading of earlier Marxist anthropology,[1] which is used rhetorically to suggest that an interest in social class is, *a priori*, an interest in impersonal 'structure', which eschews the study of intermediaries, empirical detail or the human scale (James 2011).

And yet only the most prejudiced observer of Kinshasa (or indeed many other African cities) could deny the importance of social class. Anyone who does not pick up at least some of the class-based differences in styles of dress and speech, locations of residence, occupation and the rest has not observed the city, or the wider DRC, in any detail, as plenty of non-Marxist scholars have noted (e.g. Schatzberg 1980; Pype 2007). Nor is this a question of discounting local representations – indigenous taxonomies of class are widespread (see also Nzongola-Ntalaja 1970).

A somewhat more complex point concerns the kinds of conceptual oppositions – class versus patronage being the crucial one – that are embedded in the 'anti-class' argument outlined above. But this supposed incompatibility between class and patronage contains no basis – patronage ties are often the *medium* through which class is realized. As I will show in this chapter, patronage implies coercive monopolistic control (gatekeeping) – no one needs a patron when you can get it by yourself. Retaining such control relies on the help of others who stand in a similar position vis-à-vis the resource in question. In this context, 'clientelistic' economic practices rely on two distinct forms of prestation. One kind is generous and advantageous and is given to those who are within the same class, while the other kind is paltry and enfeuding, and is given to those outside the class.

Historical Trajectories of Gatekeeping

Dupré and Rey (1980) argued that in the more stratified parts of pre-colonial West-Central Africa, above all on the lower Congo, a class of 'elders' was dominant. This dominance was based in their rights over the labour of others – slaves of both sexes, most women, and male 'cadets' – dependants who were held in various states of social immaturity. These elders did not appear to have very strong control of the means of production – land was plentiful and the chief factor of production was the labour of the young. They nevertheless managed to enforce their dominance via their control over 'social reproduction'. This was effected through exchanges in prestige goods. Such exchanges determined the destinies of slaves, women and cadets, and were pivotal in allocating labour between corporate groups. The prestige goods were obtained from European merchants at the coast in return for various commodities – including slaves, ivory and rubber – through chains of exchange monopolized by elders. Thus, via 'articulating' between the 'capitalist mode of production' and their own 'lineage mode', the elders were also able to control the surpluses others produced, extracting tribute or labour from subaltern groups by manipulating an ideology of descent and holding out the promise of social advancement to a select few.

Dupré and Rey probably overestimated the stability of precolonial forms of social stratification and overstressed the idea of 'the lineage'. This was at the expense of other, much wilder, more unstable exchanges, which were tied to a network of funerary, jural and therapeutic ritual (see Trapido 2016). And, whatever its previous status, in the contemporary context the lineage is no longer the locus of significant social power. But with the collapse of the centralized state controlled by post-independence ruling classes, a new class – what I term a 'gatekeeper class' – was able to maintain some grip on production via its (very partial) control of certain quite precise forms of exchange.

My use of the term 'gatekeeper' in this context relates to its use by Cooper (2002) to describe the colonial and immediate postcolonial period. In such 'gatekeeper states', power was exercised via control of a capital city through which loans, aid and the resources of the interior had to pass. The model of the state Cooper describes came under strain in the 1980s, when many economies in Africa began to contract. In Zaïre, where the contraction was particularly serious, there was a particularly serious fragmentation of power – in place of a single gate, which was controlled at the apex by a state elite skimming rent from industrial enclaves, numerous smaller 'gates' proliferated.

The system was still hierarchical and violent, and the capital retained much importance, but power was much more diffuse and uncertain. Control of these gates, as in precolonial times, was dependent not just on connections to the outside and on being the beneficiary of rents from foreign owned industrial enclaves, but also on extracting the labour of underlings in various noncapitalist ways. At the heart of this was a renewed reliance on arduous forms of nonindustrial labour, such as artisanal mining and peasant farming (see De Boeck 1998; Raeymaekers 2010).

But the social and political economic effects of this change were certainly not restricted to these sectors. The top-down patronage networks and bureaucratic institutions of the postcolonial state, which previously had dispensed substantial resources over a wide area, turned into quasi-familial cells connected to the wider society via a dominant individual who was able to act as gatekeeper for the passing of patronage to the rest of the cell. The most important 'passing points' in this web of connections became class thresholds. In music this change also had notable effects. In the past, maximizing sales to mass markets had relied on a relatively limited set of connections – to political patrons at the apex of the state pyramid and to Western record labels that handled Zaïrian artists in the rest of the world. In the 1980s and 1990s, this changed – the mass market was displaced, as were the international record labels.

In their place emerged a patronage system that relied not only on a few 'gros légumes', but on a myriad of potlatch patrons, each trying to establish his dominance in a deeply unstable system of ranking. Links to the outside world were still crucial to this new patronage network, and these links were still restricted and still favoured the strong over the weak. But, unlike the system that immediately followed independence, the setup from the 1970s onwards featured much more decentralized power relationships, reflecting the 'parcelized' forms of authority that came to characterize this social formation (see also De Boeck and Plissart 2004: 89). In this situation the power of *présidents* within the *orchestre* was strongly connected to their ability to act as gatekeepers over access to resources and, above all, access to Europe.

Via gatekeeping activities, *présidents* and other powerful individuals were able to act in a way that had some resonances with the precolonial elders described by Rey (1971). In other words, by their control of access to the outside world, a control that relied on a kind of class solidarity among gatekeepers, they were able to regulate access to social reproduction and, via this regulation, they were able to exploit the labour of social subordinates. Likewise, the position of these subordinates within the social unit was not like that of a 'worker' in a capitalist firm, but was much more comparable to the precolonial 'cadet'. In the first section of this chapter I place the gatekeeping practices of the *président* within the context of this broader societal reorganization, showing how rank-and-file musicians relate to a much broader category of labour in Kinshasa. In the second section I shall look at a specific set of examples concerning how *présidents* tried to act as gatekeepers over access to Europe and the social struggles that arose from this.

Inequalities, Gatekeeping and Social Dominance within the *Orchestre* and Beyond

The starting point for our analysis is the very considerable income inequality between the *président* and his followers in a successful *orchestre*. A very rough tally I made in the period 2006–7 suggested that in one case I was able to identify payments to the *président* of nearly one million dollars (see Table 5.1). While it was difficult to be precise, it seems plausible to argue that his real income was several times this, given that I excluded many of the most profitable sources of income that *présidents* are reputed to receive – above all, secret payments from politicians,[2] which, especially during the election period of 2006, would have been very large.

Table 5.1 Some payments that I was aware of, received by an *président d'orchestre* during a rough twelve-month period, 2006–7

$250,000 *Mabanga* Payments in Concert

This figure comes from a single, admittedly profitable, concert given in Paris in 2006. I stood near the front with a Congolese friend as we attempted to calculate the amount of money paid over by patrons, keeping a tally on paper. Both of us came up with very approximate figures of €300,000. Assuming we had both overestimated, I set this as a quarter of a million dollars. The *président* in question must have played other profitable concerts in 2007 and, a few years ago, during *le temps de l'argent facile*, such cash monsoons were more common than they are now. In other words, the annual calculation given here for concert *mabanga* is clearly an underestimate.

$100,000 Beer Sponsorship from One of Kinshasa's Major Brewers

This figure was given to me by a senior member of staff at the brewery and is lower than other figures alleged by various less well-connected informants.

$380,000 *Mabanga* for the Album Produced in that Year

There are at least 160 names cited on the album. I have assumed for the sake of argument that only one hundred of these were paid for in cash, while some would have been thrown in free for reasons of friendship, political protection, radio and television airtime. Others will have been paid in goods (see Chapter 3). We arrive, then, at a figure of $600,000 – six hundred dollars per *mabanga* was given to me as the standard price for this *orchestre*. So, if we deduct five *mabangas* – i.e. $15,000 – for each of the fifteen other members of the group, as is standard practice on any album, we arrive at a figure of $375,000. We then add on the $10,000 dollars for the *président* who is listed as the author of two songs on the album, both of which are dedicated to individuals. The standard price for such a *dédicace*, given to me by members of the *orchestre*, is $5,000.

$25,000 Private Album Fee

This was the price paid by a Congo-Brazzaville politician for the recording of a private album for his wedding anniversary. The fee was in fact double this, but it was shared with the *arrangeur*. I was present at the negotiations and although I did not follow the entire event, I was told by several people who had been closely involved that this was the figure arrived at. The *président* undoubtedly received many such payments during the year from politicians in the DRC and the neighbouring countries. Having no means of calculating these other payments, I have excluded them from my estimates.

$20,000+ *Cachet d'artiste* for the *Président's* Next Album

While no one would give me a figure for this, I have chosen $20,000 because it was the *cachet d'artiste* given to Madilu by the producer KTC (see below). Madilu was a very well-respected artist, but his popularity and his political clout was much lower than that of the *président d'orchestre* in question. Therefore, it seems reasonable to assume that Madilu would have been given a smaller *cachet* than the *président* under discussion.

$50,000+ *Cachets* for Performing Live

I was informed that a top Congolese artist could command a $10,000 *cachet* for a live performance in Europe. The *orchestre* of *président* X played concerts every weekend for several months. Many of these concerts took place in regional French and Belgian centres with smaller Congolese populations, so it is possible that in some cases the *cachet* was more modest.*

All these figures are at the lower end of estimates and exclude almost all income from acts of political largesse, business interests, illegal sources, noncash transactions, etc. As we have seen, these are, or in the recent past have been, very important. In addition, the income from *mabanga* given during a concert only represents the income from one event.

---

* How much of an underestimate this probably is can be demonstrated by the fact that a single *fara-fara* – face-to-face – concert between Werrason and Koffi Olomide, which was to take place in Paris in 2007, was advertised as having a *cachet* of €70,000 to be split between the two artists, though in fact this concert never took place. Concerts in Congo demonstrate more variety, ranging from vast paying concerts in the national stadium *Le Stade des Martyrs* and huge free concerts paid for by breweries in various open spaces to quite expensive concerts in bars and hotels in the centre of the city. While I was in Kinshasa, J.B. Mpiana and Werrason were offered $100,000 each to perform *fara-fara* at the *Stade des Martyrs*, though this concert was also cancelled, this time by the town hall, which cited fears for public order. A producer in Kinshasa told me that producing a paying concert in Kinshasa included a *cachet* of $900–$1,200. This fee refers to an 'average' concert where an entry of around $10 is charged; *orchestres* will play dozens of such concerts a year. A few times a year, small but very expensive events take place – on Valentine's Day, for example, the big stars perform concerts in the city's luxury hotels that command fees of up to $100 a ticket (field note, Paris 12 February 2007). It would seem likely that such events entail a higher *cachet*, though unfortunately I seem not to have asked this question of anyone.

Contrast this with the fact that rank-and-file musicians are most often not paid a salary at all. While all the major musical organizations claim to pay their members, my interviews with musicians confirmed that, of the three *orchestres* that have dominated the Kinshasa music scene since the 1990s, only one pays a regular and even modestly adequate salary ($300 a month) to its members, while the other two made mention of salaries of around $140, but it was clear that these 'salaries' – which in any case do not represent a living wage – were only paid sporadically or not at all.

This inequality and exploitation of retinue is of a piece with wider remunerative practices in Kinshasa, where a broad range of jobs pay out a semifictional salary. Those 'salaries' paid to musicians are entirely typical of remuneration in the wider society. In 2007 a civil servant's basic salary was one hundred dollars a month, while ordinary police were paid forty dollars. And these salaries were often *not* paid – a friend who worked in the tax office was not paid for seven months out of twelve in 2010. In this context, a broad range of jobs are valued not for their salary, but rather as positions from which to negotiate patronage. The civil servant will scrape by, perhaps, on the bribes he demands for supplying paperwork, while the policeman will extract a fee from taxi drivers as he directs traffic, or he will rent his uniform to criminals, or rob members of the public himself, occasionally hitting the jackpot when the upturned card is a Western graduate student. Thus, rank-and-file musicians fit into a much broader group of the Kinois population. This group is better off than much of the population – generally speaking, they are the children of those who really were paid salaries in the 1960s and 1970s.

All this did not happen in a vacuum. As the output from industrial enclaves declined, the wage-earning classes – the state bureaucracies and the industrial and agricultural proletariat – atrophied. In numerical terms, these wage earners were always a minority of the labour force, but they were an important mediator between the comprador political class at the top and the lumpen and peasant majority (Nzongola-Ntalaja 1970). In this shift, other class structures emerged. A crucial unit in the deployment of labour under this new dispensation was a series of quasi-familial corporate bodies. Absorbent of people, hierarchical and yet unstable, dependent on logics of wealth in people that partially reproduced the structures of the lineage, these bodies negotiated power using a vocabulary of eldership and seniority (see also De Boeck in De Boeck and Plissant 2004).

Such structures had always been part of the Kinois scene – gangs, mutual associations and *orchestres*, to name but a few. Yet conditions enhanced their value. This was in part perhaps because certain social activities that lent themselves to this form of organization – artisanal mining, religious prayer groups, judo dojos, gangs – moved from the margins to the centre of social life. But this was far from all. As economic growth disappeared, these kinds of structures began to colonize characteristically 'modern' sectors of the economy. Ostensibly bureaucratic organizations have reorganized themselves in this way and what appear to be large centralized institutions are in fact nests containing many of the hierarchical quasi-familial corporations described above. Often these cells are in competition with each other.

Small parties based around a police station, a local tax office, a town hall, a professorship or a television station will extract unofficial fees, generally cultivating a further network of clients below them – like students, property owners or taxi drivers who need their services – and patrons above them, often more senior individuals within the organization, but also other powerful figures. The distribution of such monies within the cell will be negotiated according, once again, to vocabularies of seniority and eldership. Just as bureaucracy has reorganized itself into such structures, so there has been a migration of bureaucratic language into some surprising new contexts. Terms such as *cabinet*, *bureau* or *staff* no longer refer to the conventional spaces or relationships that the Western observer would associate with them. All are now deployed by a wide range of nonprofessional groups – street gangs, parties of artisanal miners, work parties – and such terms refer to an entourage, not to a physical space. Such organizations also bristle with *présidents*, treasurers, secretaries and other such titles. These titles mean little beyond their power to persuade interlocutors, perhaps, that the individual in question is the person who should be the conduit for resources.

Clearly not every point where a 'gate' has been established marks a class division, but at the more important points – between, say, a minister or senior civil servant and his retinue, between a senior pastor and his congregation or between a *président d'orchestre* and his rank-and-file musicians – there is a categorical difference in income and opportunity, underwritten by relations of exploitation. It is also the case that the retinues being exploited, such as rank-and-file musicians, are very far from the bottom of the social pyramid. Their parents were often part of the decayed bourgeoisie and they have generally competed fiercely for the positions they occupy. They also have at least a shot at achieving the kinds of socially recognized adulthood that totally elude most Kinois. But it is precisely this relative possibility that grants the *président d'orchestre* (and others like him) his power. By manipulating access to social reproduction, the *président* is able to appropriate the labour of cadets voluntarily.

In negotiating these payments, there is a very considerable emphasis on personal ties. Part of this is a simple response to informality – 'bribes', which shade imperceptibly into 'patronage', are often forms of payment for dealing with the complexity of certain situations, which can spare one from the intricacies of the wider process or of constantly having to handle demands for payment from everyone within the unit. In contrast to the social and aesthetic value generally placed on crowds and clamour, transactors insist that deals or, indeed, any form of payment be conducted in private with the same, favoured intermediary. The individual dealt with becomes 'my man' – *mutu na ngai* – who can, for a reward, handle the complexities of the situation. Obtaining a form, getting a relative sprung from detention or paying 'supporters' to attend a political rally all involve paying one individual identified as the leader of an informal corporate group.

The secrecy of such dealings and the desperation of the participants mean that, where the stakes are low, legitimacy is openly contested. A good example would be political rallies. The bulk of the crowd at political rallies in Congo are made up of the sub-proletariat, who are expecting a payment at the end of the meeting. While the crowd may appear an amorphous mass, it is in fact composed of a great many corporate units. Boxing clubs and Judo dojos, both of which are popular with the urban poor, often form the units upon which political fixers recruit crowds, and it is to the head of the club that they hand out t-shirts or very small envelopes of cash at the end. It is for this reason that political rallies in Kinshasa invariably end in fights, not between rival political factions, but *within* various dojos and boxing clubs who all suspect that their club *président* has sold them short.

Alongside convenience and questions of retaining accumulation, prestige plays a role. The grander the *grand* with whom one deals, the more one is part of the 'top table' oneself, and actors will often make theatrically secret deals with an important personage, seizing them by the hand and leading them into a corner, where everyone can see – but not hear – that *bazobeta kop*, they are striking a deal. This is reflected within *orchestres*, where far more patronage is given to the *président* than to other members of the *orchestre*; the more public an act of largesse, the more likely it is that it will be made to the *président* himself rather than to other *orchestre* members. In studio work, where the exchange of money is relatively discreet, *mabanga* will flow into the recording from all the musicians – the drummer, the bass guitarist and the rest. During a concert, where, by contrast, patrons press money on musicians in a highly theatrical way, almost all monies are given to the *président*, with perhaps a smattering of notes dispensed to one or two high-profile singers. Prestations to instrumentalists during a concert are rare.

Another motivation for dealing with one regular *mutu na ngai* is based on the interest established gatekeepers perceive in maintaining an ethos that is supportive of established gatekeepers. Just as the baron, whose position depends on deference to authority and hierarchy, may actively support the authority of the country squire in relation to the hoi polloi, so a patron who has accumulated wealth by being an established gatekeeper for others will respect and try to deal with the established gatekeeper 'be he ne'er so base'.

Established *présidents d'orchestres* will generally try to obtain *mabanga* on private visits large patrons, calling by their offices. Over a beer in Bandal, the home district of many of Kinshasa's top musicians, I met with a certain star's *pettit ya confiance*. He told me how he had found out that it might be promising for the star to visit a certain well-connected lawyer in negotiations over the dedication of a song. As is his habit, the star in question did not insist on a sum of money, but rather told the man to 'lakisa munene na yo', 'show his bigness'. The lawyer gave him an envelope, which the star did not look into until he was back in the car. When he did look, he exclaimed: 'I didn't realize lawyers made so much money!' Such private, low-key or even secret personal exchanges will take place frequently between those who consider themselves to be in the same social class, while the retinue, even of a quite stable long-term kind, will only see money on certain, carefully stage-managed occasions.

This dialectic of secrecy and theatre became apparent to me when I tried to pay over $100 that I owed to a friend of mine who was a television station owner. Not being *au fait* with the conventions pertaining to such transactions, I discussed this transaction in front of his employees and, to his immense discomfort, handed over the money in public, in the car park. This immediately prompted a mass petition for money from the very poorly remunerated staff and he was forced to hand over all of the money then and there. Making the best of a bad job, he handed over a small number of bills to each in turn with a benevolent air.

This rather comic performance was both revealing and atypical, in that it was a kind of ludic imitation of the real thing. As I soon discovered, the television station owner was an amiable fantasist who was trying to perform on a scale his finances could not really sustain, and I was just one of a number of 'props'. To my dismay, he had told all and sundry that I was his accountant and business partner. In line with the notion of bullshit explored in Chapter 3, this performance was in part to bolster his own less-than-secure hold on the status he wished to occupy. A more genuine example of this type of exchange relationship was well illustrated by a small musical commission I witnessed in 2007.

Mutu na ngai, *or How Tintin Got His Shout*

It is around 11 pm and I am in a recording studio. In walks a small man in late middle age, who we will call Figuero, a well-connected individual from Congo-Brazzaville. Figuero has commissioned one of Kinshasa's most popular *orchestres* to make an album. A private commission, the album will not receive a general release and is to be played only once, at the birthday party of Figuero's wife, to be held in Brazzaville several months hence. Figuero is here to supervise the insertion of *mabanga* onto the album's introductory track. He has already paid for the album, so this is not the pay-per-shout that occurs with a normal recording and he is including all the names he wishes – in this case passing on the names of all the notables who have been invited to the birthday celebration. The list quickly turns into a catalogue of the great and the (not so) good of Congo-Brazzaville. At one point, Figuero stops the singer, who is halfway through reciting the name of a minister. 'Oh just call him Tintin – that's what we all call him', he says.

The story of the album quickly filters through to me from various sources – Figuero has paid $50,000 to make the album. Despite the fact that the songs for the album were written, performed and arranged by the rank-and-file members of the *orchestre*, along with a few of the Paris-based studio musicians, this money was taken by the *président*.[3] I ask a musician friend who, despite intense hours spent on the album, has received nothing why he does not ask Figuero directly for a share of the money. He replies that this is not how things work: 'People like that, they only deal with one person.' Several other musicians concur that to ask Figuero directly would only invite ridicule or real trouble. And, indeed, it is natural that Figuero should adhere to this kind of *mutu na ngai* logic in dealing with inferiors, as that is exactly what he himself relies upon in dealing with superiors.

Figuero is from the south, near the centre of the Congo-Brazzaville oil industry. In the precolonial period, this area was part of Luango, one of the most powerful slave-trading kingdoms in Central Africa, but since then the fortunes of the region have declined. While the oil wealth of the country is on their doorstep, control of these resources now runs through the capital, Brazzaville. A series of bloody civil wars, wars in which French oil interests were deeply implicated, pitched youth militias of 'Cobras' and 'Ninjas' from the north and south against one another (Bazenguissa-Ganga 1999; Englebert and Ron 2004; Faligot and Guisnel 2006; Shaxson 2007). Sassou Nguesso, a northerner, emerged victorious and became President.

While the general perception is that one must be a northerner to succeed in any business endeavour in Congo-Brazzaville, the truth is that all but a tiny handful have been cut out. Most northerners are desperately poor, while a few, well-connected southerners have done well. Figuero is one of these. He has been implicated in several scandals, stretching back to the 1990s, when – so well-informed Brazzavillois allege – he was involved in the importation of toxic waste and in negotiating corrupt contracts with a European petrochemicals company. Needless to say, he has never been charged with anything and derives power, wealth and impunity from being Sassou's *mutu na ngai* in the region.

In addition to the approach work related to the patron, a very considerable effort is expended by the gatekeeper in maintaining his own position. A friend, Josué, who works as a taxi driver in Paris, made regular payments to a singer in one of the major *orchestres*. The two were close friends, and while Josue never handed over huge amounts by the standards of the time, he paid $600 every few years and received *mabanga* shouts on several albums. The *président* became aware of Josue as a source of income and approached him personally, saying that Josue should pay his money to him and not bother with underlings. Thus, while it is true that being a member of an *orchestre* can get you into a patronage network, the *président* is not above trying to lock you out of it again.[4]

Access to Europe: Power in the *Orchestre*

As was noted before, all of the gatekeepers described in this chapter did not simply receive patronage allocated from above. Gaining such patronage was dependent on extracting labour from subordinates and this depended on retaining their allegiance. For this reason, it is an essential part of the gatekeeper's power that, despite his exactions on the rank and file, he can hold out the realistic prospect of social advancement. During the 1990s and the first half of the 2000s, patronage in Europe was the richest source of income to musicians and for this reason, it was also the area where the attempts of the *président* to act as gatekeeper were most apparent.

As has been outlined in previous chapters, the 1980s and 1990s saw an increasing drive by Congolese to migrate. Successive European governments have made migration more difficult, with an increasing number of migrants attempting to *kobuaka nzoto* – literally to 'throw' one's body, but here to claim asylum – once in a European country. The hardening of visa requirements culminated in 1991 with the implementation of the Schengen Agreement, which introduced stringent stipulations for Central Africans in all the signatory countries, including France and Belgium, then still the two major centres of migration for Zaïrians.

In this period, however, musicians' visas remained relatively easy to negotiate. A *président d'orchestre* who was able to demonstrate that he had a contract with a European-based promoter and access to a lawyer who could negotiate with the French Embassy could secure a fairly large number of visas. Up until the late 1990s, the deposits demanded for each visa by the embassy in Kinshasa were relatively low – around $500 in 2000.[5] This situation granted a relatively large number of *orchestres* access to travel to Paris. Clearly this differential access to visas between successful *présidents d'orchestres* and ordinary Kinois was a source of authority to a *président* in several ways. First, within the *orchestre*, travel to Europe could be held out as a reward for loyalty, while the threat of withholding access could be used to enforce discipline. Second, this access to visas was in itself a considerable source of funds to a *président d'orchestre* via the trafficking of illegal migrants, known as *ngulu*.

Ngulu primarily means 'pig'. The reason why this word is now used to refer to people-smuggling is not entirely clear. Among the possible origins for the term, some informants put forward the idea of the poor 'pig-like' living conditions endured by illegal migrants. But this seems somewhat unlikely given how Europe was generally fetishized. A somewhat more likely explanation relates to some sort of (possibly humorous) reference to the idea of the *Mundele Ngulu*. According to Kinois lore, the *Mundele Ngulu* was a European who, it was said, took Africans to Europe and brought them back to Congo as tinned meat. Adding a further layer of confusion to this already unlikely etymology, the meat identified is generally corned beef, not spam. In the Kingabwa district of Kinshasa, the *Mundele Ngulu* is identified with a Belgian expatriate who lived there until the 1980s, but again this cannot be the origin of the belief, which dates back to at least the 1950s. The idea of Africans going abroad and being consumed is itself almost certainly related to earlier beliefs about European cannibalism connected with the slave trade (see Thornton 2003), in which sense it fits into a wider set of ideas about eating, sorcery and wealth that are recurrent themes in Central African ideologies of power.

Be this as it may, making a journey to Europe is something that musicians dream about, but that most never achieve. Most *orchestres* never leave Kinshasa, while the level of decline in once great *orchestres* like King Kester's Victoria Eleison were identified in the popular mind by the fact that they no longer travelled. As we saw in Chapter 3, Victoria Eleison were mocked for travelling to Kikwit in Bandundu and coming back with cassava flour rather than going to Europe and returning with cars. Even those *orchestres* that do travel always leave some members behind so that just getting on the plane is a considerable demonstration of favour from the *président*, and the threat of giving or withholding this is one of the most powerful disciplinary measures that the *président* possesses. Musicians that are just starting with an *orchestre* will frequently be left at home, while others that are considered unreliable – for example, Werrason's veteran singer Adjani – generally do not make it on to the plane.

Yet despite the mythical status accorded to the rich North, when these migrants get to Europe, their life is, in fact, far from easy. When *orchestres* tour Europe, rank-and-file musicians are paid nothing for the entire duration of their tour, which can last several months. The musicians of Wenge Maison Mère were on tour in Europe for over six months in 2006–7 and, on their return, were given a 'fee' of around $400. During tours of Europe, the *président* will stay in a hotel, while members of the *orchestre* will throw themselves upon the hospitality of the Congolese community, raking up a series of *debts morales* that will have to be paid via *mabanga*. The dancers are reliant on prostitution – Fifi Motema, mentioned in Chapter 3, is one of several female procuresses in Europe who are known to act on behalf of the dancers in touring *orchestres*.

Male musicians can also suffer visibly during the earlier stages of a tour. I knew several members of Wenge Maison Mere in Paris in 2006–7 who were sleeping in very makeshift circumstances for extended periods. This kind of scenario was especially common with the less experienced travellers in the party who have not established good connections with the community or, as was the case with Wenge BCBG in London in 2005–6, when the *orchestre* has no history of long-term sojourning in a city and the rank-and-file musicians rented in an incredibly fleabitten set of digs in Tottenham.

This contrasts strongly with the opulence of the *président*'s living arrangements. Such arrangements could range from the moderate extravagance to something much more extreme. When Werrason was in Paris for a considerable number of months in 2006–7, he stayed in a midrange chain hotel in Saint-Denis near Studio Marcadet, with the costs of this hotel borne by his producers, the 'duo d'Enfer'.

When J.B. Mpiana came to play a concert in Paris in 2005, after many years' absence, one of his patrons paid for him to stay in the George V, one of the most expensive hotels in Paris. J.B. was interviewed returning to the hotel from the concert by journalist Djo K. Kabongele, who is fanatically pro-J.B.. During the interview, J.B. was dressed in a three-piece outfit with hood and cape designed by the Japanese designer Kasamoto that he wore for the concert. Some excerpts from the interview are fairly evocative of this ritual marking of status.

As they enter the hotel:

Djo K.: Here we are in a class apart, we are in the very luxurious Paris, because here, where we find ourselves, a room costs €2,500 a night.

J.B. Mpiana: No, 4,500!

Djo K.: Excuse me! 2,500 is for when they are doing a promotion! But tell me why are you staying here, when most Congolese musicians will accept any old hotel?

J.B. Mpiana: Because we have advanced.

(Maisha Park Vol 4 Ricardo Productions Paris, 2005)

Later on in the interview, J.B. claims, rather fantastically, that he is only the second global star, after Michael Jackson, to stay in the hotel.

Some more quantifiable breakdown of these inequalities in conditions can be seen in a rough cost list that I was given by the producer KTC, who produced the album *Le Tenant du Titre* by the artist Madilu System and the 10 man *orchestre* the *Tout Puissant System* in Paris. KTC cited his own business interests as diamonds and import-export.

Table 5.2 Total cost breakdown as listed by Jossart Balezi, aka KTC, for the production of the album *Le Tenant du Titre* by Madilu System and the *Orchestre le Tout Puissant System* released in 2005:

Cachet d'artiste **Madilu = $20,000**

ICA Studio in Kinshasa (one month) = $200 per day

Studio Harry Son in Paris (two months) = €400 per day

Hotel for the artist while in Paris (two months) = €100 per day

Hotel for the producer while in Paris (two months) = €100 per day

Restaurant bill for the artist (two months) = €30 per day

Restaurant bill for the musicians = €1,000

Transport for the artist (including flights, visa arrangements, etc.) = €2,400

Transport for the producer = €2,400

Car hire in Paris (two months) = €60

Payments to musicians performing on the album = €100 each
(x ten performers = €1,000)

Instrument hire = €1,000

Mastering studio Top Master Paris = €550

Fees to SACEM (French performing rights body) = €5,800
(on production of 10,000 CDs).

Cost of reproduction = €1.30 per CD on a production run of 10,000

Total promotion costs spent over a period of eighteen months from album's release = €12,000

Graphic designer's fees = €850

Posters = €1,500 (2,000 copies printed)

Arranger Maika Munan's fee = €3,000

Sound engineer's fees = €8,000

Camera rental (for video clips) = €300

Filming costs (for video clips) = €450

Editing video clips = €200

Clothing for video girls = €480

Technician's fee [I am not sure what he meant here] = €300

As we can see from the list KTC gave me, he estimated paying $100 a day for two months for the *président*'s (Madilu's) hotel. Over the same period, he did not include any money at all in his budget for housing the ten other musicians. This can partly be explained by the fact that some of these musicians were Paris-based, although many were not. He budgeted $30 a day for restaurants for the *président*, coming to approximately $1,800 over the two months. Over the same two-month period, he spent $1,000 on feeding the other ten musicians. Madilu was given a $20,000 upfront fee, as well as getting the lion's share of *mabanga* on the album – the album includes a song dedicated to Angola's very wealthy Dokolo family – while the other artists were given $100 one-off payments. Such disparities are not unique in Congolese music and I strongly suspect that KTC was in fact far more scrupulous and generous to musicians than were other producers. Certainly it seems suggestive to me that he was the only one who did not refuse me a breakdown of his costs.

Rank-and-file musicians will be required to perform in the studio and at concerts, and the *président* will take almost all the profits from these events – on all occasions that I was able to verify, the *catchet* for the performance was paid up front to the *président*. Very often the compositions of ordinary members of the *orchestre* will also be appropriated by the *président* during recording and claimed as his own (see Chapter 8). Nevertheless, after a sojourn in Europe, the musician can hope to return to Kinshasa sufficiently laden with goods to become a modest somebody – perhaps owning a car, attracting a following of admiring *petits* who follow him around in the *quartier* of Kinshasa where he lives, and attracting women.

A good example of this modest success story was the musician Franklin, who plays in one of the major *orchestres*. He had joined it in 2005 after many years of being unemployed. During his first years with the *orchestre*, his income was very restricted and he received little in the way of salary. He was given a few *mabanga* shouts to sell on an album that the *orchestre* recorded in Kinshasa. In addition, he was given crates of beer each month, passed on to him by Wenge Maison Mère's sponsor, Primus, which he could sell. He also received a small amount of rent from rooms on the family plot, amounting to around $50 a month. In addition, he got some monies from acts of *matolo* – charity/solidarity – from supporters of the *orchestre* and from occasional remittances sent by relatives in Europe.

Franklin was one of the musicians who worked on Figuero's album, all for no reward. He had entirely arranged the major hit on the previous album and had received nothing for his pains. Then he *was* allowed to contribute a song in his own name to the album recorded in Europe in 2006 and was paid $5,000 for the *dédicace* by a patron. He was also given *mabanga*, each worth $600, to place on that album. He spent the entire $5,000 on a new Renault and on having it shipped.

Such a modest step on the path to social reproduction is something that the *président* is generally happy to grant. It represents no real threat to his own power; indeed, it shores up his reputation as a source of good things, while the musician continues to depend on him and other gatekeeper figures in myriad ways. Indeed, Franklin's car illustrates this well: he entrusted his car to a Congolese shipping agent in Paris, who dispatched the car without the correct paperwork and who himself disappeared before the car arrived in Congo. Franklin was then obliged to pay a considerable amount in bribes to officials, as well as calling in favours from various patrons with political connections, in order to free the car from the port of Matadi.

A second level of social reproduction might be attained by a musician gaining independent access to Europe. This is far less convenient for the *président* and, as a rule, he will try to throw obstacles in the path of a musician who tries to make this move. Most musicians who choose to leave one of the big *orchestres* will try to wait until they are on a tour of Europe. Almost all tours of Europe will leak one or two musicians or dancers, while some tours will positively haemorrhage personnel. Such defections can mark a real threat to the power of the *président*. The reasons for this are not only that it represents a loss of skilled and popular musicians, but also that the *président*, or his producer, will have paid a considerable deposit to obtain the visa, which can only be recouped when evidence is presented that the musician has returned to the DRC (though ways can be found to get around this – see below). In addition, if such defections become known to the French authorities, they may jeopardize future visa applications, as may have happened to J.B. Mpiana, who was refused a long visa to the Schengen Area for five years after a mass defection of junior musicians during his tour of 2001.

Yet while losing musicians in Europe is almost always inconvenient for the *président*, not all defections carry the same threat. The musician who claims asylum, probably on his first or second trip to Europe, represents far less of a challenge to presidential authority than other defections. This is because anyone who claims asylum is signing away any hope of an independent musical career, resigning himself to years of being snarled up in the asylum system and, by implication, stuck in Europe – the 'graveyard of musicians' (see Chapter 3). Indeed, the fate of the many musicians who claimed asylum in the last ten years can be said to have had a disciplinary effect on rank-and-file musicians from touring *orchestres*.

Musical Travellers' Tales

Sampras plays bass. He came to Europe in 1999, with an *orchestre* put together by a musician who had broken from Koffi Olomide in the 1990s. After the concerts, the *orchestre* fell apart and it seems that the *président* actually encouraged his musicians to claim asylum. With no right to work and his asylum application rejected, Sampras is now forced to accept piecework in the studios. It was Sampras, along with Franklin and a few others, who wrote and arranged most of Figuero's wife's birthday album. They were hoping to be given something for all this effort, but nobody was in a position to insist, least of all Sampras, who has no papers.

Most months Sampras is able to send home $100, the only money his family has to live on. A great many ills, typical of the *sans papiers*, assail him. Accommodation is extremely hard to come by in Paris and doubly hard for those who cannot present documents or work contracts, let alone find money for a deposit. When he was turned out of his apartment near Marx Dormoy Metro Station, he was homeless, sleeping on floors, then sharing my apartment for months, until a friend sorted him out with a room in a squat in Saint-Denis. He hates his position and would like to return to Kinshasa, but his family is dependent on the money he sends home.

A much greater threat to the *président*'s authority would be the musician who remains with the *orchestre* over several journeys to Europe and who, via one expedient or another, has managed to acquire papers while at the same time continuing to work for the *orchestre* – thus travelling between Kinshasa and Europe, and remaining in the public eye (see Chapter 3). The canniest and most successful underlings were generally able to do this in the 1990s and early 2000s, and these would include current stars like Fally Ipupa and Ferre

Gola. Such a musician represents a risk to presidential authority for two reasons. First, he is less reliant on the *président* in general terms. He does not need the *président* for a visa, and the right to residence in Europe gives him a kind of retirement plan. Under such circumstances, the threat of expulsion from the *orchestre* is not backed by the menace of a plunge back into indigence. Clearly the individual in such circumstances is a less malleable opponent. Second, as discussed in Chapter 3, access to *both* Kinshasa and Europe has become the *sine qua non* of independent musical success, so that underlings stuck in Europe are even less of a threat to the *président* than those stuck in Africa. Musicians with independent access to both continents, on the other hand, have a much easier path to an independent career.

Musicians are reputed to be especially successful with women, and it is notable how male musicians will often rely on the patronage of women. Many of my informants came to rely on apartments in Paris that they shared with lovers from the Congolese community. Some liaisons provide much-needed material support, while others, such as those with famous courtesans, can give considerable impetus to a career. Yet another advantage of such relationships concerns the search for First World papers. It may be possible to persuade women who themselves have papers to marry. Perhaps the more popular, or at least the more symbolically potent, way of gaining papers is to produce offspring. Musicians will boast of the children they have in Europe, sometimes mentioning them in television interviews.

Celeo, a popular *atalaku*, formerly with Wenge Maison Mère, included among his praise names *Tata ya Mapasa Français* – 'Father of French Twins'. And it is true that musicians do seem to have quite a number of children. Yet the mythological cachet associated with such an expedient – combining Europe and giving birth, two areas of massive cultural prestige – can obscure the facts about birth and migration. Historically, French citizenship was based on the principle of *jus soli*, under which those born on French soil are French citizens. Since the 1992 reforms to the law, this is no longer the case;[6] allocation of citizenship or residence rights for both the child and the parent are dependent on the citizenship or residence rights of a second parent – a similar requirement to that which pertains in the UK and Belgium. Gaining residence rights in this way is neither quick nor straightforward, and it turns out that many Congolese musicians with French or EU children, including Celeo, do not in fact have residence rights in France (see below). Over and above the normal problems that applicants face, rank-and-file musicians with Congolese *orchestres* face an additional hurdle. Establishing that you are the father of a child, or indeed participating in a host of other bureaucratic procedures, requires identity documents – and, as we shall see, the musicians rarely control these items.

We saw in Chapter 4 that the *président*, who is up to his neck in informal and criminal practices, can have little recourse to legal instruments, such as contracts, to control his musicians when in Europe. On the other hand, the *président* does have recourse to several other expedients to retain his authority. Perhaps the most important of these concerns the control of passports. On arriving in Europe, it is standard practice for the *président d'orchestre* to retain the passports of all the musicians.

Passport Control and the Cascade Experience

In the summer of 2006, rumours spread about the imprisonment of a certain singer who was then in Europe on tour with a major *orchestre*. He was stopped by the police and asked for an identity document during a check at Cologne in Germany. He produced a document purporting to show that he was a French citizen, but was taken into custody when he had difficulty remembering his own birthday. It later transpired that the document belonged to a relative of the singer. This practice of travelling on the documents of another, known as *cascade*, is common among the Congolese in Europe. But a mystery remains: all the musicians in the *orchestre* had visas for France. France and Germany are both signatories to the Schengen Agreement, which, among other things, allows free movement between these countries. This has not abolished passport checks entirely, but it does mean that a visa granted for France will also take you to Germany or Spain. So why did he not simply travel under his own passport?

An answer emerges when we look at the case of another musician, the aforementioned Celeo. Throughout the sojourn of Wenge Maison Mère in Europe during 2006–7, rumours spread of a deterioration in the relationship between Celeo and *président* Werrason. As the *orchestre* prepared to return home, it became clear that Celeo was avoiding contact. When Werrason left for Kinshasa with most of the group, Celeo was not on the plane. Werrason went back to Kinshasa, taking Celeo's passport with him. Unbeknown to Werrason, Celeo had booked a ticket to return to Kinshasa for later in the month. Alone in France, he gave several interviews to the Congolese press and television. As the following example shows, he accused Werrason, in thinly coded terms, of theft – and demanded the return of his passport:

It is the *président* Werrason who keeps my passport. Because, according to the information given to him, I wanted to participate in the making of Lacoste's Album [an earlier breakaway from Werrason] or to take part in a marriage to a white [I suspect this 'en marriage une blanche' is an error of transcription by the journalist. 'Une marriage en blanche' means 'a marriage of convenience', which seems more likely]. There you have it, the reasons given for holding my passport. In any case I don't know what intentions there are for blocking my passport [that is, not giving it back]. A good father to his family, he should understand me. (*Multi Media Congo* 2007)

What was unusual about Celeo's case was not that Werrason retained his passport, but Celeo's warlike response. Passports are routinely held by the *président*, and this is why musicians with a visa will travel on false documents. So what specific benefits accrue to the *président* from such a course of action? By retaining passports, the *président* may be able to present them at the French Embassy in Kinshasa as evidence that the musicians have returned to the DRC, and he will be able to recoup the deposits he paid to obtain the visas in the first place. A passport can also be sold on, though the resale value of a Congolese passport per se is not particularly high. But the main benefit to the *président* is the value that such a document has to its original owner – the musician – and the controlling and disciplining function that retention can exert upon a subordinate.

The value to such a musician of his original passport may be summarized as follows. A passport with entry and exit stamps is in itself regarded as an asset, since exit stamps are believed to be a sign of reliability, which will be taken into account by embassies. In addition, for the musician who has succeeded in marrying or impregnating a woman with EU residence rights, the lack of a passport presents a real obstacle to regularizing his situation. Sorting out such matters is a time-consuming endeavour, even where the papers are in order. If identity documents are missing, the process will be hugely delayed. The *président* will rarely release passports for any reason. When he does so, it is seen as a privilege for a particularly valued musician. Thus, when Wenge Maison Mère returned to Kinshasa in 2007, its lead guitarist Flamme Kapaya, who has several children born in France, was allowed by Werrason to remain behind to sort out his residence rights.

One cannot help but think that this reflected Werrason's relatively weak position in this case. Flamme is a skilled guitarist who gets Kinshasa to its feet whenever he plays, and one suspects that Werrason felt that he could not replace him and thus had no choice but to indulge him. In fact, Flamme did defect soon after and many years later, Werrason has still not found a guitarist of similar abilities. Another musician, an *atalaku* who played with Werrason some years ago, has also had several children in the EU. He was not given his passport to regularize his papers and tried to negotiate matters on his return to Africa, first from Kinshasa and, subsequently, from Luanda. But this merely complicated his application. Obtaining a new visa for the EU, without money for a deposit and without his initial passport, was now impossible, while coordinating with his children's mother over the presentation of his dossier, when he was in Angola and she was in France, was extremely difficult. To the best of my knowledge, the situation has still not been resolved.

Beyond the *Orchestre*: Trafficking in People

Within the *orchestre*, travel to Europe could be held out as a reward for loyalty, while the threat of withholding access could be used to enforce discipline. But the *président*'s gatekeeper status also had another advantage – access to visas was in itself a considerable source of funds to a *président d'orchestre*, via the trafficking of illegal migrants, known as *ngulu*. The connection of musical performance with illegal migration is etched very strongly onto the public consciousness. One *tata ngulu*, or people-smuggler, is said to have organized several 'orchestres' composed entirely of prospective migrants. Nothing if not thorough, he would rent instruments and a hall, and organize obligatory rehearsals. Thus, an assortment of unemployed law graduates, civil servants and doctors would get together once a week and thrash about for several months before the big day. Not content with this, he would rent a concert venue in the suburbs of Paris. When the group arrived in the French capital, he would require that it give one public performance, after which its members would scatter to the four winds.

Setting aside the literal truth of this particular case, such accounts indicate the imaginative link made between music and migration (see Sumata 2002). This is also evident in the fact that in a large number of cases, the document forging workshops – known as 'embassies' – had as their frontman a series of figures who were famous for their connections with the world of music; indeed, such connections could be important in drumming up business. One such figure, who subsequently became a regional deputy under Kabila, is commemorated in a song by J.B. Mpiana. In the song, J.B. sings from the point of view of a stricken woman who has received medical advice that she will die 'within 48 hours' if she does not get to see her beaux.

Arriving at a precise estimate of the numbers of migrants who travelled with famous musicians is impossible, but certainly it represented a very considerable source of income to all *présidents*. The practice of musical *ngulu* was clearly well established – all Congolese in Europe who I have met can think of at least one acquaintance who was brought to Europe in this manner, and I certainly know of several. It is also common knowledge that in the past, *ngulu* was practised by all of Congo's touring *orchestres*. A story told to me by a member of the Ndjili airport staff indicates how widespread knowledge of such practices was in the early 2000s. On realizing that a person departing with the entourage of one of the major *orchestres* was unfamiliar, he was able to blackmail the *président* into paying him to let the incident pass.

Places for *ngulu* seem to have been in heavy demand and securing a seat on the plane required at least some connection to the entourage of the *orchestre*, once again reinforcing the idea of the *président* as one who draws people towards him. Certain individuals seem to have hitched a free or subsidized ride. Many of these people would have been pre-existing kin of the *président*. Others were taken because of their absorption into the familial-corporate structure of the *orchestre*. *Ngulu* clearly reinforced the capacity of the *président* to act as a source of patronage to subordinates, and it seems that prices for *ngulu* could reach up to $5,000, though fees of $2,000–$3,000 were more often quoted to me, and this is also a figure given by Tsambu-Bulu (2004).

It is interesting to note here that alongside *présidents d'orchestres*, Pentecostal pastors were also very strongly linked to migration in this period. Pentecostal churches often had a strong ideological orientation towards Europe, offering its members *pambola poto* – 'Europe blessing' – and members of congregations who managed to make the journey were held as an example of the spiritual efficacy of particular pastors. The achievement of such blessings was not left to prayer alone and, rather like *présidents*, pastors were well known as people-smugglers. A key technique seems to have been to gain visas for revivalist conferences held in various European or North American locations. As with musicians' visas, those with a conference invitation found obtaining access considerably easier than did a normal applicant. The delegates would then pay several thousand dollars to the pastor to attend the event, from which the delegates would never return. As with *orchestres*, such places were keenly sought, and being part of the pastor's entourage was a clear advantage in securing a berth. One informant who had been close to a pastor well known for his activities as a *tata ngulu* (he was later arrested in Sweden for human trafficking) remembered accompanying him to an internet café in downtown Kinshasa, where he spent hours researching and applying to the various Christian conferences taking place.

The arrest and subsequent convictions of both Papa Wemba and Nyoka Longo in 2003 on charges related to people-smuggling, and the subsequent tightening of visa requirements for musicians, removed an important source of revenue from the *présidents*. The peregrinations of Pentecostal *tata ngulu* also seem to have been curtailed at much the same time. But, as in other cases, the imposition of greater scarcity gave a comparative advantage to established gatekeepers. Because of this, the results of the so-called *affaire ngulu* were not entirely detrimental to the power of the established *présidents d'orchestres*. Each musician's visa requires a deposit paid at the embassy which issues it and, in the aftermath of the scandal, the price of deposits went up considerably to around $5,000 per visa – a price extremely discouraging to all but those with the deepest pockets.

Other comparative advantages accrued to established *présidents* in the crackdown that followed the events of 2003. In the strange logic of bureaucracy, those with a track record of receiving visas, that is, those who had profited most from *ngulu* in the past, were given preferential treatment. Meanwhile, many musicians were refused visas outright. Others faced severe restrictions. The young star Fally Ipupa had a contract to play the Olympia, a prestigious venue in central Paris. When, after considerable negotiation, he was given a set of visas for barely two weeks, the number of visas issued was markedly fewer than had been requested and several members of the *orchestre* had to be left behind. During the same period, Werrason was able to obtain twelve-month visas for seventeen musicians and dancers.[7] The other big fish, Koffi Olomide and J.B. Mpiana,[8] were also able to negotiate visas for significant periods in the EU for most members of their *orchestres*.

Conclusion

I have established that the capacity to act as gatekeepers was a crucial element in the power of *présidents d'orchestres* over rank-and-file musicians and that these power imbalances were also central to the dynamics of how the *orchestres* operated. I have also suggested that the *orchestre* was but one example of wider social changes, in which hierarchical corporate units came to the fore. As 'modern' institutions and state patronage networks became less and less able to provide for people, smaller, more fragmented organizations became central to patterns of social dominance. The majority of these organizations offered very small rewards to their members, and even the most successful were quite exploitative. The most successful, however, were able to offer some possibility of 'social reproduction' to favoured subordinates. During the 1990s and 2000s, the possibility of access to Europe was the most powerful offer a gatekeeper could hold out to followers, and the association with Europe was central to the appeal of both *orchestres* and Pentecostal groups. While the *président* could be happy to see junior musicians return laden with goods and with their social standing enhanced, he was less happy to grant them independent access to Europe that would allow them a degree of independence that would be detrimental to his authority. It was only the canniest and most successful of subordinate musicians who were able to make this momentous step and, in general, the increasing difficulty of obtaining visas seems to have worked to reinforce the authority of established actors.

The notion of the *orchestre* as an example of a quasi-familial corporate body – which draws people to it, is organized hierarchically and allows 'elders' to secure the labour of underlings through acting as gatekeepers to the outside (and to the prestige goods coming from there) – is clearly reminiscent of precolonial political formations. It was part of the argument of Rey (1971, 1973) that the elders and cadets that made up those precolonial political formations were, in fact, social classes. This claim is often considered outlandish today, where talk of class in noncapitalist situations is generally dismissed as some sort of category error. As we argued at the start of this chapter, this dismissal generally relies on assumption rather than argument, with the over-reliance on metaphors of the 'horizontal' and the 'vertical' leading scholarship into all sorts of blind allies (see also Tilly 1999).

As in precolonial Central Africa, control over social reproduction via restricted access to the outside was the major mechanism of social dominance. Individual 'big men' cannot achieve or maintain such primacy acting alone, and gatekeepers at various points in the social formation show basic forms of class consciousness – only performing exchanges with other gatekeepers in a logic we have called *mutu na ngai* or 'my man'. Such forms of solidarity were not in general based on elaborate strategic visions, but instead were rooted in rather local and immediate imperatives to gatekeepers. I believe that such solidarity is also generated by forms of subjectivity related to music, which we will investigate in subsequent chapters. Subordinates did not accept this lying down and the present set of power relations within the *orchestre* are the result of hard-fought social struggles between the *président* and the rank-and-file musicians over control of social reproduction. Such struggles were not restricted to *orchestres*. In the next chapter we examine how a broader class of subordinate youth struggled to access social reproduction.

Notes

1. Whatever is said now, neo-Marxist studies in anthropology showed a keen interest in intermediaries and on specific empirical details. Wolf's essays of the 1950s and 1960s are particularly striking in this regard (e.g. Wolf 1956). Asad's (1972) essay on the Pathan is not, as is often argued, a denial of client ties in favour of class; rather, it is a demonstration that, in a place where the patrons are the landowners, client ties and class structures are mutually constitutive. Dupré and Rey's famous (1980) argument about 'articulation' describe a series of dyadic ties – 'horizontal' ties between trade partners leading to and from the coast, and vertical ties between 'elders' and 'cadets'. Much of the presumption that French Marxist writers were peddlers of abstract theory and uninterested in empirical detail comes from the fact that it was only their shorter, programmatic writings that were translated into English, while their lengthy empirical writings are only available in French. Monographs by Rey (1971) or Dupré (1982, 1985) defy the characterization of French Marxist anthropology as uninterested in empirical detail or the human scale.
2. To some extent, politicians would be included in the *mabanga* payments, as the names of politicians were frequently shouted. But payments from campaign songs – i.e. songs commissioned by politicians that are explicitly for political campaigns rather than love songs – and wider support, such as the frequent informal payments by politicians to musical figures, have been excluded.
3. And split down the middle with the studio arranger, who had done very little, but had made the initial contact with Figuero.
4. Though, in fact, in this case Josue kept on giving his money to his friend, not to the *président*.
5. Private communication with music producer, 20 August 2007.
6. If both parents are foreign nationals, it is only when the child reaches thirteen that he or she can apply for citizenship. Obviously, for the parents to stay in France for thirteen years, and prove that they have done so, requires that they have some other form of residence rights in the country.
7. Some of his musicians – like J.R. and Micha Bass – have EU passports.
8. J.B. has had some visa problems and has been granted admission to the UK with only brief visas to the Schengen Area. In the last two years, London has effectively become out of bounds, but J.B. seems now to have regained access to the Schengen Area.

– Chapter 6 –

MIKILISTE ECONOMIES

This chapter is about the resources and relationships connected to *mabanga*. It shows how various actors – the *mikilistes* in Europe, Congolese diamond miners in northern Angola (called *bana Lunda*), the younger members of the ruling class, and musicians themselves – came into contact in the context of music patronage. As the exchanges introduced by the *mikilistes* became ever more culturally central, they were taken up by those whose wealth was tied to the extractive economies in the interior – like diamond dealers in Kasai (south-central Congo) and northern Angola or the ruling class in Kinshasa. In Europe itself, successive waves of migrants, first in Paris and Brussels and later in London, vied to make the most impressive displays of wealth and style. As the Europe-based criminal economy went into decline – an economy that had underwritten *mikiliste* exchanges – the classes of people tied to the extractive economy, above all the rulers in Kinshasa, have come to dominate the kind of potlatch we have described. This eventually led to several trends, which I outline towards the end of this chapter. Certain *mikilistes* have been able to use their cultural capital to integrate into this elite milieu and become part of the political/business class themselves, also drawing on their cultural virtuosity to facilitate the successful performance of potlatch rituals by their sponsors in the political/business class. Another, larger group of migrants has been unable or unwilling to make this transition and has turned to attacking the musicians and journalists whom they once patronized. In this context, transnational flows of goods and praises have turned into exchanges of violence.

The *Mikiliste* and Wider Politics: Resistance?

Music and power were strongly associated in both precolonial and postcolonial polities. The typical *ambianceurs* of the post-independence state were members of the political and business elite, who cultivated a sense of joyous folly, courted scandalous women in bars and dispensed resources on musicians. The rituals of the *mikiliste* were clearly a variation on this earlier theme, yet because the *mikilistes* came of age in the 1970s and 1980s and were excluded by their elders, their largesse suggests imitation, not membership, of the ruling class. What such imitation might mean is controversial. Justin Gandoulou argues that the *sapeur* – a social figure largely continuous with the *mikiliste* – 'accepted the social system as it currently exists' (1989b: 174, my translation). We might align this idea with Perry Anderson's more general description of what he calls 'personal projects', which are 'inscribed within existing social relations and typically reproduce them' (1980: 19). Certainly, the actions of the *mikilistes* were personal in the sense that their concentration was on the well-dressed person and was aimed not at social change, but at a set of individual psychological goods – essentially to shake off their status as 'little men'.

But whatever their intentions, the *mikilistes* could not simply recreate the social world of the earlier generation – almost everything about 'the social system as it currently exists' was in the process of being violently disassembled. In their attempt to integrate with the old, they created something that was rather new. The ludic dress sense of this younger generation is in some way emblematic of this process. In their exploded suits, foot-long crocodile-skin shoes and *Hermes* umbrellas opened indoors, the *mikilistes* referenced – but went way beyond – the sartorial habits of their parents' generation. What was true of clothes was true more widely: improvising on an old theme in a new context, they produced a set of rituals that were far wilder and more desperate than those of their salaried forebears.

By the late 1980s, the regime faced broad-based opposition in Kinshasa (see Turner 2007). But this political challenge was accompanied by a much wider crisis of authority. Power in DRC has been exercised 'mostly outside the spheres of formal politics' (De Boeck 2004: 89) and the *mikilistes* challenged the symbolic primacy of the elite in many of these informal spheres. Nor were they alone. In the 1980s and 1990s, there was an upsurge in other social movements, where subaltern groups sought wealth in a series of increasingly desperate ways. This can be seen in the waves of looting that swept Kinshasa and later Brazzaville in the 1990s, and the departure of large numbers of young men to become *bana Lunda* – artisanal miners – in northern Angola (De Boeck 1998; Bazenguissa-Ganga 1999). The wealth thus acquired was spent in acts of wild dispersal.

Aware of the *mikilistes'* non-elite status, Gondola (1999) has written that their practices constituted a 'hidden critique' of the powerful, while Bazenguissa-Ganga and MacGaffey in their book *Congo-Paris* (2000: 3) contend that transnational Congolese traders 'on the margins of the law' – a group in which they include the *mikilistes* – drew on a 'second economy' to 'resist an oppressive state' (2000: 5). While the latter analysis does capture the anti-authoritarian nature of *mikiliste* practices, the rubric of resistance, derived from James Scott (1990a, 1990b), is rather misleading. In fact, the *mikilistes* came into regular contact with members of the ruling class in Europe and seem to have cultivated such ties. As we shall see, many *mikilistes* profited from such connections and even if the majority did not, they seem to have accepted being represented alongside the rulers in various ways.

Most striking in this regard is *mabanga* itself – the names of *mikilistes* regularly appeared in songs that also named members of the ruling class, and individuals in Paris or London were apparently content to be named in close proximity to some of the most notorious regime figures, men like Kongulu Mobutu or the army general popularly known as the 'Roi des Bêtes'. Musicians were in close contact with regime figures and with the *mikilistes*, and while this was eventually contested, it was years after the period described by the authors of *Congo-Paris*. Such contestation also took place after, and probably because of, the collapse of the clandestine *mikiliste* economy. Bazenguissa-Ganga and MacGaffey, by contrast, argue that the resistance of Congolese was enacted precisely via recourse to a clandestine 'second economy'.

But placing resistance at the centre of our conceptual schema creates even more fundamental problems. It encourages not only the wrong answers but also the wrong questions. Ideas of resistance or acquiescence, while sometimes useful, impose simple binary questions on a multilayered historical process and lead us to confuse actual behaviour and/or economic structures with ideological opposition. What I mean by this can be seen in the case of the *bana Lunda*. There seems little doubt that many of those who went to mine diamonds in northern Angola were hostile to Mobutu (see Mbiki 2008), yet the diamonds they mined provided a key resource to the Zaïrian ruling class in the late Mobutu period. This was crucial in economic terms – the diamonds were smuggled via Kinshasa and made money for key regime figures. But the benefits were not only economic. The export of diamonds via Zaïre from União Nacional para a Independência Total de Angola (UNITA) territory (in breach of a UN embargo) allowed the United States to keep its support for UNITA's anti-Soviet counterinsurgency 'off balance sheet'. Allowing diamonds to be smuggled via Zaïre thus gave Mobutu a chance to win back credit with his American allies, who had become disenchanted with their increasingly useless client.[1]

Even where popular action was undertaken in the service of an ideology that challenged the ruling class, the optic of resistance leads us to confuse intentions with effects. This is particularly apparent in the case of the two great street-level lootings or pillages that swept Kinshasa in the 1990s.[2] Both had paradoxical effects, but here I shall look particularly at the second, which took place in 1993. This event was sparked when Mobutu tried to pay soldiers using a new 5,000,000 Zaïre note (christened the *Dona Beija* by the Kinois, after a popular Brazilian soap opera character). The note was refused by shopkeepers, which triggered widespread looting by the soldiers. They targeted businesses and private homes associated with the regime. But, whatever the intention, the pillaging spree had a series of effects that were not entirely unhelpful to the regime.

Undirected by any kind of hegemonic leadership, the soldiers also targeted ordinary people and, unlike the first round of looting in 1991, in which the masses had participated, this second pillage of 1993 was also inflected by a clear sense of intimidation directed against the general population. For similar reasons, the soldiers made no attempt to do anything that would harm the ruling class permanently, such as arresting regime members or seizing broadcasting infrastructure. Lacking such direction, the major effect of the pillages seems to have been to ramify the already extant elite pattern of jettisoning infrastructure and concentrating on core networks of predation and resource extraction (see Reno 1998). It is as if the stormers of the Bastille had arrived to find the king already selling the stones for building materials.

This brings us on to my most important point – by the end of the 1980s, Zaïre was entirely caught up in the dynamic of potlatch. Escalating instability (Jewsiewicki 1992) meant that ever more dramatic displays of authority were demanded, actors sensed that resources tomorrow would be less than they were today, and individual enrichment was secured in ways that degraded the means of production and led to aggregate impoverishment.

As we have established, the optic of resistance does not help us to understand this dynamic, but there are also limits on the power of other explanations that stress elite strategy as the driving force, as to some extent is the case with Reno (1998). Rulers did better than others, and intentional strategies were important, but these intentional strategies were the most frantic and short-term kind of improvisations, whose wider effects were often perverse. It was beyond the control of any one social group, but it was not a force of nature and there were a number of people whose actions were critical in adding momentum to the dynamic. In this context the glory and fame contained in the *mabanga* transaction and the legendary returns of *mikilistes* to Kinshasa, where money was dispensed in wild rituals, were clearly a model for other social movements. Many of the prominent *bana Lunda* diamond dealers went to Angola intending to raise capital for trips to Europe (see below), while the rituals of largesse in which they participated – where years of hard labour could be distributed in weeks of wild living, music patronage and womanizing (see De Boeck 1998) – clearly drew on the *mikiliste* template. Underpinning these dispersals was the ideology of 'breaking rocks' or *kobeta libanga* – the idea that the wherewithal for such events was to be accumulated by any means necessary.

The *Mikiliste* Economy

As we have seen, *mikilistes* were able to access the resources necessary to perform various kinds of potlatch ritual. How were they able to do this? In one sense the answer is simple: they stole them. As we have shown in Chapter 2, creating a threshold around designer clothes was central, and in the early days the *mikiliste* methods to obtain these items was fairly direct. As one informant remembered:

> If you were going back to Kin, people would go shoplifting for months. There would be one person who would just spend weeks stealing [designer] socks. Imagine, weeks all day just on socks. Well, then they would arrive in Kinshasa and [making a throwing gesture] it would be like 'Parisien aye' ['(the) *Parisien* has come'].

Paris was the centre of this operation. The large number of pieces put into circulation, and the growing connoisseurship among Congolese, led to a system in which the equivalence of clothing with conventional currency became semiregularized. Most people did not steal clothes themselves, but, then as now, clothing was hawked ever more widely between the various *nganda*[3] and within *mikiliste* social networks. These networks of stolen clothes were known as *kula*. As we noted in Chapter 2, *kula* or *nkula* was a word frequently used to refer to red substances used to adorn the skin in ritual contexts, notably during male initiation – camwood, which was used to make this red paste, was a major valuable in precolonial Central Africa. A degree of haggling was involved in the selling of items, but this was mainly to catch the uninitiated, since an underlying agreement meant that prices were effectively set at half the retail cost. The knowledge of clothes and prices became a serious social advantage, and many Congolese would scan catalogues and trawl shops to obtain the required information. This cultural virtuosity, with its system of cash equivalence, made prestations of clothing, including those used as payment for musical patronage – *mabanga* – a far more quantifiable kind of transaction.

Stealing clothes was far from the only criminal activity undertaken by the *mikilistes*, and designer clothing was progressively integrated into a wider criminal economy. Drugs were (and are) an important part of this economy, with migrants acting both as dealers and as mules. However, probably the most important aspect was cheque fraud, or *chekula* as it is known in Lingala. As one former *bon vivant* put it: 'Ezalaka facile, ofungoli compte, ozwua chéquier' ('It was easy. You open an account. You take a cheque book'). And, as he might have added, you start issuing cheques. Initially this seems to have been the most common form of cheque fraud. One would open an account in a false name, using an item of fake identification. Later, in the 1990s, cheque books and cards were obtained or stolen using a variety of expedients. Sometimes the identification was produced in Europe. More often it would be the product of craft expertise in Kinshasa, where international vaccination cards or student cards were particularly economical and popular choices. From the 1990s onwards, credit card fraud also became extremely important, with the credit card itself being known as a *minduki* – or gun – because, in the words of one informant, it was like a gun: 'Whatever you want it will do for you.' A great deal of the money raised by these means went into the remittance economy, thereby staving off disaster in Kinshasa. Much of it was also spent on music patronage. Informants described how through the 1980s, *mabanga* became an increasingly monetized and formalized transaction. Many musicians were vague about prices at this period, but one confirmed that in 1989 a *dédicace* – where the patron is sung as the object of desire in the romantic narrative of a love song – cost around $4,000, a figure not so far removed from today's prices of $5,000–$6,000 from a top musician.

Bana Tshangu

The earliest *mikilistes* – like Niarcos and his friends – were associated with the *orchestre* Viva la Musica and their space at the Village Molokai in Matongé, near the centre of town. While they were coming of age in a society that promised them less and less, they came from families that had been relatively privileged, with salaried relatives and houses in older areas of the city near the colonial centre. One of the social tendencies that gathered weight as the 1980s progressed was the migration of the inhabitants of Tshangu, known as *bana Tshangu* (children of Tshangu – the singular is *mwana*). Composed of the vast and densely populated communes of N'djili, Masina and Kimbanseke, Tshangu is the largest and most crowded of Kinshasa's poorer outlying areas.

Migrants from Bandundu, the neighbouring region to Kinshasa, predominate in Tshangu, giving the area an ethnic mix that is different from the melting pot of the rest of the city. Living far from the centre, the *bana Tshangu* had not been members of the Village Molokai, located far away in Matongé and close to the colonial city centre. Nevertheless, *bana Tshangu* like Modogo Gian Franco Ferre and his younger contemporary Titi le Vallois became amongst the most prominent of *mikilistes*, admired for their dress sense and known for their name checks on record. Like their compatriots from the richer parts of town, the *bana Tshangu* came to Europe to escape an economy that struggled to provide for them. But while those who had left relatively affluent households could imagine that their family members were still doing reasonably well, the *bana Tshangu* could not entertain such illusions. Friends from more affluent districts in Kinshasa remembered how in the 1990s, as the economic noose began to tighten around the necks of the middle class, their relatives in Europe had sporadically sent back a few hundred dollars, while all around them in the money transfer offices, the relatives of migrant *bana Tshangu* who were abroad received regular packages of hundreds of dollars. Clothing remained hugely prominent among the items of largesse dispensed by migrants. Clothes were carried by migrants on return visits, but they were also sent back via informal remittance companies. One informant claims to have sent a parcel of designer clothing that cost £700 in postage alone. Often these clothes were sent in a way that appears very close to the manner of sending cash remittances.

The forms of solidarity and dispersal shown by the *bana Tshangu*, who were remembered by all informants as particularly extravagant distributors of resources, probably also exaggerated status competition beyond their milieu. Certainly the largesse of the *bana Tshangu* in Europe gave a certain inflection to existing social hierarchies. Several informants from more affluent backgrounds remember going to Tshangu before important social events and making cash offers to people in the street who were wearing the designer clothing sent by their relatives. An informant whose father was in the diplomatic core in the 1980s remembers stopping his car in the middle of the street and trying haggle a *mwana Tshangu* into parting with his *Jean de Marithé et François Girbaud*[4] jacket. Fairly soon afterwards, migrants from more affluent backgrounds also began to send designer clothes home to their families. One informant who was studying in Brussels and being heavily subsidized by his father said:

> I used to go to Matongé [in Brussels][5] and buy clothes for my sisters, who were still at school [in Zaïre]. And I can say that they were at school with the children of generals and cabinet ministers, but they were better dressed than all of them.

This underlines a further point: the migration of various *mikiliste* groups happened in parallel with a considerable elite migration, as throughout the 1980s, the ruling class increasingly sought to relocate their assets and families to Europe, above all to Brussels.

The imperative to secure clothes led to contacts between the ruling class and the *mikilistes* that would not have been made back home. The elite in Europe began to seek out the *mikilistes*, following them into areas like Matongé in Brussels and Château Rouge in Paris, as it was they who had access to *kula*, the circuits of cheap designer clothes. This drew many children of the elite into the milieu of the *ngandas* (see Bazenguisa-Ganga and MacGaffey 2000: 137–65) – the small, frequently illegal bars where musicians, *mikilistes*, famous courtesans and others hung out. Clearly, this implied that the *mikilistes* controlled the terms of access, which drew the rich kids further into accepting the forms of subjectivity that the *mikilistes* embodied.

Female *Mikilistes*

Women faced somewhat different challenges and opportunities compared to other *mikilistes*. They were in the minority in the *mikiliste demi monde*, perhaps because – a point touched upon in Chapter 1 – operating as a woman in this kind of environment means accepting a loss of respectability as a *mwasi ya libala*, a 'woman of marriage', and being dubbed a *ndumba* – a prostitute or courtesan. This sacrifice could grant another kind of reputation – as a scandalous sex symbol. Part of the cachet of these women was generally related to the fact that they had been lovers of famous musicians and that their names were often sung on record. Once in Europe, the women could access all the resources open to the men, and also had access to some other opportunities that were specific to women. Bar owning is often seen as a woman's job, and a charming and glamorous female patron of an establishment is certainly a big draw. Many of the most popular *nganda* in Paris were run by established sex symbols, women like Mere Malu or Laurisse la Congolaise.

The imperative of seeing and being seen in high-status locations meant that these illegal bars could charge way above the going rate for drinks (see Bazenguissa-Ganga and MacGaffey 2000), and the women also often engaged in romantic liaisons with the clientèle, with a flow of prestations from male to female (see Chapter 7). Such *basi ya success* – 'women of success' – were also involved in other activities that drew on their connection to the world of music and the bar. A good illustration of this is found in the story of Fifi Motema, a woman we last saw giving money to Werrason in Chapter 3.

Fifi Motema grew up in the Lemba district of Kinshasa, where she was a famed judo champion. She also seems to have had an irresistible sexual allure, being courted by musicians, footballers and glamorous crooks. She was born in Matadi and came to Kinshasa as a young girl, where she was taken in by the family of a general, whose name she now uses. Already rather a handful, she left his home reasonably young. She was always popular with men and rumours about her reputation seem to have started from the time of this move. Her enthusiasm for martial arts led to an affair with her judo master, with whom she had a child. Her life as a minor celebrity began through an affair with the goalkeeper of one of Kinshasa's main football teams. When he left to play for a team in South Africa, she began an affair with a *tata ngulu* – a people-smuggler – of some repute. Crazy for her, the *tata ngulu* spent lots of money on her, buying her a house and a BMW. From this time, musicians also began to sing the name of Fifi in concert, spreading her fame.

With a *tata ngulu* as her man, getting into Europe was a simple matter, and Fifi went to live in Switzerland with her beau in 1996. Fairly soon after arriving, she fled her *tata ngulu* boyfriend and went to live in Paris. She fell in with another man who was both a *tata ngulu* and a participant in several other unspecified forms of criminality.[6]

Her name, by now, had been sung by a great many musicians. Most recently, she has been romantically linked to one of the *atalakus* in the *orchestre* Wenge Maison Mère. Like many famous courtesans from Kinshasa, she also acts as a procuress, connecting her patrons with girls. Many of these girls are *sans papiers* for whom such transactions represent one of the few avenues of advancement open to them. She is also said to play a similar role with the female dancers from the DRC's popular *orchestres* when they tour Europe. Like other members of the *orchestre*, the dancers face great financial hardship when they arrive in Europe. Fifi will offer them a place to stay and will also play go-between with the many men in the diaspora who want introductions to the dancers, extracting recompense when these women obtained patron lovers.

Bana Londres

As the 1990s progressed, an important new destination for Kinois fleeing economic collapse and an upsurge in political violence was London. The reasons why people came to London specifically were diverse. There was a perception that London was less racist than Paris or Brussels. Informants also cited the fact that work was easier to come by there, and that, with changes that took place in the wake of the 1990 Schengen Convention, it was more difficult to obtain visas to signatory countries, which included France and Belgium. The discontinuation of many grants available to foreign students in France and a progressive tightening of checks made before the issuing of student visas by the French and Belgian Embassies also played a role. Student visas had been one of the principal modes of entry for Zaïrians (Tipo-Tipo 1995).

A reason of undoubted importance was the ease of identity fraud in the UK. The period stretching roughly from 1990 until 2000 is obliquely referred to as *le temps de l'argent facile* – the time of easy money. The universal perception among informants, many of whom had lived in France or Belgium prior to coming to London, was that fraud had been considerably easier and more lucrative in the United Kingdom than in other European countries. The United Kingdom appears to have been slower to address the weak points in its banking and benefits systems, leading to a period of 'easy money' that lasted considerably longer than in other European countries. The United Kingdom was also behind France and Belgium in introducing fingerprinting for asylum claims, without which the practice of routine multiple applications could continue for longer. As in France, *chekula* was the most widespread form of fraud. In the United Kingdom, syndicates working out of the post office were central. During the service-sector boom of the 1990s, work in postal sorting offices was easy to secure.

The *mikiliste* in the sorting office would throw aside anything that looked like a chequebook. These cheques would then be made out and signed, after which likely locations for cashing them were sought. Often a syndicate would have a specialist, who would spend all his time driving around post offices and small bank branches in his regions of operation, cashing cheques. Another common strategy was to make use of *bureaux de change*, on occasions striking a deal with the owners for sharing the profits. Soon certain Congolese from London started using this wealth in extravagant ways, attending concerts in Paris and decisively outdoing their rivals in potlatch rituals, as they dressed in fantastically expensive clothes and showered money on musicians.

A less common but more dramatic theatre for these displays was Kinshasa itself. Many of the potlatch events associated with the return of *bana Londres* to Kinshasa have passed into popular legend. Luxury cars were a particularly important area for the display of rank and by the mid-1990s were being shipped back in large numbers, and migrants began to send home 4x4s for use during the few weeks of the year that they spent in Kinshasa. One famous London *mikiliste* bought a Jaguar, known as an *ngubu* (hippopotamus) by the Kinois,[7] and had it shipped to Kinshasa. When he learned that a rival already had such a vehicle, he took a large rock and beat his car with it – implying that it was nothing to him, whereas his rival would not dare mistreat his car in this way. Another *mikiliste* took to letting his Rolls Royce be used as a taxi. Taxis are the cheapest form of transport in Kinshasa and the majority are dilapidated old bangers, so the implication was that this Rolls Royce was a thing of no account to a man such as its owner. These stories mark extreme instances – as we have argued, the potlatch was more about display and distribution than destruction – but such logics of theatrical destruction are fairly widespread. It is common at concerts and in bars for individuals to remove expensive jackets and throw them on the floor. The reasoning here, recounted to me on several occasions, is that the jacket is *eloko pamba* – a worthless thing – to 'one such as myself'.[8]

This extraordinary wealth has been interpreted by the Kinois in a striking way – London is seen as a city dominated by witchcraft and many expressed great fear about Congolese who had returned from London. One reported that 'you have to pay attention when you see these *bana Londres* going past in their Jeeps. They are very dangerous'. One of the reasons why London has become so associated with witchcraft is the reports circulating in Kinshasa about London's large Indian population. Local beliefs equate Hinduism with devil worship and I was told repeatedly that Indians operate shops selling *ba talisman* 'on every street corner' in London. But, more fundamentally, such beliefs about the wealth of the *bana Londres* must relate to older Central African political and economic theories. And given that the *mikilistes* reproduced many aspects of an earlier potlatch dynamic, it is perhaps not surprising that such prosperity was understood with reference to the local political tradition. In the context of economies based around violence and gatekeeping, to become wealthy or powerful has often been thought to necessitate the mystical sacrifice of others (see also Harms 1981: 251). Sudden surges of unstable wealth are clearly a recurring motif of Central African modernity and have tended to be viewed as *mbongo ya nkisi* – money from *fétiche*.

In the expanding displays of ritual authority, *mabanga* was probably the single most important device. Used for creating a reputation, it allowed status and rank to be depicted and conceptualized through the romantic narratives of the songs and the implication of a connection to a glamorous world. The wealth of the Congolese in London was key to the further development of *mabanga*. The means to achieve this were pioneered by Koffi Olomide on his 1993 album *Magie*. Advances in recording technology meant that by the 1990s, in well-equipped first-world studios, upwards of forty musical lines, or *pistes*, could be recorded separately and mixed into the same song. Overwhelmed with requests for *mabanga* by Congolese in the diaspora, above all from London, Koffi Olomide devoted a separate track just to reading off names at any point where a space in the music would allow it. Early on in the record, Koffi acknowledges the provenance of much of this new support, saluting the 'Bana Magie oyo ya Londres': literally, 'children of Magie, those ones from London'. From this moment, *mabanga* came to be the principal source of revenue for most musicians. As we will see, it is also around this time that *mabanga*'s shift from the margins to the centre becomes perceptible. What was once a practice associated with a chic but disreputable subculture would soon become a central aspect in the expression of power relations for the political elite.

Bana Lunda

The *bana Lunda*, the Congolese who went to Lunda Norte Province in Angola in search of diamonds, were another important vector of migrant capital. In the 1980s, significant deposits of high-quality diamonds were discovered in northern Angola, a country that was by then in the grip of a civil war between UNITA, a rebel group backed by the United States (and its proxies in Zaïre and South Africa) and the pro-*Soviet* Movimento Popular de Libertação de Angola (MPLA) government. Since UNITA lacked direct access to the outside world, diamonds mined in the territory it controlled were exported via Zaïre. This offered an important economic resource to the Zaïrian ruling class. Many of Mobutu's inner circle ran planes into Lunda Norte, ferrying in supplies (which sold for a fortune in the besieged territory) and carrying out diamonds. Key smugglers included Mobutu's son, Kongulu, aka 'Saddam', his security chief and ethnic *confrère* Honoré Ngbanda (Mbiki 2008), and Bangala businesman Bemba Saolona, a key ally of the regime whose daughter later married another of Mobutu's sons, Nzanga (Bemba Saolona was also the father of Jean-Pierre Bemba, leader of the Uganda-backed rebel group and the Movement du Libération du Congo (MLC) political party, who is currently on trial at The Hague).

The town of Cafunfo at the centre of the region changed hands several times, but the surrounding country was controlled for most of the period by UNITA. The instability generated by the war meant that extraction was a largely 'artisanal', pre-industrial production process, for which a massive influx of Zaïrians from across the border provided the majority of the labour force (De Boeck 1998; Monnier, Jewsiewicki and de Villiers 2001; Mbiki 2008). Like the *bana Tshangu*, with whom there was a considerable degree of crossover, the majority of these migrants had roots in Bandundu, a province with historical and geographical ties to northern Angola. By the early 1990s, the *bana Lunda* had acquired a distinct identity in Kinshasa, spending dollars gained in Angola on the kinds of potlatch with which we are now familiar. Much of this money was spent on *mabanga*, with musicians in Kinshasa mythologizing the *bana Lunda* in praises to rival those showered on the *mikilistes*.

While the lion's share of the wealth generated from mineral extraction has been made by expatriate-owned *comptoirs*, local figures have been significant links between the resources of the interior and the Kinshasa-based political elites. In the case of the Lunda Norte economy of the 1990s, undoubtedly the most important such figure was Tshatsho Mbala 'Kashoggi'.[9] Tshatsho Mbala was born in Kikwit, in the province of Bandundu. Like many Zaïrians, when he finished his studies in the early 1980s, he set off to look for diamonds. His first excursions into the diamond trade seem to have been in Kasai in the south of the DRC, around the towns of Kananga and Tshikapa. Later on he went to Lunda Norte in Angola. Having already acquired a knowledge of diamonds, he arrived relatively early in the boom time there and was able to strike up a strong relationship with Jonas Savimbi, leader of UNITA. Named the 'president' of the Zaïrian miners by UNITA and eventually head of UNITA's diamond corporation (Mbiki 2008: 100), Tshatsho dealt in diamonds himself, but was also able to create a gatekeeper role as fixer or *passage obligé* for Zaïrians in Lunda Norte, who were vulnerable to the whims of the UNITA regime. Such vulnerability principally concerned the 'little people', who were subjected to exemplary beatings for the most trivial offences and could be summarily executed at the whim of a local UNITA *delegado* (see Mbiki 2008). But on occasion the vulnerability extended up the political network.

In this context Tshatsho was able to do something inconceivable on the other side of the frontier – that is, to resist the will of Mobutu's son, 'Saddam'. In the early 1990s, Tshatsho and Saddam were in conflict. I have not penetrated the details of the dispute, but it seems that for a time Tshatsho was able to restrict Saddam's access to the diamond fields of Lunda Norte. Tshatsho, ensconced in Angola, was safe, but the conflict could not have come at a worse time for what was then Zaïre's most popular music group, Wenge Musica BCBG. Why? Well, they were about to release an album, *Pleins Feux*. The album was larded with praise shouts for Tshatsho Mbala, and one of the standout tracks, 'Tshatsho Mbala le monde est méchant' (Werrason 1995), was dedicated to Tshatsho. The song has a rather lightly articulated narrative, where Werrason sings as a woman who has overcome doubters to live with Tshatsho Mbala. The main idea conveyed, however, is that those who are far away from Tshatsho are not qualified to judge him, yet say bad things about him: 'Batekisa finga na yo soi-disant ozali mabe' – 'They trade insults about you saying you are bad'. Yet those close to Tshatsho know what a good soul he is: 'Mais na vandi pembeni namoni seulment le contraire' – 'But I have stayed close and I see only the opposite'. The lyrics sound as if they were deliberately written to take Tshatsho's side in the dispute, though in fact this was entirely accidental. The album seems to have been recorded in Paris before the dispute emerged, and Wenge Musica BCBG had already had enough experience of Saddam to know not to cross him.

And in general the interplay between the Mobutu regime, the diamond miners, UNITA and high-living fixers like Tshatsho was shot through with ambiguity. As Mbiki's account makes clear, hostility to the Mobutu regime and UNITA among the miners was fairly widespread, yet at the same time the former *bana Lunda* I spoke to remembered Tshatsho with real warmth, even though his dealings depended upon and enriched those groups. Tshatsho was petitioned constantly and greatly admired (Mbiki 2008: 100–2). The admiration was connected to his lifestyle, which included constant handouts to his retinue and expenditure on *mabanga* with Kinshasa's most popular musicians. The number of young women surrounding Tshatsho was legendary and, at one point, he was served by a staff of young women known as the 'Tshatshettes'.

Among the most prominent diamond dealers in Kinshasa more recently is Didi Kinuani, self-proclaimed *sauveur de l'humanité* – saviour of humanity. Like Tshatsho, Didi was born in Kikwit. His main business is still in Cafunfo (the capital of diamond mining in Lunda Norte), though he is frequently in Kinshasa. Didi arrived in Lunda Norte in the early 1990s and, at the start of his career, worked in Cafunfo for a Frenchman who ran a *comptoir* – an official buying point for diamonds. Didi is said to have an excellent eye for diamonds and quickly became a trusted employee, travelling to Antwerp, where the highest quality gemstones are cut and traded. The French company liquidated in the late 1990s and he took over the *comptoir* address book – including, it is said, his contacts with the Antwerp diamond houses.

When in Kinshasa, Didi is famed for his acts of largesse. One informant remembers a social occasion to which he was invited. He was called over to the main table, given a handful of dollars and instructed to give each guest at his table $200, then to take $300 for himself. When Didi had done the same for all the tables, he took his briefcase and went outside, where a crowd of street children were waiting in the hope of receiving a few dollars. He opened his briefcase, throwing $5,000 over the throng. In the recent past he was also the largest single music patron in Kinshasa, with songs dedicated to him by, among others, Kester Emeneya, Madilu System, Werrason, Mirage, Jus d'Eté and Papa Wemba. One musician he has not received *mabanga* from in recent years is J.B. Mpiana – wagging tongues in Kinshasa attribute this to the fact that Didi married J.B.'s former wife Amida. Unlike Tshatsho, Didi has excellent connections with the MPLA and it is alleged that he sells diamonds for the President's wife.

Mabanga and Younger Members of the Political Elite

The desire by the *bana Lunda* to emulate the *mikilistes* was part of a wider trend in youth culture. From the 1990s onwards, younger members of the political and business elite in particular began to participate in the *mikiliste* mode of success. The reasons for this trend have already been discussed – *mikiliste* subjectivity was a variant on the well-established model of the *ambianceur*. The *mikilistes* came into contact with members of the elite in Europe (see also Bazenguissa-Ganga and MacGaffey 2000). *Mikilistes* were able to establish designer clothes as a central medium of exchange/prestige and were able to control access to the circulation of these clothes. Meanwhile, potlatch returns to Kinshasa, and above all *mabanga*, established the *mikiliste* sensibility as the dominant form of prestige among the young.

From the 1990s onwards, the names of younger members of the elite began to appear on record. A range of military and political names could be cited, but most prominent among these was Kongulu 'Saddam Hussein' Mobutu. In the increasingly lawless milieu of Zaïre in the 1990s, Saddam was enormously powerful. Aside from his father's wealth, he made large amounts of money from diamonds. Using the security forces to do his bidding, he was famous for his enthusiasm for *ambiance*, establishing a new variant of the *ambianceur* as violent sexual predator (see Biaya 1997). One of the fruits of his enthusiasm for this world was the establishment of his personal production company, Yosshad, which dealt with different aspects of music production.

Yosshad Productions

The following story, showing the trajectory of one *mikiliste* and his interactions with Yosshad Productions, gives a good indication of how the elements of music, access to migration, and informal economic and political power began to recombine into something close to their present form. Jean Mutombo was born and grew up in Bandalungwa, more often known as Bandal, a central district of Kinshasa. He went to primary school there, then to high school in the Institut de la Gombe. Bandal was also the home *quartier* of Wenge Musica, the *orchestre* that dominated the Kinshasa music scene in the 1990s. Still in school, at this time, was Blaise Bula, who became one of the main singers of Wenge Musica. Several other members of the *orchestre* probably also attended. Like most *bana Bandal*, Jean was a great fan of Wenge

Musica and was well known to several members of the *orchestre* from long before they became famous. Even as a young adult in the late 1980s, Jean lived the life of a minor star – *vie de vedettariat*. He dated several girls, he liked music and was also something of a thug – 'un homme fort ... pomba'. For the Kinois, such a lifestyle requires the use of *fétiche*, and Jean was said to be quite enthusiastic in his use of occult devices.

Jean's father had a good position at the Agence Central de Transport and in around 1989, he assembled the funds to send Jean to Europe to study. Jean did not do much studying. Arriving in Europe and continuing with the kind of life he had enjoyed in Kinshasa, he hung out in *nganda*, going to concerts and living the life of the *mikiliste*. When Wenge Musica came on their first tour of Europe, Jean met up with the group. Also during this tour, Wenge experienced their first split. A group of musicians, including the bassist Aime Buanga and the singer Marie Paul, remained behind in Paris and formed an *orchestre* called Wenge Musica el Paris, though shortly thereafter, following a dispute with Wenge Musica BCBG, they became Wenge el Paris. Jean had himself named a kind of honorary *président* of the *orchestre*, a role somewhere between a patron and a manager. Quite how he pulled this off is a bit of a mystery, as most of those who knew him from Bandal said that he did not have especially deep pockets at this time.

What Jean did have, however, was a lot of daring and an excellent set of contacts, and it is probably this that convinced Marie Paul and others to take him on in this prominent role. In his capacity as manager, Jean organized the return of Wenge el Paris to Kinshasa, doing so in collaboration with Yosshad Productions. Whether Jean had known Saddam before this collaboration is unclear, and Saddam's backing of Wenge el Paris relates to a set of rather murky incidents. At a certain point in the early 1990s, the then main faction of Wenge – Wenge Musica BCBG[10] – fell foul of Saddam, an occurrence that is subject to a number of conflicting accounts. According to one version, Saddam was angered by J.B. Mpiana's adoption of *le Maréchal* as a praise name, given that this was one of Mobutu *le père*'s own titles. According to another, he was angered by the group's appearance on television wearing ties.[11] A third story concerns a conflict over one of J.B. Mpiana's girlfriends whom Saddam wanted for himself and eventually acquired. A fourth has it that there was a dispute over musical equipment belonging to Saddam, which had been damaged during a performance by Wenge Musica BCBG. Whatever the truth, there seems to have been a history between Saddam and the *orchestre*, and he decided that Yosshad productions would back Wenge el Paris.

There was also the aforementioned conflict between Saddam and Tshatsho Mbala, in which Wenge Musica BCBG were also caught up.

Be that as it may, by 1993 Jean was working as part of Yosshad productions. According to several informants, he was also a *tata ngulu*, taking money to smuggle people into France – we may speculate that the musical and political connections he enjoyed would have been useful in this line of work. He continued to operate within Yosshad, growing closer to Saddam until he eventually joined FROJEMO (Front des Jeunes Mobutistes), an organization that contained several ambitious, politically minded young men, many of whom passed smoothly into the current political setup, among them the young Vital Kamerhe, once secretary of the PPRD, the party of Joseph Kabila, and presidential candidate for his party, the Union pour la Nation Congolaise, in 2011.

As the decade progressed, it became clear that Wenge el Paris had been the wrong horse to back. While Wenge Musica BCBG released a series of albums that took Kinshasa by storm, notably *Kalayi Boeing* (1994) and *Pentagone* (1996), Wenge el Paris stagnated. The former made several successful tours of Europe, while Wenge el Paris, despite its name, stayed in Kinshasa – which, for the Kinois music fan, is synonymous with failure. Even Saddam switched his allegiance, and Wenge Musica BCBG reciprocated with a song dedicated to Saddam, entitled 'Le Tempête du désert', a song that clearly casts Saddam as a kind of *mikiliste*. Singing as a smitten woman awaiting the return of her beloved to Kinshasa's N'djili Airport from Europe, the song stresses Saddam's dress sense: 'soki alati kitoko, il faut tala presence' – 'If he dresses beautifully one must behold his presence'. It is also larded with praises for real *mikilistes* in London, Paris and Switzerland. Acclaiming him as a Zaïrian aristocrat, the song continues: 'Essence na ba bourgeois Saddam Hussein' – 'The essence of the bourgeois[12] Saddam Hussein'. The female lover has also bought a 'bouquet of flowers' and the 'perfume of love' so that, on the day he comes, she can anoint Saddam 'Ndenge bapabolaki Jesus na Bethanie' – 'As they anointed Jesus in Bethany' (Massela 1994).

During this time, Jean's stock was naturally somewhat reduced, but he retained several aces up his sleeve. One such was his French citizenship; during an interview for the popular music/showbiz gossip programme *Karibou Variétés* in the 1990s, he even took out and brandished his red French passport. As we shall see, whatever his travails, Jean still had a bright future, bringing the *mikiliste* arts into contact with the ruling class.

Instability

The mode of success adopted by the *bana Lunda* and many members of the ruling class closely resembles that of the *mikilistes*. This is hardly surprising – the *bana Lunda* seem to have set out very consciously to imitate the *mikilistes*. Indeed, a great many informants have used Angola as a springboard to European migration, and informants close to Didi Kinuani and Tshatsho Mbala said that initially both had intended to use Angola as a way to raise capital for journeys to Europe. Likewise, ruling-class involvement with *mabanga* and designer clothing was explicitly based on *mikiliste* models, to the extent that they often bought *kula* from *mikilistes*.

The alacrity with which these forms were adopted is, of course, related to common predecessors. What is interesting is that the forms of production relied upon by the *bana Lunda* and the ruling class displayed far more material similarity with the economies of the Central African past than did the *mikiliste* economy itself. The *bana Lunda* economy, based on violence, nonindustrial productive systems and an external demand for a raw commodity, shows a striking similarity with the economies of the eighteenth, nineteenth and early twentieth centuries in the region, organized around the violent appropriation of such items as slaves, ivory or rubber (see Harms 1981; Vellut 2004). For the *bana Lunda* and the ruling class based in Kinshasa, the crucial importance of the gatekeeper/intermediary is one with clear echoes in the precolonial past, although in the modern context, access to the capital and to the 'resources of sovereignty' this grants (Englebert 2003) have now replaced access to the coast as the ultimate guarantor of rentier income.

This connects with the analysis we presented in Chapter 5. As in the past, 'parcellized' forms of sovereignty contain aspects of hierarchy both within and between political units. The one who connects the local economic unit with the outside is recognized as 'big', or 'heavy', is acclaimed as 'Kashoggi' or 'Sauveur de l'humanité' and is surrounded by the 'empty' – followers, lovers, petitioners and acclaim. Long-distance political allegiance (like almost everything else) is shifting and unstable, but as a first attempt at generalization, we could say that it tends to follow a logic in which those further away from a connection to the capitalist outside world are in a subordinate relationship to those who are nearer to such a connection.

A complicating factor concerns the quality of connection with the outside world: those who are in a real alliance with the capitalist classes beyond Central Africa, such as UNITA, though they were relatively cut off, tend to be more powerful than those who effect 'pirate' forms of articulation, such as the *mikilistes*, who connected directly to the resources of the capitalist mode of production, but in ways that were not legitimated by the dominant classes in Europe.

The need to meet capitalist demand from noncapitalist forms of production and the insatiable demands for displays of ritual authority mean that these relations of production imply all the political and economic instability of the precolonial potlatch dynamic. As certain authorities collapse, various subordinate gatekeepers are quite suddenly thrown into confusion. One musician friend described working on a production funded by Tshatsho in 2002, when news came through of the assassination of Jonas Savimbi. 'My God he was furious', the informant remembered, 'but what could I do? It wasn't my fault Savimbi was killed.' When this fieldwork began, it was very widely asserted by many informants that, in the post-Savimbi world, Tshatsho was 'finished'. The success of Fally Ipupa's song 'Associé' (quoted in Chapter 7), dedicated to Tshatsho, and his further investments in Fally – including $14,000 spent on equipping his *orchestre* – seem designed to allay this impression.

Exceptional here are the *mikilistes* themselves. They not only travelled to Europe, but had their resource base there. Far more sustainable forms of capitalist accumulation would have been possible. But this was not what happened. The imaginative and emotional universe of the *mikilistes*, generated in the collapsing Zaïre of the 1970s and 1980s, reproduced the logic of potlatch. For although recent immigrants are commonly involved in crime and although the Congolese were far from being the only ones involved in benefit and cheque fraud, the logic of potlatch meant that, unlike other migrants, they rarely accumulated capital. As one London-based informant put it: 'The Indians and Jamaicans they were all doing it too, but they started shops. We spent it on shoes.' For the *mikilistes*, banks were places to defraud rather than places to keep money; a culture of keeping money in banks is almost as absent among *mikilistes* in Europe as it is for the Kinois, where the banking system has collapsed. A great many informants in any case have terrible credit ratings arising from unpaid overdrafts, as well as convictions for fraud, making banking difficult or impossible.

Even in the field of criminal endeavour, the short-term nature of the *mikiliste* search for fame seems to have left him behind. The incompetence and lack of ambition of many Congolese criminals in Europe is often satirized by the Congolese themselves. One well-known Paris-based drug dealer is so often in jail that he is referred to as 'Mandela' and Papa Wemba gave him the praise name of *bakanga ba cracra balemba* – 'they tired of putting handcuffs on him' – under which name he has received several shouts on record. Even Stervos Niarcos, in many ways the model of a *mikiliste*, died in prison in the mid 1990s. It is common to hear *mikilistes* speak in awed tones about Nigerian gangsters or Cameroonian *feymen*; many of the more profitable scams brought to my attention in recent times were efforts coordinated by Nigerian or Cameroonian gangs in which a *mikiliste* had played a peripheral role.

Increasingly draconian immigration regimes throughout the 1990s have also meant that being caught carries with it the threat of expulsion, while their lack of involvement with the formal economy makes acquiring permanent resident rights difficult. The dilemma of being trapped between the potlatch and the police in this declining economy is well evoked by Papa Wemba in his song 'Kaokokokorobo' (Wemba 1995), where Wemba recounts in very slang-inflected Lingala how they broke into the designer clothes shop 'Ligal ya Caluggi na ya Comme' – 'the stall of Caluggi and Comme [des Garçons]', to get the gear he was going to 'kotelema' – 'stand up in' at a concert. But the house where he lived and where the stolen goods were stored got raided by the police, his 'pal got pushed [deported]' to Congo 'masta batindika ye'. Now that he has lost everything, his girl has moved on – 'abendana' – taking his clothes by 'tshatche [Versace]' and 'Ba Miyake [Issey Miyake]' along with her. Her parting shot is that, in his reduced state, 'he is not down with the hip crowd' 'alobi ngai nayebi movement te'.

As the new century has progressed, *le temps de l'argent facile* has come to an end. While the criminal and informal economies are still important in the community, increased security – police raids, video cameras installed in postal sorting offices and tighter controls on benefit allocation in France, Belgium and the UK – has meant that simple forms of identity fraud, so often practised by the *mikilistes*, are barely worth the risk. 'Monde wana esili', as many informants commented – that world is finished.

All of the most famous *mikiliste* that I was aware of were given prison sentences, some of them substantial. Even more importantly, with the economies of fraud all but dismantled and the exuberant nightlife a thing of memory, many of the *mikilistes* seem to have accepted that their time was over. When the police came for Jean Marie, he knew he was going away. His famous wardrobe had been financed through his membership of a syndicate that stole cheques from the post office. Always a charming man, he persuaded the police to let him change into his Jean Paul Gaultier outfit before he was taken to the police station. Eusebio, who had been a close confidant of Papa Wemba and Stervos Niarchos, served nearly two years in prison and emerged to find the world changed. He moved in with a very devout Pentecostal woman, who had banned alcohol and 'worldly' music. Using me as an excuse, as much perhaps for himself as for anyone else, Eusebio would buy in large amounts of beer, nodding in satisfaction as I finished it – obediently he didn't touch a drop – and talked animatedly of days gone by. Like many others, he believed the particularly spectacular decline of the London scene was a consequence of the extreme use of magic devices by the London *mikilistes*. 'Ye wana!' – 'That one!' said Eusebio of one London-based star who had long since vanished from the firmament. 'Nganga azwui pin number na ye!' – 'The *nganga* took his pin number!'

The knock-on effects of this within the Congolese communities of Paris and London were far-reaching. The hordes of young men who, when I started fieldwork, clustered in and around the small shops selling CDs and African foods in Chateau Rouge were *commissionnaires*. Their near-constant hanging out, which I had found so convenient as a junior ethnographer, was not aimless. They were waiting for a commission – to cash a bad cheque, dispose of stolen goods, etc. Walking the same streets today, one is struck by how few of them remain. The number of small bars decreased sharply, as did the diasporic media outlets – financed as they were by handouts from *mikilistes* who paid to appear in productions. Deprived of the income from cheque and other forms of fraud, and of the freedom it gave to spend long nights hanging out in bars with other *mikilistes*, all forms of potlatch expenditure by migrants have declined.

New Trends: The Winners

Divergent trends have emerged among the *mikilistes*. The first trend is integration into the political system, with certain *mikilistes* drawing on their cultural virtuosity to instruct members of the political elite in the arts of *ambiance*, while at the same time becoming part of the political elite themselves. These figures managed to shift their source of finance from the dying migrant criminal economy to the rent-seeking of the rulers. Jean Mutombo once again provides us with a revealing example. After the fall of Mobutu, he again used his contacts to befriend key members of the regime's inner circle, many of whom liked to hang out in the bars in Bandal, living the good life and listening to music. The nightclubs of Bandal were Jean's natural habitat and he took the opportunity to make contact – bringing with him gifts of designer clothing, using his sense of style and his access to the circuits of *kula* to help the former guerrilla fighters who did not know their *Comme des Garçons* from their *Yohji Yamamoto*. The connection was extremely useful to Jean, who moved into several import/export activities, undoubtedly with powerful help. During the elections of 2006, he stood as a candidate for the presidential party, the PPRD (Partie du Peuple pour la Reconstruction et la Démocratie) in the national elections and is now a deputy in the National Assembly.

A number of journalists who had formerly lived in Europe and depended primarily on the largesse of the *mikilistes* now moved back to Kinshasa and began to integrate into the political class. Zacharie Babababaswe had been a celebrity and music journalist who presented his programme *Feux Verts* from Belgium. His previous income, like that of many other European-based journalists, came from *mikilistes* who paid to appear on his programme. In the mid 2000s he returned to Kinshasa and, alongside new broadcasting interests, also became a Deputy in the National Assembly for the PPRD. Sam Mpengo Mbey, the editor of the magazine *Grands Lacs* – originally a kind of *Hello!* magazine for Congolese in the diaspora – followed a similar trajectory. Sam started the magazine in the UK and made money mainly from *mikilistes* who paid to appear in it. In 2006 he and the magazine returned to Kinshasa, and the content changed sharply. Having previously been given over to profiles of musicians and to *mikilistes* posing in their finery, it now became a kind of political review, along the lines of *Jeune Afrique*, with most space being taken up by Congolese politicians, above all from the *Kabiliste* stable. His new clients, like his old ones, paid to appear. I have heard plausible rumours that he made a million dollars from the election of 2006, though this cannot be confirmed.

A number of female *mikilistes* have been able to use their charms to effect a similar form of integration into the political class, in a way that reproduces the earlier relationship between the 'scandalous beauties' and politicians. One example would be the aforementioned Fifi Motema, whom we left in Paris. Fifi also had business interests in Kinshasa, where she had a boutique selling clothes in Matongé, one of the major commercial areas of Kinshasa, though this now appears to have been sold on. It is said that she visits Kinshasa fairly regularly, where it is asserted that she is romantically linked to one of the most prominent politicians in the city. I was sceptical about this, but several informants assured me that two high-level politicians, including one who was then a very senior cabinet minister, were known to be involved with her.

This is part of a wider, reiterating pattern: as in earlier times, 'scandalous beauties' from the world of the bar have become integrated into the ruling political business class. Wivine Moleka, a celebrity journalist, onetime lover of Papa Wemba and, more recently, of Laurent Kabila, was elected a PPRD deputy in the National Assembly in 2006. Tshala Muana was another lover of Laurent Kabila and was one of the few musicians to gain significant patronage from him. She was a member of the (appointed) National Assembly of 2000 and more recently became President of the PPRD Woman's League. This account from Gerard Prunier is rather evocative:

> When presidential chief of staff Aubert Mukendi asked the famous singer Tshala Muana the reason for the payment he was supposed to make to her, she burst out laughing and answered, 'I give very special night concerts to the Chief and that is a very expensive service.' (Prunier 2009: 165)

The echoes of the earlier post-independence relationships described in Chapter 1 travel down the decades as effortlessly as love songs.

The Losers

A second, much larger group of *mikilistes* were unable to integrate themselves into the political system and, as the economy that had underwritten their former largesse was eroded, feelings of financial exclusion began to feed into a new kind of Congolese nationalism. After the 1980s, the opposition to Mobutu among the Kinois and Kinois migrants to Europe had been led by the UDPS (Union pour le Démocratie et Progrès Social), which was one of the few political groups with a pedigree of integrity and nonviolence. After the fall of Mobutu, the new regime fairly quickly alienated a large section of the Kinois population (and by extension much of the Kinois diaspora in Europe), offering little by way of material improvement in their lives and often seeming to imply that the Kinois had been complicit in Mobutu's rule. Despite this, a succession of strategic errors by the UDPS – above all its refusal to participate in the peace accords of Sun City or in the elections of 2006 – probably misread the popular mood and certainly left the party excluded from the sources of patronage that accrued to all those participating in the transitional government (Van Woudenberg 2006). At the same time, oppositional political networks associated with former Mobutistes were extremely active, associating themselves via the media with ideologies about the Congolese war that combined anti-imperialism with stridently xenophobic narratives.

Chief among these was the MLC, a rebel movement backed by Uganda, which took part in the transitional government established by the Sun City Agreement and also participated in the elections of 2006. It was led by Brussels-educated Jean-Pierre Bemba, the son of Bemba Saolona, the wealthy member of Mobutu's inner circle. Also significant was APARECO (Alliance des Patriotes pour le Refondation du Congo), an extreme nationalist party based in Europe and led by Mobutu's close ally and ethnic confrère Honoré Ngbanda. The diaspora in Europe, in particular, was a centre for the dissemination of stridently racist narratives, which drew on the same kinds of 'Hamitic hypothesis' that had been a factor in the Rwandan genocide (see Taylor 1999). Since the ADFL/RPA (Alliance des Forces Démocratiques pour le Congo/Rwandan Patriotic Army) takeover of Congo in 1997, there had been growing popular resentment at the quasi-colonial behaviour of Kagame's Rwanda. Kinyarwanda speakers living in the DRC were subject to harassment and pogroms, and an ideology emerged, heavily indebted to colonial racial theory, that opposed noble *bantus* (here applied to Congolese) to jealous *nilotiques* (here applied to Rwandans), who were in league with Westerners in their quest to pillage the DRC.

Like many of the most dangerous tales of national grievance, this account contained an element of truth. 'The West' has clearly backed Joseph Kabila, and acted deaf and dumb in relation to clear evidence of war crimes committed by, among others, Rwanda. That said, the narrative contains some pretty crude conspiracy theories, while many of those who propound these theories – Ngbanda, Bemba and others – are in a position of extreme hypocrisy. Bemba, as guerrilla leader, was backed by Uganda and almost certainly also 'took his dossier' to Rwanda (Prunier 2009: 204); Ngbanda, like Bemba's father, was a central figure in the late Mobutu regime and a huge smuggler with UNITA. And the Zaïrian ruling class's role in the Angolan war fits far more neatly into the 'Western stooge' category than the chaotic layers of competing and coalescing global and local interests that characterize the Congolese wars of the late 1990s and the 2000s.

Once he had broken with his RPA minders, Laurent Kabila and his entourage certainly used this anti-Rwandan feeling to their own ends, as did Joseph Kabila, especially while the Rwandan-backed rebel movement/political party RCD-Goma appeared to be his principal political rival. But perhaps the most energetic exponents of this rhetoric were the ex-Mobutistes. In the aftermath of M'zee Kabila's assassination, the emblematic allegation was that Joseph Kabila was not really his father's son, but was rather a Rwandan Tutsi called Hippolyte Kanambe. Meanwhile, the politics of post-Laurent Kabila Congo came to revolve around a split between Lingalaphone 'westerners', who were mostly hostile to Joseph Kabila and his newly minted party, the PPRD, and Swahiliphone 'easterners', who were mostly supportive. Those in the west were reluctant to believe, as the – admittedly unreliable – projections from the 1983 census seemed to imply, that the Swahiliphones were more numerous. Some I talked to even suggested that the Rwandans/*nilotiques* 'began at Kisangani', the Congolese town that straddles the border between Lingala and Swahili as the main vehicular languages.

As the media presence of the abovementioned ex-Mobutiste political networks grew and as the narratives they championed gained purchase, they increasingly came to replace the UDPS as the primary opposition and the most popular political movement for the Kinois and the Kinois diaspora in Europe. Perhaps the most notable aspect of this has been a series of attacks on prominent individuals associated in some way with the current regime. In 2004, a press conference with Vital Kamerhe, then PPRD Secretary-General, was attacked in Paris by Ngbanda's APARECO. In 2006, Shé Okitundu, then Cabinet Secretary to Kabila, was assaulted, stripped naked and filmed on a mobile phone during a private visit to London between the first and second rounds of the Congolese election campaign. As this shows, politicians have been targeted, but more often this violence has expressed a distinctively *mikiliste* set of priorities. Most attacks have been directed against musicians and celebrity journalists – individuals who had lived hand in glove with the *mikilistes* and had previously relied on their patronage.

The motive for such attacks by *mikilistes* against their erstwhile colleagues was the support shown by these figures for President Joseph Kabila. After a period of relative austerity post-Mobutu, the regime in Kinshasa began to offer increased financial opportunities to popular *orchestres* and others in the public sphere. A notable example took place in 2004, when the Rwandan occupation of Bukavu sparked huge amounts of popular unrest in Kinshasa, causing roadblocks to be erected at the entrance to N'djili, a poor outlying area of Kinshasa, part of the district of Tshangu discussed earlier. The high-profile journalist Zacharie Bababaswe, then based in Belgium, introduced several prominent musicians, alongside politicians such as Vital Kamerhe, on his programme *Feux Vert* (produced in Belgium, but screened in Kinshasa on RTNC 1) to call for calm. Werrason himself, noted for his close connections both with the youth of Tshangu and with President Kabila, went to N'djili in person and persuaded the protesters to dismantle their roadblocks.

Another marker of this new closeness between the regime and musicians was the series of events known as 'les accords de Maisha Park', hosted by the Luba folk singer Tshala Mwana, mentioned above. These agreements were ostensibly established to curtail the forms of ritual insult – *polémique* – between musicians. The agreement signed by the musicians established a new 'Amicale des Musiciens', which pledged peace between the rival *orchestres* and, performing a kind of imitation of the transitional order, established a 'constitution' with a president and four vice presidents. While the organization imploded almost immediately after allegations that a large sum of money donated by the Ministry of Culture had been appropriated by some of the more senior members, it seems to have been successful as a vehicle through which musicians were able to strengthen their ties with the new political masters. In any case, it is from around this time that it became clear where popular musicians had cast their support.

This increased largesse coincided with the collapse of the *mikiliste* economy in Europe. In the buildup to the elections, eventually held in 2006, the PPRD, violently unpopular in Kinshasa and the Lingalaphone west of the country, invested ever more heavily in musicians. This included payment for *mabanga* on record, but also offered other opportunities. During 2006, several of the major *orchestres* – among them Quartier Latin, Wenge Maison Mère and Wenge BCBG – all performed at the wedding of Joseph Kabila to Olive Lembe, receiving unspecified amounts of money to do so. Finally, many of the country's most prominent artists performed songs in support of Kabila's election campaign, for which the *présidents d'orchestres* involved are alleged to have received $20,000 each. Most of these musicians would have faced severe difficulties had they refused these monies. Also, these payments came along just as the terminal decline of the *mikiliste* economy was taking place, on which prominent musicians had so relied – though the acceptance of the money in itself hammered another nail into the coffin. Wenge BCBG was based in London for much of 2005–6, and a few days after the attack on Shé Okitundu, a crowd of Congolese advanced on the boarding house where they were staying. According to several reports given to me, the intention of the crowd was to beat and strip naked the *président d'orchestre*, J.B. Mpiana – the fate already meted out to Okitundu. I was told by several *orchestre* members that a tipoff had been received and J.B. had arranged for a number of hired 'Jamaïcains' to act as bodyguards.[13]

During the same period in 2006, several informants reported that Koffi Olomide was shown a gun when he arrived in London and was told never to return. Such confrontations also occurred in France and Belgium. In July 2006, at the Elysée Montmartre in Paris, Papa Wemba performed to a virtually empty concert hall. From October to December 2006, Wenge Maison Mère was in Europe, but was prevented from performing any of its scheduled concerts because of threats from, and confrontations with, migrants. Eventually Werrason did face down the crowd to perform in front of a packed hall in Paris. But death threats continued, with London being the primary source. In 2007, Kester Emeneya, then in Paris, received a telephone call threatening him with death if he set foot in the United Kingdom. But while members of several prominent *orchestres* confessed to me that they were too frightened to visit the United Kingdom, trips to Paris and Brussels continued without significant incident. Since then, attacks appear to have once again increased in intensity. In 2009, Tshala Muana was attacked in Brussels.

These developments were not separate from events taking place in Kinshasa, where the public sphere, ever more polarized between the television stations favourable to the opposition MLC and those favourable to the government,[14] itself became a zone of violent contestation. It is striking that in an election campaign marked by arson and violent conflict over the media, the first sites to be attacked were the large open-air bar, the Samba Playa, owned by Werrason and the home of his Orchestre Wenge Maison Mère, and the church of Sonny Kafuta, a Pentecostal pastor who, like Werrason, was a prominent supporter of Kabila. These sites were set on fire during a march led by the main opposition leader, Jean-Pierre Bemba. What is notable about this violence is how it drew upon, yet inverted, the logic of the *mikiliste* exchange. Until recently, the *mabanga* transaction had incorporated the patron into a narrative in which love, transnational flows and material abundance were entwined.

Now, ritualized, often ludic violence sought to close these channels by specific attacks on musicians and on points of access to the public sphere. It is also notable that several of the most prominent figures among the assailants, latterly known as *les combattants*, had been enthusiastic participants in the *mikiliste* economy of largesse. Just as in earlier times, when the *bana Londres* had been the most excessive participants in the *mikiliste* potlatch, they now became the most implacably hostile, issuing death threats and banning musicians with even the most tangential connection to the regime from performing in London. The manager of the Double Club, a Congolese-themed bar in London, was prevented from having any prominent Congolese artists perform at the venue. At one point, he tried to book the singer-songwriter Lokua Kanza, an artist living in Europe with no regime connections. *Les Combattants* told him that this would not be accepta-ble, because Kanza had performed a 'featuring' on the song 'Diabolos' on the most recent album by Koffi Olomide.

By 2011–12, these forms of contestation had become even more widespread and one sensed that new forms of authority were being exercised within migrant communities. One example would be the *combattants* in South Africa, where they enforced a three-month music ban following the elections of 2011. This ban, justified as an act of 'national mourning',[15] applied to all secular music performed by Congolese and included a ban on an amateur band made up of Congolese living in Pretoria, fronted by a lead singer who worked during the week as an electrician. Statements made by the *combat-tants* frequently seem to teeter on the edge of the absurd in a way that suggests that at least something of the *mikiliste* folly has been retained – one group, for example, appeared on YouTube banning Koffi Olomide from entering Australia, a country he has so far shown no indication of wishing to visit.

According to several reports given to me recently by contacts in Kinshasa, this has been reciprocated, with police and officials at N'djili Airport allegedly subjecting *bana Londres* to intense scrutiny. So we see that while the exchanges of money and music were un-dertaken within an ideology that saw access to Europe and Kinshasa as central to social reproduction, the exchanges of violence and in-timidation have reversed this logic, as their aim is to restrict access by enemies to the sources of social reproduction.

Conclusion

I have argued that the *mikilistes* and the wider social forces that they partly inspired are poorly understood through the rubric of resist-ance. I believe that the later twists that the story takes bear this out. Forms of violent nationalism only really took off after the economy of fraud, upon which the *mikiliste* way of life depended, had found-ered. As we noted at the start of this chapter, the *mikilistes* seem to have been content to have their names cited alongside figures from the Mobutiste regime and continued to pay for *mabanga* well into the Kabila period, by which time their names regularly appeared on record alongside figures in the new regime (who were quite often the same people with whom they had 'rubbed names' earlier).

The *mikiliste* mode of social action emerged in imitation of the free-spending ruling classes of the late 1970s, whose largesse had been based on receipts from a series of industrial enclaves that were in a state of vertiginous decline. The context in which the *mikiliste* came of age meant that capitalist forms of rationality – concerning wage labour or accumulation – no longer made any sense. In this context the forms of imitation that the *mikiliste* embodied ramified and exaggerated certain elements of elite behaviour, producing forms of subjectivity that began to reproduce the precolonial potlatch dynamic.

The *mikilistes* were imitated in their turn by various powerful groups in Congo who not only reproduced this potlatch sensibility but also depended on relations of production that bore some resemblance to precolonial modes of production – value was extracted using various nonindustrial techniques, and central control dissolved into various localized forms of sovereignty, where social dominance resided with a gatekeeper figure who could make an alliance between his socioeconomic unit and wider forces. Hierarchy existed both within and between these localized forms of sovereignty, with a general logic that saw surpluses and authority flow towards the site of articulation between the local mode of production and the capitalist mode. In the postcolonial world, the capital, rather than the coast, is clearly the key site of articulation, a role it has retained through the various incarnations of the post-independence state.

As in the past, this articulation was underpinned by an alliance between local and external classes. Such alliances are based on some kind of coincidence of interest (see Rey 1973). These alliances have ebbed and flowed – in 1996, unlike during earlier rebellions, Western powers did nothing to save the regime with which they had had so many dealings in the past. That said, the continued role of the capital as the primary site of articulation between elites and various dominant classes outside is founded on a real community of interests, albeit one that is based on rather different economic imperatives, as we will see in Chapter 8.

While the *mikiliste* mode of social action reproduced the logic of potlatch, the resources it used to do this were derived from Western banking and welfare states, and were resources supported by the productivity of advanced capitalist economies. The kinds of connection they effected with the capitalist mode of production were not based on an alliance with dominant classes in the West, but on illicit appropriation. The *mikilistes'* assumptions about wealth and accumulation meant that they eschewed capitalist forms of investment. This made their situation rather precarious, but in a way that differed markedly from the vulnerability of those back home who had imitated them.

Benefit and cheque fraud was, in the last instance, a crime of Europe's 'little people', and dominant classes in the West had no interest in protecting this form of value extraction. Indeed, once they awoke to the problem, they invested heavily in stamping it out. Whatever the rhetoric about benefit cheats found in the popular press, my fieldwork revealed to me how effective this investment was – *all* the informants whom I knew to be involved in benefit fraud were eventually caught and the *mikiliste* economy is a grim shadow of its former glory. As we will see in Chapter 8, little effort has been expended on controlling other, flourishing forms of revenue evasion. It is in these forms of value extraction – tax havens and the wider infrastructure of elite revenue avoidance – that the dominant classes in Congo, 'the West' and the BRICS countries find their principal community of interest.

Had the *mikilistes* perceived their position within Western society more accurately, perhaps they could have built some kind of shelter from the storm that eventually arrived – started more shops and bought fewer shoes, to paraphrase my informant. But this is to misunderstand the nature of what potlach was about. The *mikilistes* did not have as their real aim to resist the state or even to insert themselves into a better position within the social order, though these things might, on occasion, have been byproducts of their actions. Rather, they were trying to access a certain sensibility, an ideal of human flourishing, which was connected to their idea of rank and the individual. It is to this that we now turn.

Notes

1. As the 1990s wore on, however, even the value of this compliance began to erode as Cold War exigencies receded and it became apparent that the oil-rich MPLA were not developing policies likely to threaten U.S. interests.
2. Identifying such acts of looting clearly with an oppositional project is in any case problematic – some informants remembered how crowds during an earlier act of popular looting in the 1980s shouted 'Mobutu! Mobutu!' as they robbed West African traders, associating their appropriations with the forms of elite appropriation that had

taken place under Zaïrianization. Traders from Guinea-Conakry I talked to who were looted in postelectoral violence in 2006 also attributed the looting to popular starvation, not any specific hostility. This raises serious questions about the degree to which abstract political motivations were 'add-ons' to what were at root survival strategies.

3. Congolese bars, frequently illegal.
4. A French brand: I have never seen it in the United Kingdom apart from on Congolese immigrants. In France it is expensive but not that exclusive, like Adidas or something similar, yet it is wildly popular in Kinshasa.
5. An area near the Porte Namur in Brussels that is full of Congolese bars and food shops and very different from the posh suburbs where Mobutiste cadres took houses. It is named after the original Matongé in Kinshasa, which was formerly the main entertainment district.
6. My source spoke of 'biznes assez inconnu' – *biznes* in Kinshasa refers to criminality.
7. After Koffi Olomide, who owns a Jaguar, began to refer to his car in this way. Why he called it that I have no idea.
8. Very similar references to 'bad things' are made by name holders in the potlatch societies of the American northwest coast.
9. After the Saudi arms dealer, Adnan Kashoggi.
10. BCBG: *Bon Chic, Bon Genre 4X4 'tout terrain'*.
11. Ties were banned under the strictures of *Authenticité*, Mobutu's programme of cultural nationalism. The wearing of ties was unbanned after the liberalization of political parties in 1991, but it was often construed as symbol of support for the opposition.
12. Kinois would perceive no contradiction in describing Saddam as nobility in one line and the essence of a bourgeois in the next. Both words are common praise titles that do not carry the Western meaning, but rather imply personal abundance – much as they would take the names of designer clothing or expensive cars. I was often amused by how my decidedly unbourgeois Congolese friends in Paris would use 'bourgeois' as an epithet to describe themselves, when all around them bourgeois bohemian Paris vigorously repudiated the term.
13. That is, black Anglophone Caribbeans. The term is used by U.K. Congolese as a byword for delinquent.
14. Kinshasa at this time had over forty television stations. Important pro-government stations included the state broadcaster RTNC 1 and 2, and Digital Congo, owned by the presidential family. Owning a television station has become a badge of honour for prominent parliamentarians. Notable pro-regime television stations are very numerous, but include Antenne A and RTGA. Most notable among the opposition stations are those owned by opposition leader Jean-Pierre Bemba – Canal Kin and CCTV. Later in the campaign, Bemba's studios suffered very serious fires. In the aftermath of the elections, Joseph Kabila initiated an attack on Bemba's bodyguard, which had resisted integrating into the national army (in part because they feared for their safety), killing around 300 in downtown Kinshasa (see Stearns 2011: 323). Bemba is now on trial at The Hague.
15. Though, as we have seen, music is fact an integral part of funerary ritual in Congo.

– Chapter 7 –

LOVE AND MONEY

Ba diamants ebele Lokola pare-brise arrière ya car epanzana, opesa pe bolingo te?
[You have] many diamonds, it is as if the rear window of a car had shattered, won't you give some love?

—Fally Ipupa, 'Associé

So begins Fally Ipupa's song 'Associé', written for the diamond dealer Empereur Tshatsho Mbala Kashoggi, mentioned in the last chapter. This chapter considers the romantic themes of popular music and the way in which *mabanga* payments linked to popular music interact with the lyrics. Romantic love is important to our study for several reasons. Terms such as 'social reproduction' or 'wealth in people' do not imply an abstract struggle for power, but one for meaningful goals. The world of the bar and of the potlatch is related to the notion of *ambiance* – a cultural nexus that includes wild expenditure, beer, music and 'romancing scandalous beauties' (La Fontaine 1970) at its heart. In this way romantic love is closely related to the nexus of ideas about retinue and largesse that we have been investigating.

For academics, it was a particularly common story about romantic love that it was attached to the process of modernization and emerged in parallel with, or was part of, the emergence of individualism (see, for example, Stone 1990; Giddens 1991). More recent scholarship confirms the intuition of the common man that such claims cannot be true. While some argue that individual love was thwarted by wider kinship structures (see Hirsch and Wardlow 2006; Vaughan 2009), others assert that it was generally incorporated or perceived as compatible with premodern institutions (Cole 2009; on Congo, see Laman 1953–68, vol. 2: 26–31), there is abundant evidence of love in non-Western and premodern contexts (for a general critique, see MacFarlane 1979; see also Jankowiak 2008).

Part of the reason why scholars have been drawn to the view that love does not exist outside the West is that Western ideology associates love with a series of oppositions – of individualism to kinship, of domestic to public, of reason to sentiment, of gifts to commodities and of love to money. Such binary frameworks are well represented in literature on intimate relationships in Africa. Jennifer Cole, drawing on Zelizer (2005), notes that an extensive literature on 'transactional sex' in Africa has continued the analytical tradition of seeing 'economic activity' and 'intimate social attachments' as 'hostile worlds' (Cole 2009: 110). This is dangerous ground to tread upon and will perhaps appear to apply cultural relativism to coercive sexual acts. I do not think this is in fact the case – it is merely to make the obvious point that many affective and sexual relations involve transactions.

This baggage means that, when confronted with the confluences of power, love and money that we see in Fally's song, it appears to us as a contradiction in terms. Such a profession *must* be insincere, or confused, or contradictory. This chapter argues that in the Kinois world under investigation, there is no systematic ideological opposition recognized between the two things. In the song 'Mbongo' – 'Money' – one of the great poetic lyricists of Kinois music, Simaro Lutumba, wrote of money and women as 'children' born of the same mother, and a wealth of empirical examples show that affective and political economic forms of attraction are often perceived as congruent and complementary rather than contradictory.

Love and Theories of the Individual

Jonathan Parry (1986) argues that the divide between a quasi-sacred sphere of purely disinterested gifts and a sphere of antisocial and purely self-interested exchange is a product of modern social relations. 'True love' is, of course, the supreme example of this quasi-sacred sphere of purely disinterested exchange, the conceptual opposite of the cash nexus and the market. Webb Keane (2007: 221) suggests that Protestant Christianity has carried an ideal of a subject whose actions are 'abstracted from social and material entanglements'. A certain reading of Habermas (1992) might also propose this ideal subject as the domestic counterpart of the public individual of liberal theory – a subject whose most valued quality is 'freedom' defined as 'proprietorship of one's own person' (Macpherson 1964: 142) and who engages in contractual relations with others within a 'possessive market society' (see also Povinelli 2006; Cole 2009).

We are, of course, in the realm of ideology. In fact, people's actions transgress these conceptual oppositions all the time – from the attractions of playboy millionaires or the sincere expressions of love embodied in forms of mass consumption to the calculations made during processes of inheritance or divorce about the monetary value of emotional contributions (see Miller 1998; Zelizer 2005). Likewise, in the DRC, very different ideologies of love are belied by practice all the time. Here, the notion that love and money are complementary *is* a powerful assumption, but it is also an assumption stretched taut by underlying contradictions.

Different notions of the person are often characterized in anthropological literature as a split between modern 'individuals' and premodern 'dividuals' (see Niehaus 2002 for an overview). This literature has produced some important observations – above all, that the boundary of the person is often seen as porous in non-Western cosmologies – but it is also a very problematic example of 'west v. rest' reasoning. The individual and the market is equated with the West, the 'dividual' and 'networks of reciprocal exchange' belong to the rest. But this fits rather badly with what we find in Central Africa.

To be sure, one can find scholars who have claimed that the individual did not, or does not, exist in Africa (see Friedman 1991: 106–7; Chabal and Daloz 1999: 44). But, as we shall see, this is rather at variance with the facts on the ground and with the conclusions of most scholars. This book argues that Central African peoples exhibit highly developed notions of the individual, but it is a notion of the individual that is not defined in terms of personal autonomy; rather, the more one can draw others to one in a network of rights and obligations, the more self one is considered to possess (Miers and Kopytoff 1977; Guyer 1993, 2004; Barber 1995, 2007a). This is indeed related to a theory of the person where the powerful individual overspills the bounds of the physical body (see Niehaus 2002). But this 'overspill' is the characteristic expression of this kind of individualism, not its negation.

This overspill can be expressed in the display and dispersal of material goods, but it can also be conceived as metaphysical forms of abundance that are believed to emerge from the person. These forms are conceptualized locally as substances, such as spittle or breath. While the moral origins of such abundance may be questioned, the individual who 'overspills' – dispersing largesse and acquiring lovers and dependants – is clearly an aspirational figure. In this framework, affective ties and economic flows are not placed in separate categories, but are seen as commensurate and complementary (Cole 2009).

Here I should offer a methodological note. This chapter concentrates on song lyrics and, while the understandings I reach draw on my fieldwork, the style of analysis is more literary here than in the other chapters. In this context, the evidential claims being made should not be misunderstood. Cultural productions like songs are not a transparent window onto social reality, and in this chapter we are attempting to gain one rather specific kind of insight into an ideological form. Such a predominantly textual analysis is intended to complement the ethnographic focus used in the rest of this book.

Modernity and the Individual in Congolese Music

Any notion that the individual is not a central preoccupation in Kinshasa today is quickly dispelled by a cursory examination of Congolese music. A striking feature of Kinshasa's popular music, evident from its earliest expression in the 1940s until the present, is that the narratives are always sung in the first person. Thus, Antoine Kolosoy – 'Papa Wendo' – sings of his passion for Marie Louise: 'eh solo eh ngai na yo' – 'truly me and you' (Wendo and Bowane 1948/1996).

This concentration on the first-person perspective becomes ever greater, with a strongly empathetic and psychological emphasis that is more and more forceful in subsequent generations. While romantic love has been the predominant theme of Congolese music, the reflective, first-person narrator is employed in almost all songs. This is illustrated in the case of Tabu Ley's 'Mokolo Nakokufa' – 'The day I die' (Ley 1970/1997), in which the singer muses, as if in a dream, upon the day of his death. He then goes on to imagine himself as various individuals in turn, at the moment of death. In each case 'he' is 'I'. First he is a poor man who thinks of his wife and his children, and rejoices that the pain of the world is left behind. Next, he is a rich man who thinks of his money, his compound, his lorries and the children he has sent to Europe. Then he is a drunkard – *moto ya kwiti* – who thinks of his cup of beer and of the end of the month when he drank with his friends. Last, he is the prostitute/courtesan – *mwasi ya ndumba* – who thinks of her wig, her clothes and of Ley's *Orchestre African Fiesta* whose performance, this implies, she attended (the support of fashionable courtesans being very important to the success of musical ensembles).

The figures Ley chooses – the poor man, the rich man, the drunkard and the courtesan – are important in that they are representative figures in Kinshasa's urban mythology, and Ley's project in the song is nothing less than an empathetic identification with the city of Kinshasa *as a collection of individuals.* The ambition of Ley's project – identification with the entire city – prevents a more detailed engagement with the emotional states of the individuals presented, but such engagement is present in the majority of songs, which deal with one individual.

In many songs, metaphors of the individual human life and fate entwine with ideas about love. A common image in Lingala songs is the path. It is used in proverbs and in countless songs in a manner related to the notion of individual human destiny. It seems that 'the path' in question is probably a path in the forest. Cosmologically the forest is often associated with the land of the dead (MacGaffey 1986), but also with the city of Kinshasa (see Tsambu-Bulu 2004). To lose one's path – *kobunga nzela* – in the 'city forest' is to lose oneself in hostile territory, both metaphysical and mundane. 'The hunt', associated with the 'city forest', is also an intense area for the production of meaning and affect. Deciding on the correct route as the path forks assumes a quality of destiny, as can be seen in the following song, which talks of the protagonist's relations with a partner, using the metaphor of the *mboloko* (an antelope), which must choose the path to take in order to avoid the hunter. After describing how he tires of imploring the beloved, he remarks:

Ata mboloko alembaka kokima	Even the *mboloko* tired of fleeing
Ye akopema na kati ya zamba	He rests in the forest
Kokanisa nzela nini aleka	To think what path to pass along
Noki akutana na mobomi niama	For fear of meeting the hunter
Atie vie na ye na danger de mort…	Throwing his life into mortal danger

He then addresses the woman more directly:

Yoka ngai mawa, zongisa mabanzo	Have pity on me, think again
Tobokolo bana toboti	Let us bring up our child

The song then returns to the theme of the path:

Banzela ngai nalekaka se kombo na yo	All the paths I take is your name
	(Show Musica, personal recording, 13 November 2007)

Similarly, the idea of the boat in the river is a repeated motif, implicating love in the flow of human life. In Petit Prince's 'Sango ya mabala Commission', which is a lament over a marriage contract broken because of his poverty, Prince sings:

Ebale na ngambo na ngambo masua ememangai Etikingai na kati kati ya ebale
In the river from side to side the boat carries me leaving me in the middle of
the river

(Prince, P. 1982/2008)

Another example is Koffi Olomide's song 'Ngobila', another melancholy evocation of a relationship ended, in which he evokes his
sadness as the boat carrying the beloved travels away while:

Nga na libongo lokola bakatingai makolo   I am on the dock as if my legs
were cut off

(Olomide 1991)

Central to this metaphor is the tumult of the Congo River (which
carries more water than any river other than the Amazon). Like the
boatman, we, the postcolonial subject, try to steer a course, but mostly
we are swept along and away by forces much greater than ourselves.[1]
Love, then, in all its pleasurable agonies, is depicted as integral to
the project of human life, entwined with notions of fate rooted in the
Central African past. Likewise, love is depicted as central in the dis-
appointments of human projects. The predominant emotional tone
of the singers during the slow *rumba*[2] section in Kinois music is one
of melancholy.

A common story about modernity is that it is characterized by
various forms of angst – anxiety, melancholy, disorientation – emotions that are rooted in the consciousness of rupture or alienation.
This sort of story has some purchase in the context of Kinois music,
where the melancholy relates to alienation in the postcolonial city
and to the resignation of the individual to this state. Romantic love
has often been theorized as a way of transcending the rupture of
modernity (see, for example, Giddens 1991), yet the versions of love
sung of in Kinois music are rarely presented as actually offering
this resolution. At the most obvious level, the idea of failure in love
is invoked as a particularly urban kind of misery. Until the 1980s,
popular songs regularly invoked the idea of returning to the village
after an unhappy love affair – for example, Bitshou's song 'Infidelité
Mado' (1970):

Mwasi ngai nalingi aboyi ngai na makasi nakozonga mboka...
The woman I love rejects me utterly, I will return to the village

(Bitshou 1970)

The idea of a return to the village sits comfortably with Western
European notions of romance (see also Fabian 1997: 23), where the

individual sees in romantic love the lost unity once found in premodern forms of solidarity such as kinship. This appears to link alienation, interiority and intimacy with modernity. But this is misleading – Kinois popular music also frequently draws a comparison between failures in romantic love and precolonial forms of alienation. Slavery, for example, is often evoked as a paradigm of alienation (see Patterson 1982).

The song 'Synza', written by Koffi Olomide (1978/1998), for instance, is sung from the point of view of a man to an unhappy female interlocutor called Synza. First the narrator describes her unhappiness in terms that are relatively familiar to Western invocations of the lovelorn – physical deterioration, 'crying and crying' by herself in the night: 'yo moko na kati ya butu'. But the singer then evokes Synza's unhappiness in love in a stark and unfamiliar way:

> *Mwana yango mowumbu, babwakela ye soyi te na bomwana, akola na kobanga*
> This child is a slave, they did not spit on him in childhood, he grows up to fear
>
> (Olomide 1978/1998)

Spitting on someone's head is a traditional form of blessing all over Central Africa, usually given by politically powerful elders to the young. Koffi's adage makes it clear that the conception of being a slave is not about belonging to someone, but precisely about *not* belonging to someone (see Miers and Kopytoff 1977). Without the metaphysical sanction of the elders, the slave lived outside of the network of reciprocal rights in others and could be alienated in a radical fashion – sold on or sacrificed. Struck by this line and its apparently oblique relationship to the rest of the song, I was surprised that informants thought the connection obvious, to the point where my questions bemused them. Several informants stated that the comparison is made because Synza is unhappy – *malheureuse* – like the offspring of a slave.

A similar figure occurs in the song 'Zando ya Tipo Tipo' – 'Tipo Tipo's Market' – by Michel Boyibanda (1974/2000), which makes repeated reference to the famous Zanzibari slaver Tipo-Tipo, who controlled large swathes of the Congo basin in the late nineteenth century. The island of Zanzibar, one of the most significant markets for Congo Basin slaves in the nineteenth century, is also repeatedly invoked as a metaphor for the singer's state of separation from his wife.

In this song the metaphor of slavery is partly related to the mercenary behaviour of the in-laws, *bokilo*, but the primary point is that the alienation of abandonment is clearly related to the alienation of the slave who is held in Zanzibar. This comparison of love with preco-lonial alienation is reinforced by the song 'Mère Supérieur' by Papa Wemba[3] (1977/1998), in which the singer – 'I poor wretch, a slave to love' – feels that love itself is a foreign country – 'mboka mopiaya'.

This is particularly interesting, since not only is unhappy love equated with slavery, but love, in the mind of the unhappy lover, is a 'foreign country'. The association between the stranger and the slave is a recurrent theme in ethnographies of the wider region (see Miers and Kopytoff 1977). In these two songs, as elsewhere, the metaphor is clear: the unhappy lover is a slave, while the loveless state is like being stranded in a strange or foreign place without the ties of belonging noted above. Many authors have commented on the fluid position of the slave within the lineage societies of the Congo Basin (see Miers and Kopytoff 1977). Socioeconomic inferi-ority was a kind of junior status of which slavery was an extreme form, a perspective that resonates in contemporary social relations in Kinshasa, where terms like *vieux* and *yaya* ('elder') can be used to establish client status. Historically, polygamy in much of the Congo Basin also corresponded with social and economic stratification (Hilton 1983), and the association between love and money is still a strong one. In contemporary Kinshasa, where forms of sexual and affective success still appear very strongly associated with wealth and hierarchy, the link between poverty, slavery and lack of love has great resonance.

Beyond this, there is a far wider range of references to a sense of alienation connected to the lack of love. There is not space to analyse each in detail, and some of them are quite oblique; nevertheless, I cite some of them below, simply to give a sense of the richness of prover-bial and metaphorical allusions that relate failed relationships and lovelessness to a broader sense of alienation:

> *Na tikali ngai lokola mwana soso, wana balé mama na ye na bonne anée*
> I am left like the chick – the one whose mother was eaten at new year
> (Olomide 2008a)

> *Zamba oyo ezangi niama ezali lokola mwasi abotaka te zelaka elaga pona kotumbi ango*
> This forest without game is like a woman who does not give birth, wait for the dry season to burn it
> (Emeneya 1982/2008a)

Boni bokotsie ngai pene ya moto lokola ba koita mbisi na motalaka
How can you put me near to the fire like fish [for smoking] on a wooden
frame?

(Prince, P. 1982/2008)

Kinois popular music has always presented love as a difficult and often unrequited thing. But while songs from the 1950s and 1960s – a period of high hopes for the Congo – sometimes couch this in the idea of folly, from the late 1960s, the object of love becomes ever more distant, cold or unreciprocating, as in Teddy Sukami's (1978/2005) 'Pachalabran', in which a woman cries that her children go hungry and patch their clothes while her husband is only interested in drink. It is almost never love mutually consummated, but rather a litany of miseries such as love scorned, abused, wished for but not achieved, marriages ruined, and drunken husbands chasing other women or buying the same wax cloth for wife and mistress.

One of the most powerful indicators of a preoccupation with psychological depiction is, paradoxically, the way in which many songs evoke a public façade. First-person protagonists often describe their situations in a way meant to maintain appearances, but at the same time projecting a sense of inner torment. In the song 'Sans Préavis', by Kester Emeneya, the female narrator affects a cool indifference to the callous behaviour of her lover, chastising him only for providing insufficient warning 'préavis' of his intention to leave her:

Bimisa ngai na ndako/Ndako ya yo moko
Throw me from the house/The house is yours alone

Okomi na mbongo ngai nakomi mabe/C'est la la loi de la nature
You have come into money. I become bad/That's the law of nature

This façade becomes less convincing as the lyrics advance and it is finally abandoned; she admits to her darling 'Motema [literally heart]' she is surprised by his rejection and that happiness 'will await her nowhere', before ending on the despairing couplet:

Mokili ekomi nango indifferent/Ata moi ebimeli ngai a nalala o
I become indifferent to this world/The sun rises but just I sleep

(Emeneya 1982/2008a)

The above song illustrates some of the most powerful themes in Kinois music, which make a connection between private emotion and public comportment. Numerous other songs connect the anguish of abandonment to the shame of public derision arising from a separation. Maintaining the intimate self is inextricably tied to the externalized public image. None of this is specifically Congolese, but it is important to note that this public construction of the interior emotion, the relationship between 'interior and exterior', has been used to argue that 'reflexive individualism' did not occur in Africa or that it was peripheral to the African experience.

In his book *The Structural Transformation of the Public Sphere*, Jurgen Habermas argued that the 'closed' bourgeois household, having cleansed the domestic space of both economic activity and extended kin, became a zone for the growth of 'interiority' cultivated by certain kinds of reading, particularly of letters and sentimental novels. The affective equality of cultivated individuals 'as it emerged from their spheres of intimacy' (Habermas 1992: 54) and became the ground for rational interaction in the public sphere.

Explicitly or not, this kind of consideration underpins the argument that 'self-reflexive' styles of affect are not part of the African experience. For example, Breckenridge (2000: 337–48), quoting Karin Barber, argues that love letters sent by migrant workers in South Africa are 'about individual self, but not interiority', because the letters were composed collectively and read aloud by the recipient (see also Barber 2007b).

The Kinois musician, by this measure, would likewise fail to demonstrate interiority, as composition is often a collective process and the paradigmatic space of reception is the bar. The argument that such forms cannot be evidence for interiority, despite the considerable supporting fact of the texts themselves (and the way they are received), merely because of their collective composition, is surely to accept one of modernity's myths about itself – one that predicates interiority on silent reading and the solipsistic privacy of an imagined bourgeois interior. Even in Europe, such a picture is at the very least an oversimplification, if not entirely false. As Reddy (2001) and Schama (1989) have shown in the case of France, the new concentration on sentiment born during the eighteenth century was, initially at least, related to public associations, such as the salon and the mason's lodge. Rousseau – whose literary and autobiographical works were among the foundational texts of this sentimental revolution – envisaged and encouraged a new age of virtue in the 'republic of friends' where public figures would dress humbly and weep openly.[4]

Such accounts of sentiment in Africa are perhaps unsatisfactory for another reason, since, closely adhering to the story about modernity told in classic accounts such as Habermas (1992) or Stone (1990), they privilege literacy. Without wishing to dismiss literary forms, novels and letters are clearly of secondary importance in Kinshasa, where I would hold that the music playing in the bar has always constituted a far more important element in the 'domestication of modernity' (see Jewseiwicki 2003). In Kinshasa it was precisely in this public arena of bars (and also churches) that the inward, empathetic sensibility was cultivated. This equation of privacy and interiority has also been linked to the post-romantic conception of the 'lonely artist', which again appears culturally specific rather than as a general feature of modernity. The Kinois conceive of the artist as the epitome of sensitivity and interiority, but they also see him as an emphatically social figure. Indeed, sociability is considered so integral to artistic production that accusations of personal autonomy – calling an artist 'proud' or 'stubborn' – can amount to an aesthetic critique.

This is not to dismiss the relevance of Habermas' thesis. The rise of the novel in Europe, where male authors write in the first person as female heroines (like Clarissa or Eloise), and in the process create a new concentration on sentiment and a new kind of subjectivity, does seem to offer some suggestive parallels with the development of popular music in the Congo.

Voices

In the music, melancholy is the main emotion associated with this interiority. Melancholy is not conveyed by the words alone; vocal techniques play a crucial role in communicating emotion. The high, fragile-sounding voice of Tabu Ley, with a tremble in it that conveys further emotional anguish, was cited as a model by many singers I spoke to. Kinois popular music is composed of one or more cycles based on two or three chords. Against this, and within a roughly established melody, each singer will improvise his own melodic line. Watching singers in the studio is rather like observing method actors at work. The singer will frequently ask about the emotional state in which he is to sing, and others will offer a great deal of advice about how a line should be sung, though in fact much of this is extremely unhelpful, as patrons will take it as their right to hang around a studio, proffering distracting and ill-informed suggestions.

It often struck me that there was a relatively limited set of descriptive terms compared to the actual diversity of voices employed, but one would regularly hear instructions for a vocal line to be sung *ya elengi* ('with pleasure'), *ya pasi* ('with pain') and *ya charme, ya brutalité, na couleur mosusu* ('with a different colour'). Stress, volume and intonation are varied dramatically to convey the correct feeling, and singers will cultivate a catch or a rasp in the voice, or even sing a little above their comfortable range to convey pain and melancholy. In conversation, singers and fans alike will emphasize the importance of a melancholy quality in the voice – comparison is frequently made with Julio Iglesias, who is considered a master in the communication of this emotion. Other foreign singers, such as Céline Dion, who can belt out a lachrymose ballad, are also greatly appreciated by Congolese audiences.

The voices most valued in Congolese music are high, and are known as *première voix* and *ténor*. Then there is a somewhat lower and less-appreciated voice known as *deuxième voix*. *Ténor*, which in Western terms is a kind of counter-tenor voice – one that uses the highest registers available to the male human voice, using a predominantly falsetto technique. *Deuxième voix* approaches the operatic baritone, while *première voix* is equivalent to the operatic tenor. The capacity of high male voices is particularly appreciated, in part because it requires considerable virtuosity to hold a tune while singing at this pitch, but also because this voice is seen as the best at conveying pain and melancholy.

It is interesting to ponder why voices in the higher range are so much appreciated by the Congolese. One might regard the question as ethnocentric owing to the assumption that lower pitches, often favoured by Western popular musicians, are more 'natural'. However, the high voice seems not to be a fixed cultural preference, but a trend. There are many more singers specializing in the upper ranges now than previously. While there were some moderately high voices in the so-called *première* and *deuxième générations* of Congolese music – including Tabu Ley or Josky Kiambukuta – the voice now denoted by the term *ténor* is appreciably higher than those singers. This voice seems to have emerged in the *troisième génération* with such singers as Evoloko and Papa Wemba. The *ténor* voice has multiplied and is more prevalent than ever in the latest, *cinquième génération* of Congolese musicians. I believe, therefore, that it is quite legitimate to ask what is so special for the Congolese about higher voices.

Several informants stated that the *ténor* voice was *elengi* – pleasurable – yet at the same time, it is considered the voice most able to convey melancholy and pain. I frequently heard admiration expressed for the *ténor* voice of contemporary singer Ferre Gola, which was esteemed for its melancholy – and Ferre was frequently compared to Julio Iglesias. The idea of gaining pleasure in pain is important. Observing Congolese music as it is consumed on public occasions – in bars or at weddings, for example – it can be seen to generate emotions that belie the despairing lyrics. The *rumba* section is the occasion for slow partner dancing – a very slow marking of the beat with the hips that has a powerful romantic eroticism.

'Mr Brown' and 'Chocolat Chaud' Get into the Rumba *Section*

> Went to a party at Le Terrain in Saint-Denis. Someone told the DJ that I was a fan of old Kester songs and they put on Okosi Ngai Mfumu (Emeneya 1982/2008b). I saw 'Mr Brown' drawing up 'Chocolat Chaud' to dance. They were hardly moving as they danced, she was just rolling her bum. About halfway through the song she put her arms around his neck, relaxing onto him. (Journal, 4 May 2007)

It was around this time that I became aware that Chocolat Chaud was one of Mr Brown's many girlfriends. I am unsure if this was when their affair started, but clearly it was a moment of romantic engagement between the couple. If we look at the song to which they were dancing – 'Okosi Ngai Mfumu' – which is about an affair that has ruined lives and marriages, we see the discrepancy between Kester's pained voice, the melancholic words and the response it encouraged in the audience. After an introduction that seems to make a more general statement to the world about the female protagonist of the song, it shifts to addressing the man in the second person:

> *Amour ya mbanda ovotaki/Wapi ye lelo?/Okomi kotindela ngai/Maloba ya Bolingo/ Kobosana ngai.*

> The love for [my] rival who you chose/where is she today/you start sending me/words of love/Forget me

> *C'est trop tarde pona ngai/Na silisi mfumu ngai/na zonga libala*

> It is too late for me/I put an end to this my 'chief'/[I am not going to] return to [our] marriage

> (Emeneya 1982/2008b)

While partner dancing is considered the 'correct' response to the *rumba* section, other forms of participation are more common. Chief among these is singing along. Individuals throw themselves into the lyrics. By turns, they press their hands to their hearts and then, arms outstretched, flutter their hands as if imploring an imaginary interlocutor – gestures that singers often make when performing. More than anything else, these gestures seem to define the space of the bar as an arena where delicate passions are to be performed. The identification with the protagonist that takes place during the *rumba* section appears to elicit various types of romantic feelings in the listener, and the lyrics, the vocal tones adopted by the singer and the gestures all assert the irresistible importance of romantic love in human existence, albeit in despairing fashion.

Women and Singing

It is striking that while the singers of Kinois secular music are nearly all male, there is a strong tradition of singing in the first person 'as a woman', particularly as a woman expressing feelings of love for a man. The convention of singing as a woman has become more common. This narrative device was driven to the fore in songwriting by artists from the 'school' of musicians who emerged from the *orchestre* African Jazz, especially Tabu Ley. It was also Ley, alongside the singer Rossingol Lando from the rival *orchestre* OK Jazz, who pioneered the use of a higher, rather womanly voice. Nearly all my older informants asserted that Ley was 'more popular' with women of all social classes than his musical rivals. Ley also pioneered the kind of intense psychological identification with his subjects that we have discussed above.

One of the reasons why this might be important is the well-established idea that certain women, essentially the kind of high-profile courtesans we have discussed throughout this book, are 'leaders of opinion'. The role of such women as arbiters is a distinctive feature of the city. La Fontaine (1970) notes how politicians in the late 1950s would assiduously court 'scandalous beauties' as part of their drive to assemble political capital, and a vigorous courting of the courtesan vote was one of the more amiable aspects of the 2006 elections in Kinshasa. In a similar way, the support of fashionable *ndumba* has always been vital to the popularity of musical ensembles (see Gondola 1997a, 1997b). Support in this context can mean attendance at concerts, but it also means taking musicians as lovers. Musicians employ all kinds of strategies to court women, both as lovers and fans, and an attempt to represent female points of view is one of these strategies. Another reason why musicians might sing 'as women' and, in a stylized way, imitate the female voice is that in structural terms, their position somewhat resembles that of women in a male-dominated society, particularly the *ndumba* – that is, as 'client' in an affective transaction with a patron.

Songs also present a considerable social critique from a female point of view. As Onyumbe shows (1982, 1983, 1984, 1985a, 1985b), songs of this period present 'women of marriage' as almost uniformly unhappy, while it is only the 'other woman' and courtesans who appear to be having any fun. Yet we need to be careful about how we interpret such lyrics, which cannot simply be taken at face value as social documents.

First, it seems unlikely that the negative depictions of marriage, which were so common until the mid 1980s, were really condemning marriage. They should rather be seen as an indictment of a world turned upside down, in which, according to popular perception, the *mibeko ya bankoko* – the laws of the ancestors/elders – were cast aside for the transient anti-order of the night, the bar and the *ndumba*; the world that was so often deplored in newspaper articles by the *évolué* (see Gondola 1997b; Hunt 1991). This is expressed in the song 'Mbuma Elengi' by Djuna Djanana (1986/1998), where in the 'belle époque' love was for a thing for chiefs, while today it becomes a thing to 'kobwaka na fulu' – 'throw into the bin'.

Critiques of the wider family found in music are rarely directed at the family per se, but rather at this failure to maintain the lineage-based moral order. Grasping extended families, for example, are faulted for not living up to their side of the bargain. Paradoxically, then, such lyrics revealed the continuing strength of an ideology of marriage connected to the lineage, where anguished relations between man and woman emerge from 'incorrectly' managed relations to wider kin. A poignant example of this is to be found in the song 'Bandeko ngai ya mibale basundoli ngai' – 'My Brothers Have Abandoned Me' (1977/1995). In the song, the female protagonist laments that she has followed her brothers' advice. She married the man they chose for her after they had refused her own choice of husband. Now that she has married their choice and he has abandoned her with a child and another on the way, the same brothers accuse her of shaming the family.

Yet such an interpretation does not really explain the social meaning of lyrics relating to marriage, because it fails to account for an embedded contradiction. All the 'critiques' of marriage found in earlier songs contain this contradiction: the drunken husbands courting *ndumba* did their courting in bars where popular *orchestres* played and beer was sold, and the *orchestre* playing this music was enmeshed in these social relations while apparently condemning them. Like the *évolué* who condemned *ndumba* by day and courted them by night, music is part of the complex relationship of elites to the anti-order of the bar. The bar is a source of immorality, to be sure, but also a source of power, where all socially effective individuals must draw sustenance. And, as we shall see anon, such an 'embedded contradiction' can help us to think about Congolese music more generally, as a complex form containing a series of moral and aesthetic contradictions that lead to no moral resolution.

Through an examination of a song from this time, we can see the kinds of aesthetic, political and economic transformations with which patronage was associated. Our example is Kester Emeneya's 'Mobali ya Ngenge' (1984/2008):

> *Soki olingi ye moto ndima nyokoli bolingo na ye*
> If you love him, that man, accept the pain of loving him

> *Nasala nini po yo ndima ngai? Na mema ngambo solo nabebi*
> What can I do for you to accept me? I have messed up, truly I am deteriorating

Just after this, Kester speaks, interjecting with the names of 'two brothers' Muku Ngoma and Tumbaka Teta. An informant remembered these two figures as Luba diamond dealers, the eldest of whom was also a pastor. They were members of Zaïre's early artisanal diamond mining industry, which would soon become central in the political economy of the region. Kester signals his friendship with the brothers and alludes to their involvement in diamonds by referencing the town of Mbuji Mayi, then the centre of the industry, saying: 'We will see each other in Mbuji Mayi.'

It seems clear that some form of exchange between Kester and the brothers took place, although it is also probable that, unlike exchanges a few years later, this was a relatively informal transaction. Within the context of an expansion of clientelistic dispersal, the depiction of love is shifting. The song continues, with the female protagonist singing that she will 'cry and cry and cry' until she is dried out, declaring that: 'Even if you change women a thousand times, it is nothing.'

Love is here depicted as a power over others, a power in which the female narrator appears helpless to resist the affective domination of another. Depictions of love as a 'power over' become more common and more pronounced in lyrics of the 1980s and 1990s. The title of the song 'Moto ya Ngenge' alludes to a key term denoting this kind of ability. *Ngenge* is particularly associated with attracting both sex/love and money to oneself. While none of my informants was aware of the precolonial origins of the term, an etymology of the word *ngenge* indicates how this word is 'plugged in' to powerful channels of affect and metaphor. Janzen notes that the word *ngenge* was used by members of the Lemba cult, which operated among precolonial Bakongo peoples, and that it originally referred to a bell that was hung around a hunting dog. The bell allowed the hunter to hear the dog and find his way to game in the forest (Janzen 1982: 220). Dogs were animals of great mystical significance for the Bakongo – several of the famous nail fetishes were carved in the form of dogs. Such bells were also hung around the necks of these *fétiches* (see MacGaffey 2000: 102). Choosing the correct path in the forest, as we have seen, also appears to have been some kind of metaphor for human destiny, so the hunting bell's imputed ability to find its way in the forest carried considerable metaphysical weight. Because the forest was conceptualized as one of the sites of the land of the dead and because the hunt that took place there was a site within the culture where notions of luck and destiny crowded, *ngenge*'s etymology indicates its importance.

Ngenge is a kind of force, emerging from the person, and the phrase to 'blow *ngenge*' – *kofula ngenge* – is frequently used. Papa Wemba uses, as one of his praise titles, *mzee fula ngenge* – the elder who blows/spits/channels *ngenge*. Papa Wemba is depicted on one of his albums with puffed cheeks as if blowing. The association of *ngenge* with blowing and, by extension, breath and or spittle (synonyms for life and ancestral force all over Central Africa) is interesting in many ways, and notions of breath will be explored in the next chapter. Here we will simply note that to *fula ngenge* implies 'channelling' *ngenge* (see also Janzen 1982: 249 on similar phraseology for the nineteenth-century Bakongo).

Evidence of this 'power over' that the patron/lover possesses takes on ever more dramatic forms. In the song 'Canon ya Mofude' from the late 1980s, Bozi Boziana sings, in the persona of a woman, still in love with the man who has abandoned her with a child. The child has the 'beauty' of the departed lover so that for the female narrator:

Soki na tali mwana mai ya miso ekolela	If I look at the child tears will flow
	(Boziana 1988)

In White's (2008) monograph, he, like me, notes a transformation in the lyrical content of Congolese music. But he comes to substantially different conclusions about what these changes are and what they mean. He argues that where in the past 'the sources of love-related problems seemed clearer ... girl leaves boy, boy feels sad, boy cries for her to return', in recent times Congolese love songs have been addressed to 'no one in particular' (2008: 179–80). I believe that something like the opposite has occurred. Love songs have become much more personalized. I say this in part because in the past, songs were much more likely to invoke wider social forces as the cause of failure in love. But it is also in the simple sense that it has become much more common for real, named individuals to pay for an appearance in songs as the object of love. We see this in Bozi Boziana's 'Canon ya Mofude', cited above, where the patron/object of love, Jeannot Kannot, was a relatively well-known individual living in Europe.

This conclusion is perhaps also related to a misunderstanding White entertains about the nature of the patronage form itself. White presents a sensitive analysis of the song 'Famille Kikuta' (ibid.: 188–90), which, as he shows, is sung from the point of view of a woman abandoned with her children and left in financial hardship by a certain Didi Kikuta. But he grounds his analysis in the idea that this was a song commissioned by the abandoned woman who is the first-person protagonist. In fact, the female narrator is simply a fictional device. While patrons are sometimes placed in the song's narrative as a wise third party, perhaps a counsellor to an abandoned individual (for example, in the song 'Ikea' by Koffi Olomide (2008) or 'Amour Interet' by Ferre Gola), I know of no example where the patron is actually depicted as the 'victim', and the unnamed first-person narrator of the song is never the patron. It seems almost certain that the song was in fact commissioned by Didi Kikuta himself. This is because Didi is frequently referenced in the text in a way that is similar to the way in which other patrons are depicted in other songs, and because in an earlier recording of the same song, the title is listed as 'Didi Kikuta'.

We will soon come on to the issue of why the patron would want to be depicted this way, but first we must note that this is a very common narrative device. As we have seen throughout this book, patrons are generally sung about as the object of love from the point of view of a helplessly enamoured woman, and one frequent variant of this template is for patrons to appear in songs as the authors of unpleasant forms of abandonment. One example would be the following song from 2004 by Jus d'Été. It casts Paris-based patron Borelle in the role of a man who has seduced, impregnated and abandoned a schoolgirl.

The song stresses how Borelle met 'her' in 'na bleu blanc'/'in blue and white' – i.e. as a schoolgirl in the blue-and-white uniform of Congolese schoolgirls, and put her 'na maputa'/'Into a wax cloth', i.e. into the wax cloth worn by a grown woman. The nature of this transformation is underlined by the refrain:

Okimisi école/Okumbisa ngai pe zemi/Nabotela yo pe mwana
You made me run away from school/You also made me pregnant/I even gave
you a child

Ba facon na yo ya kotambuisa basi kitoko Borelle!
Your way of dallying with beautiful women, Borelle!

(d'Été 2004)

The song contains several other short name checks, the most prominent of which is to the governor of Kinshasa, André Kimbuta.

The song 'Chez Ntemba' by Koffi Olomide gives another airing to
what has become a stock theme:

[*Kahembe*] *Soki otika ngai kotisa ngai kelasi*
If you leave me, send me back to school

(Olomide 2006)

The contemporary musical depiction of unhappiness in love, where
the client-lover bemoans her abandonment in entirely personal
terms, does not mean that there is no concern for reputation and
gossip. Indeed, such concerns over reputation are central to the
kinds of status competition that motivate much contemporary music
patronage.

A first step to understanding this set of conventions lies in a recognition of the complex and indirect relationship between life and
art – whatever painters may have depicted, people in Renaissance
Italy did not wander around naked and crucifixion was rare – cultural products are not documentaries, and both the public and the
patrons well understand this. Adolf 'Ntemba' Kahembe – the patron
for the song cited above – emphatically rejected the idea of any link
between the song and his real behaviour; indeed, my broaching the
subject was something of a faux pas. But while this is important, it
still does not explain why a patron would want to be depicted on
record behaving in a fashion considered immoral.

Yet patrons are paying to be depicted as having abandoned
women, even as having left very young women pregnant, and this
raises certain questions. On the one hand, there is a notion of masculinity that regards impregnating many women as prestigious, so this
depiction can partly be explained in these terms. Yet while fathering
children outside marriage is a quasi-accepted part of male behaviour,
the abandonment of pregnant women is construed as both immoral
and shameful. I have heard many justifications of such behaviour,
but these were defensive in tone, not boastful, and it seems evident

that as listeners to the song, we are meant to identify with the abandoned protagonist rather than with the shadowy love object.

In crude terms I think we can say that it is because the capacity to seduce women is seen as evidence of 'substantive' powers (see the next chapter). Congolese notions of social efficacy often seem to revolve around an idea of 'overpowering' the other, and love is seen as the paradigm of this kind of invisible combat (see Tonda 2005). A wealth of sources shows that this perception of love as a 'power over' others long pre-dates the 1980s. Joseph Tonda (2005: 69–71) shows how in Brazzaville and Kinshasa of the 1960s and 1970s, the use of 'torments' (love charms) – often perfumes with presumed origins in distant sources of power, such as India or Paris, with brand names such as 'Takur' or 'Jolie Soir' – were seen as occult 'weapons' to overpower and torment the object of love. This perception was present, but it was less clearly enunciated and was less central to the song narratives before the mid 1980s.

Where earlier lyrics had often depicted the abandonment of women in quasi-sociological terms – casting abandonment within a broader narrative about grasping families who failed to respect the moral order of the lineage – songs from the 1980s onwards focus much more tightly on the individual. Central to this new template is the *moto ya ngenge* who disburses wealth, attracts followers and leaves women helplessly smitten. A trail of beauties left helpless and forlorn by a lover who can do as he wishes provides evidence of this capacity.

Embedded in this musical form is a contradiction between identification and aspiration that is quite complex and interesting, and that takes us back to the notion of contradiction broached earlier. In the slow rumba section of Congolese music, we – the audience – are clearly moved to *identify* with the protagonist, invariably the melancholic female first-person narrator. We live the alienated abandonment of the narrator in the inflections of the singer's voice and in the words. The common practice of singing along to the sad lyrics of songs, noted above, points to something deeper – the melancholic, alienated, first-person narrator is 'us', that is to say, the main intended audience, the Congolese postcolonial everyman. The fact that it is the victim who is the one depicted with tender and complex passions contradicts the strong tendency in Congolese society to disparage the masses as lacking in individuality: worthless, livestock, etc. – *mutu pamba, niama, basengi*, etc. But at the same time, implicit in the form itself is the assumption that we (i.e. the postcolonial Congolese subject) *aspire* to be the powerful love object.

In the song 'Zadio' by J.B. Mpiana, many of these issues are brought out. The song is dedicated to Kazadi, the London-based Congolese *bon vivant* whom we last saw in Chapter 2. Sung by J.B. Mpiana and other members of his band, Wenge BCBG, the song is a declaration of love by a woman to Zadio. The introductory sections stress 'her' emotional ferment, 'sabotaged' and 'pushed off course' by Zadio, who offers sophisticated tender passions:

Affection tendresse lokola mizungu
Affection and tenderness, like the whites

(Mpiana 2008)

The lyrics make a link, common in Congolese music, between Europe and love – the patron disperses tender passions, 'like the whites' (the Swahili 'mizungu' rather than the Lingala 'mundele' is used here, to rhyme with *bisou* in the next line). This link is further underlined by the next lines:

Tango midi ekoki mundele alia, ngai pe nalia epayi na bolingo
When midday comes, the white eats, I also eat at the place of love

The idea that the white eats 'at midday' is firmly grounded in Kinois mythology. This conveys two related meanings. The first is the 'rigorous', ordered nature of the white man in the Kinois imagination. Many informants related this lyric to observations of how *les flamands* (the Flemish) would always take their meals at noon. Second, eating at noon is a sign of material capacity in Kinshasa, where, even for those who are coping reasonably well, there is only one meal a day, normally in the evening when everyone has returned from a day spent wresting a living from the street. Obviously this also draws on the fertile metaphor of 'eating', one aspect of which references financial capacity. The fertility of this metaphor is further evidenced by the line 'I also eat at the place of love', which we might gloss as something like 'I am satiated with love'. The *mundele* eats regularly (in all senses) and Zadio, living in Europe, is like the *mundele*.

Metaphors of eating are a major conceptual tool in the region, used for thinking through the various ways in which money and love might be related. The metaphor of eating has been much discussed in the literature on the societies of the region and, in particular, 'eating' links (largely imaginative) cannibalism, witchcraft, wealth, and economic and political power (see, for example, Fabian 1990; Bayart 1993; MacGaffey 2000; Thornton 2003). What is less present in the literature is the fact that the erotic is also strongly linked to this 'eating' matrix, and voracious financial and sexual appetites are clearly linked. In Congolese French, they speak of the *ventre et le sous ventre* or 'belly and underbelly' to refer to financial and sexual appetites. In Lingala, the verb *kolia* – to eat – is widely used as a direct synonym for sex. A great deal of the metaphorical play connected to eating surrounds this, as a shout that accompanied the 'Techno-Malewa' dance illustrates:

> *Nalé Nalé Nalingi Nalia!* I ate, I ate, I want to eat!
> *Mutu na yo malewa! Makolo na yo malewa! Na se na yo malewa!*
> Your head is a restaurant! Your leg is a restaurant! Your 'down there' is a restaurant!
>
> (Wenge Maison Mère 2009)

Returning to the song 'Zadio', the female protagonist/lover notes that Zadio's absence from Kinshasa is prolonged, and attempts to contact him are difficult – 'is it a problem with the network or with the charger?' asks the anxious lover, noting that 'it seems' that telephones in London 'ekomi ya ngwanzu'/'come from China [i.e. are fake/no good]'. These lyrics convey a desperate awareness that Zadio is probably avoiding her calls since London, where he lives, is the centre of the affluent North, where everything – telephone networks included – functions well. As we saw in Chapter 3, this is opposed both cosmologically and practically to China – *Ngwanzu* – which is the source of cheap, poor-quality consumer goods. From talking about Europe, the song turns to the night:

> *Bachinois batonga kaka na butu, Chez Ntemba Kahembe esala kaka na butu*
> Chinese build only at night, *Chez Ntemba Kahembe* works only at night
> *Bamibale bafukwamela basi na butu Francis Kalombo abima kaka na butu*
> Men implore women at night, Francis Kalombo goes out only at night
>
> (Mpiana 2008)

'The Chinese' here have a quite different significance from that conveyed by *Ngwanzu*. The lyrics asserting that 'the Chinese build only at night' is a reference to the construction of the Stade Kamanyola, Kinshasa's largest sporting arena, now known as the Stade des Martyrs. The stadium was built in the 1980s by the Chinese government and the workers engaged on it were sent over from China. The workmen apparently laboured at night, perhaps to avoid the tropical sun, but the symbolism of the stadium that, layer on layer, advanced only at night – the time of *bandoki* (witches) and the dead – has created a Kinois narrative that links the Chinese builders, and the Chinese economic advance more generally, to occult practices.

'Chez Ntemba' Kahembe is, as was mentioned earlier, a music patron, who lives in Pretoria, South Africa. Kahembe started as a boy selling Coca-Cola on a street corner in Lubumbashi – *ntemba* means corner in Congolese Swahili – but he is now the proprietor of a series of nightclubs all over Africa. One such is the prominent Chez Ntemba in downtown Kinshasa, an exclusive locale and a key site of *ambiance*, where a bottle of whisky sells for fifty dollars. A friend of Zambia's now disgraced President Chiluba – Kahembe organized for Wenge Musica BCBG to play during his election campaign – he is also on good terms with the current regime in Kinshasa, with whom he shares ethnic origins. Chez Ntemba in Kinshasa is frequented by a cross-section of Kinshasa's elite – politicians, migrants visiting from Europe and diamond dealers, along with lots of young women. And this connection between the night, ambiance and seduction is clearly made in the lines 'men implore women at night'. When I visited the Kinshasa Chez Ntemba, several people commented that the plush interior was *neti poto* – 'like Europe' – revealing the underlying conception of *ambiance* as a series of overlapping sites: the night, opulence, Europe.

Francis Kalombo – 'who goes out only at night' – is a deputy in the national assembly and member of the PPRD, the party to which the President belongs. He lived in Europe for several years and his entry into the world of politics was preceded by a career as a celebrity *bon vivant*. A prominent figure in Kinshasa, he has continued to be strongly associated with musicians and the life of *ambiance*; several informants linked him to the use of *fétiche*. It should be noted that the figure who only goes out at night is a wider fixture in Kinois mythology related to the broader significance of the night alluded to at the beginning of this chapter – a powerful, morally ambiguous place. The night retains a rich metaphysical significance, connecting the mysteries of economic and occult power, seduction and a series of Kinshasa's 'big men', who travel back and forth from Europe.

Metaphors of Love and Wealth

White posits a 'structural tension' between 'the feelings of helplessness in the lyrics and the astounding presence of *libanga*[5] (2008: 188). He proposes that Congolese music voices an opposition between 'money and love'. This is somewhat similar to Fabian (1997), who suggests that in popular music from Katanga, feelings of alienation in love are related to 'the conditions of exchange in a cash economy'

(1997: 23). I have tended to argue the opposite – as a general theme, there is a strong feeling of congruence or even identity between exchange, material wealth and love. In this context, exchanges of cash are not placed in a separate category, nor are they seen as being particularly problematic (see also Bloch and Parry 1989).

White's argument is, I believe, at its strongest when he looks at the song 'Feux d'Amour' by J.B. Mpiana. This song, which was a big hit, is sung from the point of view of a female narrator who lives in Malweka, a very poor outlying area of Kinshasa. The narrator bewails the fact that before loving someone, the Kinois will often ask questions such as 'What family are you from?' or 'Where did you study?' At first blush, this does appear to support White's thesis about a tension between heartbreak and hunger, but while I believe he is right to note a tension, it is tension of a different kind than he envisages.

The first point to make is that the song 'Feux d'Amour' went down extremely badly in Malweka itself – far from 'restoring momentarily their dignity' (White 2008: 185), it led to street protests in the area. J.B.'s arch-rival Werrason – a man with a far surer common touch – turned up in the district and made considerable capital out of the issue. This tends to suggest that Kinois ideologies find any discussion of poverty and love problematic, and if J.B. was using the song to suggest that love and money were not natural partners, then he was going against the ideological grain.

A second issue is the fact that the female first-person narrator does, in fact, declare her love for Adam Bombole, a businessman and latterly politician based in Kinshasa, in the course of the song. And it is a declaration that takes pains to stress Bombole's wealth. This would seem to pose serious problems for White's account, problems he circumvents by seeing this point in the song as a 'complex change of register'. As we have seen, this change of register, if it were present, would be rather unusual. In most songs the declaration of love for Bombole would be the first and only theme, and congruence between abundance and love would be assumed throughout.

The closer one looks, however, the less the idea of a changing register seems to fit. The song, in fact, contains three different declarations of love by J.B. – for Jesus Christ, for his (then) wife Amida and finally, 'in character', as the poor female narrator in love with Adam Bombole. The three declarations do not fit together entirely smoothly, but of all of them, it is only J.B.'s declaration of love for Amida – whom, he says, would love him even if they only ate 'thompsons' (a kind of cheap fish)[6] – that really contradicts the idea of affect and exchange as complementary. As I stated at the start of this chapter, the dominant conception of love and exchange as complementary is an ideology and, as such, is frequently contradicted by social reality. Individuals are, to an extent, capable of perceiving and articulating these contradictions. J.B.'s comment about Amida may be an example of such a moment of perception.

And while the lyric about Amida is somewhat discordant, I am inclined to think that there is in fact no change in register in the song at all – it is simply that the point being made in the song is not the one that White identifies. There *is* a kind of structural opposition implicit in the song, but in reality it is *not* between affect and exchange or between patronage flows and love, but between styles of exchange and the notions of the moral individual that are connected to this. What is being criticized is not the idea that wealth and love might go together – this kind of connection is specifically endorsed by the declaration of love for Adam Bombole. Instead, criticism is aimed at those individuals who – unlike Bombole or, for that matter, Jesus – *calculate* before they give rather than simply giving, as the Kinois say, 'without looking'. Even Amida's acceptance of the mackerel-bearing J.B. Mpiana relates, I think, to this principle – open-hearted acceptance of the gift given and received – not to an opposition between money and love.

Congolese discourse quite often sets up this kind of opposition between the true and false people (*vrai* and *faux mutu*). The *vrai* gives freely – *afula atala te*[7] – he gives his breath/vital forces/money without looking – whereas the *faux*, if he does give money (or love, or goods), does so in a way that is calculating and instrumental. This is connected to a much wider set of oppositions. Sometimes these juxtapose goodwill and God on the one hand and calculation, bad will and, *in extremis*, witchcraft on the other. Sometimes, as we will see in the next chapter, moral judgements are more nuanced – allowing that the good leader must get his hands dirty, sacrificing a few to provide for the many. This kind of divide can be quite easy to mistake for our own more familiar opposition between affect and exchange. The possibility for confusion is well illustrated in the song 'Amour Interet' by Ferre Gola;

> Nzambe aza bolingo/alongoli ngai na bahumbu ya bolingo interet nyionso/Buzoba blandine po to pesi motema/Na mutu alingi mbongo/Bolingo te
> God is love/take me away from the slavery of interested love/It was a mistake Blandine, to give our hearts/To a person who wants money/Not love
>
> (Gola 2004)

Again, this kind of lyric would be understood immediately by a Western audience in terms of a structural opposition between money and love, but this would be incorrect. The song was written by Ferre after he and several other musicians broke away from Werrason in a dispute over money. Thus, the 'hidden' meaning of the song – immediately deciphered by the Kinois – was as a rebuke to Werrason, who, the rebels claimed, was not sharing the proceeds of the *orchestre* in a way that fairly reflected their creative input. The point of the song is thus precisely the opposite of the 'money can't buy love' idea. The implication is rather that had the lover/Werrason's love been real, he would have given money – as well as emotions and metaphysical blessings – freely and would not have been so stingy and calculating.

A second implication of this is that the rather patrimonial relationship between the musician and his boss is seen as comparable with amorous relationships. Of course, the song is a kind of metaphor, but the reason that it works so well is that both relationships are seen as fundamentally of the same kind – in both, idioms of love and munificence are used to think about value and obligation. Indeed, romantic liaisons are in some sense a paradigm of successful economic relations. Economic relations are generally concerned with extracting money from some kind of gatekeeper along the lines described in Chapter 5.

These forms of largesse are conducted via various kinds of quasi-familial social units, which emerge as individuals coalesce in their efforts to scratch a living from the unpromising environment of Kinshasa (see De Boeck and Plissart 2004: 192). These constantly emerging and disintegrating social units are, as we examined previously, structured around the relationship between gatekeepers and the wider retinue. In establishing some kind of hold on the gatekeeper, affective ties are rather desperately acted out by members of the wider retinue, and women are often the most successful operators. This can be seen even at the highest levels of the state. Important female figures within the regime – like Wivine Moleka or Tshala Muana – came into politics after relationships with powerful men, having been established as attractive and celebrated figures linked to the world of music and the bar. In a slightly longer historical perspective, many women – such as those in the famous rotating savings club the Moziki 100 Kilos – were able to establish themselves as informal traders or bar owners, owing to financial assistance or protection from figures in the regime with whom these women were sentimentally connected.

Conclusion

This is all in line with the wider argument being made here that love is not placed in a private sphere and considered categorically distinct from political economy, but rather is considered a paradigm case for the wider patronage relationships that characterize the society. In this context, certain kinds of women are seen as emblematic economic actors within an ever more informal and patronage-based economy. This is why it seems wholly appropriate that male musicians so often sing as women – as we have noted, musicians are also perceived as successful actors in the patronage economy, and the ability to charm money out of patrons is continuous with sentimental attraction.

This emotional hold is linked, in the local conception of the matter, to the idea of socially efficacious metaphysical 'substances' – like *ngenge*, discussed above. Many of these substances are imagined as emerging from the body of the successful person. This connection with the body is not accidental. Earlier on in this book, we drew attention to the way in which within noncapitalist modes of production, wealth is often stored in objects that adorn the body (Leach 1954; Graeber 2001). Equally, it seems to be the case that notions about the sources of value within such societies seem to be attached to substances that emerge from the person, like breath or spittle.

Related to this, as we saw at the start of this chapter, it was suggested that ideologies of love are connected in an intimate way to ideologies of the person. These ideologies of the person are, in turn, connected in some important way to the mode of production. Just as, in the West, love is linked to ideologies of the possessive individual and thus to a possessive market society, here also, the connection between love, notions of the person and the relations of production are apparent. Kinois ideologies of love contained in popular music tend to perceive affect and exchange as commensurate qualities. Love, or attractive force, is perceived as just one of the good things 'given off' by the person of the successful patron; like other good things – consumer goods, money or joy – love is an outward manifestation of powerful substances that the successful individual is thought to possess. In this way, love is conceptualized as a dimension of the economically and politically successful individual.

As in all complex cultural expressions, this is a set of ideas cross-cut by contradiction. One such contradiction is the fact that much of the pleasure derived from Congolese music comes from identifying not with the patron enjoying his wealth and romantic conquests, but from our intense, pleasurable-painful identification with the melancholic first-person narrator. Embedded in its most characteristic lyrical forms, Congolese music implies that it is the everywoman who is in the most profound sense and individual, who feels the intense, human passions of life most strongly. Yet at the same time this tender passion is ultimately a kind of tribute to the – far less human – love object who we nevertheless *aspire* to be. Such contradictions are perhaps inevitable in the cultural forms produced within any unequal society.

A second contradiction arises from the fact that Congolese music is in fact a kind of petition, which seeks to remind patrons of correct behaviour within a society where patronage payments are an essential social form. Songs try to hold patrons to moral norms about the good giver, which characterize true love not in terms of an opposition between affect and exchange, but rather in terms of an opposition between the false love that gives while calculating personal advantage and the true patron/lover who gives 'without looking' and with an open heart.

Thus, ideologies of love also offer an insight into how accumulation is envisaged, legitimated and contested within this mode of production. If, as we have argued in earlier chapters, rights in others represent a fundamental form of accumulation, then we begin to see that these rights in others are legitimized via the notion that the powerful 'bestow' substances on others – these can be metaphysical substances like breath or material substances like money or clothes. Such a notion of the patron as bestowing goods on a retinue, many of which are invisible, can create a notion of debt that justifies appropriation. It is to this ideological matrix, crucial in justifying the appropriation on which the system rests, that we now turn.

Notes

1. Simaro Lutumba and Tabu Ley, the greatest lyricists of Congolese music, both use this boat in the river motif repeatedly. Indeed, Simaro's song 'Ebale ya Zaïre' very closely resembles 'Ngobila' in thematic terms.
2. Congolese popular music can be divided into a slow section, called the *rumba*, where the narrative and vocal elements of the music predominate and the audience does partner dancing, and a faster section, known as the *sebene*, where guitars and ludic shouted vocals predominate, and where the audience dances on its own.
3. The song is almost universally believed to have really been written by Koffi Olomide.
4. Schama (1989) sees the Terror as the ultimate expression of this 'virtue', while Reddy (2001) seems to mourn its passing as a missed turning in modernity.

5. Following Kinois usage, I have used the plural *mabanga* to refer to patronage as an abstract noun. White follows the English convention and uses *libanga*.

6. Thompsons are a kind of mackerel named after the man who first started importing them to Kinshasa. River fish are prized in Congo and in the 1990s, thompsons were much disparaged as the food of the poor. They have gone up in price rather dramatically in recent times. Amida ran off with the diamond dealer Didi Kinuani a few years after this, though she has since left Didi for J.B. again. Amida 'Perle Noir' was the daughter of a man from the Punjab who made a living in Kinshasa doing magic at children's parties in the 1970s and 1980s.

7. The links between breath, money, music and ritual power in precolonial lower Congo receive a fascinating investigation in Janzen (1982: 248–49).

Chapter 8

CHARISMATIC FETISHISM

℮ ⌐

The strongest is never strong enough to remain always master if he does not transform force into right and obedience into duty.
—Jean-Jacques Rousseau, *Du Contract Social*

This chapter investigates a central mystery of power in Kinshasa. How are authority figures able to attract a retinue and portray themselves as 'good givers' when, in reality, their power is derived from onerous forms of exploitation? Local discourse attributes the power of such figures to occult practices and, above all, human sacrifice. Is such a widespread belief in the occult important or merely an exotic curiosity? Previous chapters have shown that supernatural powers are often attributed to those who disperse prestige goods. Is there a more substantial connection made between the occult and the control of exchange? Is the contribution of music and performance an important factor in this connection or is it peripheral to the process?

As we saw in Chapter 5, *présidents d'orchestres* rely on appropriating the labour of their underlings. And yet a variety of 'front stage' representations depict the *président* as a wealth creator. This chapter argues that the *président*'s image as a wealth creator is part of a wider Congolese theory about the creation of value that connects to perceptions of the role that 'extraordinary' individuals play in economic life. Underlying this theory are ideas about capacitating human substances that the powerful individual derives from transacting with transcendent other worlds. This theory is hardly satisfactory as a predictor of macroeconomic outcomes. Yet at another level – as an entrenched and popular (mis)representation about the sources of value – such ideologies are crucial to an understanding of how political–economic relations are perpetuated. While the power wielded by 'extraordinary' individuals is ultimately linked to their control of violence and their direct or indirect connections to powerful outsiders, their power also depends on forms of legitimacy based on the ideology to be discussed here. What this chapter investigates is the central mystery of power. How is it that an unfair social order is able to keep going?

This book has described the role of music patronage and related forms of largesse within a society where capitalism was not dominant. Central to our analysis has been the idea that, within such a society, it is the person who represents the primary form of wealth. In this chapter we will attempt to examine the ideology that relates these ideas about the person to the wider reproduction of inequality. For Marx, the capitalist mode of production was brought about by an act of violence – forcing the English peasantry from their direct relationship with the land and re-employing some of them as wage labourers. Primitive accumulation thus accomplished, the system was not sustained simply by violence, though this played a role. A rather specific kind of alienation, which Marx terms 'fetishism', meant that labourers misattributed the source of value, coming to see the products of their labour as external to them and allowing those who owned capital – itself merely a history of their accumulated efforts – to dictate to them.

In the DRC a different kind of rupture took place. Here a weakly established capitalism was broken on the rocks encountered by the post-independence state and another mode of production became dominant. Here also, class relations were not simply sustained by violence – there was also a systematic mystification of value, which justified the dominant class's division of resources. This mystification I understand via a modified version of Marx's theory of fetishism, but here it is not primarily things or money that are fetishized, but rather people. For this reason, I refer to it as *charismatic fetishism*, a form of fetishism that creates a charismatic aura around powerful individuals.

As in the previous chapter, a brief methodological note is in order. The discussion in this chapter is predominantly concerned with beliefs and ideology, and the discussion is more strongly on what people say and on myths about power than on what they do. This analysis should not be taken in isolation and readers would do well to consider it in conjunction with the accounts presented in other chapters, particularly in Chapter 5.

Magic, Charisma and the Crocodile that Eats People on Behalf of His Brother

While our theory will draw particularly on Marx, it is clear that there is a strong element of personal 'charismatic' power involved. While we ultimately repudiate Max Weber's account of this phenomenon, there are clearly some important similarities that need to be discussed. In Weber's classic discussion of charisma, he includes the attribution of magical powers to the leader, and in our discussion of 'charismatic fetishism' magical beliefs about leaders also play a key role, as the following ethnographic vignette illustrates.

I am standing, barefoot but in a suit, at *Nkamba*, the new Jerusalem of the Kimbanguist religion, in the Bas-Congo province. We are beside a concrete tank looking at a very small crocodile. A man is explaining to us that the crocodile had belonged to a once-famous *nganga*, who had converted to Kimbanguism and renounced his former life of sin. The crocodile was in fact the brother of the said *nganga*, who had been transformed into this shape so as to hunt down and eat men. Our guide explains that this crocodile has eaten a very large number of people. The vital forces of the crocodile's victims will then in some way have accrued to his brother, the *nganga*. The guide lists some prominent politicians and musicians who have benefited from the powerful *nganga*'s services. Unable to contain myself, I ask if the crocodile – which, nose to tail, is about two feet long – is not a bit small to have eaten all those people. 'He was much bigger before, when he was free' replies our guide. Looking around, I see my party, which includes several university graduates, nodding with interest and in consternation at the infamy of it all.

On my return to Kinshasa, I recounted my trip to a friend, describing an incident during the journey where our bus slid from the dirt road. 'Yes, lots of pilgrims die on that road', he replied. 'They say that they are eaten by Diangenda' (the former spiritual leader of Kimbanguism, said to have been close to Mobutu).[1]

I thought these episodes worth recounting because, despite the large number of works published on the 'modernity of witchcraft' (see below), I think it is nevertheless important to stress that I am not overselling marginal forms of folklore. In the DRC, and among Congolese migrants, belief in this kind of supernatural causation is the majority view and is massively implicated in the nexus of exchange, attractiveness, economic success and political authority that we are examining.

Recent decades have seen a revival of interest in such themes, and a great number of articles and books have been published arguing that the occult plays an important role in modern African politics (well-known examples include: Rowlands and Warnier 1988; Bayart 1993; Comaroff and Comaroff 1993, 1999; Geschiere 1997; and Chabal and Daloz 1999). This perspective, in turn, has attracted criticism. Meagher, for example, voices the objections of many when she states that:

> among a growing coterie of Africanist scholars, the occult is described as a key mechanism through which Africa engages with globalization and modernity. Undeterred by the complete lack of evidence that the occult plays a greater role in shaping contemporary African political behaviour than, say, civil as- sociations, bribery, overseas migration or mass demonstrations, the authors … [make] 'the occult' or 'the invisible' appear a more politically significant force than it is. (2006: 595)

Meagher makes a valid point about emphasis and fashion within African studies, but I find something problematic about the way this passage opposes 'the occult' to a consideration of political economy. The point surely is that, in local representations, ideas of the occult are not separated from a consideration of bribery, migration or civil society. Notions of supernatural forces, such as *kindoki*, were and continue to be central to local political and economic theory. The point is not to fetishize such local representations, but the capacity of such second-order representations to effect social reality cannot be ignored. A second point that Meagher's article makes captures what I believe is the real issue:

> More disturbing is the representation of occult practices as displays of local agency and cultural diversity rather than as cultural indicators of extreme social and economic stress in the face of decades of ruthless economic and political restructuring. Under the guise of highlighting African agency [in the form of occult beliefs], the authors collaborate in masking the desperation and powerlessness of African societies in the face of global economic and political forces. (2006: 596)

I agree that the shift in African studies from 'dependency' to 'agency' has been based on a series of flawed premises. But I find Meagher's insistence on the recent nature of occult beliefs not entirely satisfac- tory. To see why this is the case, it is useful to consider this along- side the broadly similar argument made by another group of scholars influenced by 'Manchester School' anthropology (Gluckman 1963; Worsley 1970; Comaroff and Comaroff 1999, 2001). For these writers, forms of magical and occult beliefs are the product of some kind of crisis, usually (though not always) occurring among the disadvantaged on the periphery. In these works, a belief in the extraordinary or the magical is seen as essentially aberrant, as are the enthusiasms for charismatic individuals – 'strategists of moral behaviour' (Alberoni, cited in Blom Hansen and Verkaaik 2009) – capable of manipulating or focusing popular disquiet. But while it *is* often the case that magical beliefs are linked to crisis and revolt, they are even more often linked to stasis and continuity.

The veteran Congolese politician Antoine Gizenga provides a good illustration of this. In the 1960s he was a prominent figure in the violent revolts against the Western-backed governments that succeeded Lumumba's assassination in Congo-Kinshasa. The rebel movements contained elements of Maoism, but also relied on beliefs, of the cargo-cult variety, imputing extraordinary powers to their leaders – that the bullets of the whites would be turned to water,[2] a book of magical secrets would be uncovered and the like (see Verhaegen 1966). After years in the wilderness, both literal and political, Gizenga returned to the DRC and, as head of PALU (Partie Lumumbiste Unifié), participated in the elections of 2006. Coming third in the presidential elections, he obtained a kingmaker role, bringing sufficient numbers of his Bandundu-based supporters to Kabila's camp. This gave Kabila a comfortable victory in the elections and a semi-respectable score in the west of the country, where he is generally unpopular. Informants who attended PALU meetings said that they were organized like religious revivals.

Ethnic *confrères* were told that Gizenga would make them drop dead if they didn't vote PALU, and stories of the mystic powers of *le vieux*, who is said to appear and disappear at will, abound. This is compatible with the fact that the PALU leadership, now in government, has integrated itself with depressing ease into the essentially stable arrangements of Congolese kleptocracy. A friend who attended a party thrown by PALU spoke of *le vieux* offering bricks of cash to partygoers 'for transport'. As the party progressed to an exclusive nightclub, the hospitality included a giant bottle of Johnnie Walker for each of the fifty tables. Thus, similar forms of occult power and charisma seem essential to authority during periods of relative stability[3] as well as during crises. This renders the causal attributions that the millenarian literature seeks to make between crisis and magical beliefs problematic (see also Anderson 1990).

In this vein, there is a wealth of historical evidence showing that notions of the occult are important in how Central Africans have thought about, and continue to think about, their violent insertion into the wider world, a process that dates back not merely over decades but also centuries (see, for example, MacGaffey 2000; Thornton 2003). Wyatt MacGaffey's summary of how political economy and ideologies of the occult came together for the Bakongo peoples in the eighteenth and nineteenth centuries can also provide some clues to the kinds of relationship we will be exploring here:

> The power of death [of mystical sacrifice] acquired by a chief … from matrilineal ancestors, seems to be related to the real-life function of lineage heads in regulating lineage membership by distinguishing free-born members from slaves and by trading in the latter … 'Chiefs' in this sense only emerged at nodes in the commercial network. (MacGaffey 2000: 32)

Today, the power of the *président d'orchestre* (and other social pivots in Kinshasa), like the power of the nineteenth-century chief, is tied to his position in the local political economy and the position of this economy in the global system. Extraordinary personal power, charisma if you will, is real, but it is not the random, revolutionary and 'anti-economic' force Weber posited. Rather, it accumulates in regular patterns that can be mapped onto the wider geography of exploitation. Within such networks, the dispersal of patronage is a necessary but not a sufficient foundation for authority. In particular, a set of beliefs and practices that systematically and theatrically mystify the sources of value are also required. In examining this mystification, I elaborate on the local theory of the *fétiche* and how it is expressed in a contemporary context. I then examine how this set of beliefs, rendered emotionally plausible by popular performance, is involved in processes of fetishization in something like the Marxist sense, but here the thing fetishized is not predominantly commodities or money capital, but certain people.

Charismatic Fetishism and the *Président d'orchestre*

Many of the details of presidential exploitation have been discussed in previous chapters. There we discussed some of the reasons why the president was able to maintain his power relating to his control of the 'gate' between the *orchestre* and the wider world – the gate to Europe, to political patronage and to a wider network of patrons. In this chapter we will reflect on this material again, bringing out more distinctly the ideological component of his role. One of the examples we covered in those chapters, the appropriation of compositions, brings out the ways in which the gatekeeper role is fetishized, so that appropriation and the maintenance of scarcity is made to look like munificence.

The appropriation of compositions has a long history in the Congo (cf. Chapter 4). Part of the essential context is that *orchestre* members are not paid a salary in any real sense, something that is part of a much wider set of renumerative practices in Kinshasa. The art of composition and, above all, lyrical brilliance is highly valued in Congo. Nothing will confirm the status of an artist more than his ability to create skilful compositions. A glance at most albums will reveal the *président* to be a more productive composer than his musicians, often dramatically so – because in the case of almost all top *orchestres*, at least half of their albums will be made up of songs attributed exclusively to the *président*. Yet, as the fan of Congolese music very quickly learns, the *président* is not in fact the author of many of these songs.

At times, the appropriation of songs appears relatively acceptable to all parties. For example, it seems to be accepted practice that, on being made a permanent member of an *orchestre*, a new musician is required to contribute his first composition to the *président*. In a second common scenario, a fan will pass a song to one of his idols – a practice demonstrating, at one level, the open sociability that marks such a contrast between Congolese popular music and Western variants. I was told of a song that had been composed by a youthful fraudster based in Paris. Knowing that he was going to prison, he gave his composition to his musical idol, asking in return only that his name be included on the *mabanga* for his song, so those on the outside would not forget him. All this is conceptualized within the porous, quasi-familial structure of the *orchestre*, and springs from a kind of *vieux/petit* relationship between the *président* and the composer that, for a time at least, legitimates the appropriation. At times, the exchange is of a fairly uncontroversial nature. Compositions by the young are repaid with a kind of musical apprenticeship – Koffi Olomide, for example, is well known to have written some of Papa Wemba's most famous early songs and was, in return, inducted into the music business, and Felix Wazekwa also followed a similar path.

But very often these exchanges lack any clear sense of reciprocity or fraternity. This is especially the case when a relationship develops beyond such one-off donations from a fan or a junior musician and evolves into a regular transfer of compositions.

The Ballad of Some Songwriters, and the Président with a Toad in His Belly

After playing guitar in several local bands, Sam had an audition with one of the big *orchestres*. During this audition, which included much informal music making, Sam played a composition of his own. The next thing he heard, the *président* had gone to Europe, where he was recording an album with Congolese studio musicians based in Paris. The *président* released his album and not only was Sam's song on there, it was the smash hit of the record. The song, which uses a rich poetic repertoire to talk about a failing relationship, has since become established as a classic. On the credits for the album, Sam and the *président* were listed as joint composers, though the composition was entirely Sam's own. When Sam expressed disappointment that he had taken his song without consultation, the *président* replied 'Mais non, tu est mon petit', implying that within families such actions were allowed. Sam has never received any money for the song in question.

Apart from underlings, one of the most important sources of compositions for *présidents d'orchestres* is the work of experienced songwriters. These are often musicians whose own careers are not doing so well and who supplement their incomes by selling songs. Sam well exemplifies this. After years of ill-treatment, including the outright theft of many of his songs, he struck out on his own. Though highly regarded as a composer and guitarist, at every turn his solo career has hit problems. Once, when he had found a financial backer, the same backer was then courted by his former *président* who, being a big star, persuaded the producer to drop Sam and produce him instead. Sam secured a place in Bozi Boziana's *orchestre*, L'Anti Choc, and was set to go with them on a tour of Europe, but, alone out of all the musicians, he was not granted a visa. Later, when he found a backer prepared to produce an album of his compositions, he was again frustrated. The producer began to organize for Sam to travel to Europe to record the album, but he was again denied a visa.[4]

Sam's fortunes are now at a very low ebb and he lives from hand to mouth selling compositions. According to a friend of his, Sam also composed four songs on the penultimate album of another top *président d'orchestre*. He needs to sell his songs and this represents an agreed exchange, but the informal nature of such transactions and the imbalance of power between the *président* and the songwriter means that abuse is very common – Sam, for example, is owed $400 for these works and there seems little prospect of this money ever being paid. Not every encounter is exploitative, of course: when Sam had a hospital bill to pay, another *président* stepped in to pay it, and Sam took pleasure in later making him a present of one of his best songs, but the general tenor of his relations with musical stars is quite sour.

Other appropriations are even less voluntary. When an album is recorded in Paris, it is often Paris-based Congolese musicians who do some of the work. Many of these musicians have no papers. Indeed, if and when their status is regularized, most of them choose to abandon studio work for something less exploitative – drumming at the 'African village' in Disneyland Paris was a massively sought-after gig in this regard. And the lack of papers renders these musicians especially vulnerable to having their work stolen. A friend, who has no legal status in France, twice had compositions 'reattributed' during the period of my fieldwork. On the second occasion, the arranger, who appears to have masterminded the operation, responded to his complaints with a (purely rhetorical) 'Est-que yo oza mukanda?'– 'Do you have *papers?*' His position is hopeless, not only because he cannot make any kind of formal complaint, but also because, as an illegal, he needs cash-in-hand studio work from the arranger who stole his song. The contrast is quite evident with musicians who have regular status. For example, when a famous *président* tried to extract a composition from the successful studio guitarist Olivier Tshimanga, Olivier, who has his papers in France and plenty of work, could put his foot down and insist that the composition be registered in his name.

Occasionally such practices can backfire on the *président*. Both Kester Emeneya and Guy Moller (also known as *Le Harry Potter du Congo*) released albums in 2007. Both albums contained near-identical versions of a song entitled 'Daisy', which both of them claimed to have written. The obvious conclusion is that the real author of 'Daisy' sold the song twice. This has happened several times before – in 1982, for example, Papa Wemba and Djuna Djanana both released versions of the same song, 'Parapluie', each claiming to be its author.

Sometimes the appropriation of songs appears to be simply a gratuitous demonstration of force. Franklin, who has played keyboards for many major *orchestres*, recounts having left one of them because, at the instruction of the *président*, his composition was taken from him and attributed to another musician in the group. The motivation for such an action is obscure – perhaps it is done to prevent the more junior musicians from being noticed by the public and acquiring a stronger position within the *orchestre*. Franklin himself attributed it to *jalousie*, a quality that, in the Congolese scheme of things, stands close to witchcraft and at the opposite end of the spectrum from goodwill and God.

It is important to understand what is at stake here. It is not an issue of royalty payments since, as we have seen, the body charged with the payment of artists' rights in the DRC, SONECA, is the kind of *Through the Looking-Glass* institution typical of the country. Neither authorial nor performing rights are actually paid. So what is at stake in being registered as the author? The most evident interest lies in the *dédicace*, where the composer is entitled to find a patron for his song and accept payment for it. Given the dire financial straits in which musicians often find themselves, this money is extremely important. A second factor is prestige. However indirectly, *orchestres* survive as a result of their popularity with the public. Being recognized as the composer of several songs is one of the ways in which a musician can gain the esteem of the press and the public, and this can, in turn, establish the composer as a star in his own right. Clearly the increased profile that composition can bring has advantages for a musician in terms of his position within the *orchestre* – not least when it comes to his capacity to negotiate patronage. But even above such important instrumental reasons, a musician values compositions recorded under his own name because of an understandable desire for recognition as a creative individual who is capable of generating value.

During the period 2006–8, Wenge Maison Mère recorded the album *Temps Presents*. On their previous two releases – *Témoignage* and *Sous Sol* – fifteen of the seventeen songs were attributed to Werrason. On *Temps Presents*, by contrast, out of fourteen tracks, only two are listed as written by Werrason. For most of the artists, this was the first time they had been given an attribution and, in the studio, it was noteworthy that each artist took an intense pleasure in his own song. Musicians not working on a certain day would come to the studio anyway and, during breaks, would pester the studio engineer to play the *maquette*, each for his particular song. As this indicates, the appropriation of compositions is deeply resented by musicians, though not by the wider audience.

In 2006 I was travelling on the Paris *periferique*, listening to Koffi Olomide on a car stereo. With me was a friend who had paid for a brief *mabanga* name check on Koffi Olomide's album *Loi*. Trying to elicit a debate on music, I commented that Koffi Olomide was a good composer. My friend snorted and replied that he was a good thief, commenting that he knew how to steal music from Felix Wazekwa.[5] Yet, after expressing this opinion, he went on.:'C'est comme ça, ils doivent savoir voler' – 'It is like that, they need to know how to steal.'

And the interesting thing about the appropriation of songs by the *président* is that the public knows a great deal about such practices. Indeed, the cultural template of the *président* as an amoral 'gourmand' is so strong that it leads to a conviction in the public mind that the *président* has never written a song of his own.

At times, the *président* seems little inclined to disguise the fact that he is not the author of all the songs listed in his name. On the album *Sous-Sol* by Wenge Maison Mère, for example, the song 'Enfant Mystère' is a complete departure from the band's normal style. The vocals and guitar on the song are performed by a young man who is also featured prominently on the video. Everyone I met who heard the song assumed that the young man was the composer, and in granting him such a prominent role in the performance and unveiling him as a young talent in subsequent television interviews, it appears that Werrason intended his audience to think this way.

Fans of the *président d'orchestre* of Wenge BCBG, J.B. Mpiana, will openly acknowledge that band member Jules Kibbens is the author of many songs credited to J.B. Mpiana and, indeed, Kibbens himself told me that this was the case. But this seems not to diminish their opinion of J.B. either as a leader or in some broader sense as a 'source'. Indeed, while appropriations may at times be deplored, the more persistent implication is that rank-and-file musicians are indebted to the *président*. Many other kinds of retinue beyond the world of music will similarly attribute the 'source' of their wealth to the 'extraordinary' individual who, from the outside, appears to be appropriating the surplus that the retinue has created.

While we are concentrating on concentration musicians, similarly paradoxical attributions of value creation are widespread among all gatekeepers – Pentecostal pastors, big-name media professionals, diamond dealers, politicians, members of the commercial classes and others.

This perception of dependence in the context of apparently onerous exploitation is partly enforced by the persistent context of scarcity. But it is also sustained by the fact that in the ideology of exchange that produces such notions of dependence, it is not simply material goods that are involved, but also mystical substances derived from other worlds.

This ideology can be very strongly articulated by the fans. For example, during 2007, there was a dispute between the fans of Wenge BCBG and some of their personnel. The fans wanted younger musicians to be given more of a role in the group's performances. There were rumours that some of the older musicians in the *orchestre*, unhappy with the lack of open support they had received from J.B, were preparing to launch solo careers. Included among them were several individuals known to have written many of J.B's biggest hits. Several observers expressed amusement that these musicians would consider launching solo careers and, as one informant commented, 'J.B. apesaka bango nyoso lupemba' – 'J.B. gave all of them *lupemba*.' We will come on to the concept of *lupemba* shortly, but it should be noted here that it refers to a certain quality of the person, perhaps translatable as luck or blessing – a quality that, in this context, is clearly related to ideas of occult sacrifice:

> Sometime in the 1990s the members of Wenge Musica BCBG 4X4 are all to- gether. An argument breaks out between the members about who should be in charge. The argument becomes heated, and they are all shouting and laying claim to the position of *président*. J.B. comes forward and vomits a huge toad (an animal closely associated with witchcraft, in Congo as in Europe). The other members of the band immediately stop and look on in horror as J.B. picks up the toad and swallows it again. J.B. looks around at the other members of Wenge Musica, who are now silent and cowed: 'Ngai na mema fétiche na orchestre oyo,' – 'I carry the *fétiche* of this *orchestre*', he says (Journal, 12 December 2007)

This idea of the body, above all the stomach, as a kind of container for occult animals or vital substances is extensive in Central Africa and is present as far back as historical sources will take us (MacGaffey 2000; Thornton 2003; Warnier 2007).[6] And this is part of a more widespread equivalence made between various people and things. As MacGaffey (2000: 13) has argued, the ritual device (*nkisi* or *fétiche*), the chief, the *nganga*, and the *ndoki*,[7] are all fundamentally equivalent, in the sense that they are seen as holding within themselves powerful substances, the essential component of which is a certain kind of vital substance drawn from an invisible world:

> Evoloko [a star of Congolese music from the late 1970s and 1980s, who sang in Zaiko Langa Langa and Langa Langa Stars] went to see the *nganga* and asked to be the biggest star in Zaïre. The *nganga* said to him, 'It can be done, but you will have to sacrifice your father.' Evoloko baulks at this but when the *nganga* is adamant Evoloko agrees and asks how this sacrifice should be arranged. The *nganga* tells him to watch where his father sets foot and to take the earth from his footprint, and bring this to him next week. Evoloko agrees to do this and the consultation ends. The *nganga* walks Evoloko to the edge of his compound and bids him farewell, returning to his house. Evoloko hovers on the edge of the compound, thoughts of his father tormenting him. 'My father, that is too much', he decides and as he says this he looks down and sees the *nganga*'s footprints going back to his house. Carefully he gathers earth from

one of these, and stores it in a twist of paper. Next week he returns to the *nganga*'s house, and presents the earth he has gathered to the *nganga* claiming this as earth from his father's footprint.

The *nganga* takes the earth and begins his work, but as it nears completion he sees that the face that appears in his mystic mirror is not that of Evoloko's father but his own. Thinking he has made some mistake the *nganga* repeats the incantation, but once again his own face appears. Realizing that he has been tricked, and that he is dying the *nganga* turns to Evoloko: 'I will get you in your dreams – I will get you when you sleep!' the *nganga* says before he dies. And so Evoloko never sleeps[8] [or, according to other versions of the story, he never sleeps at night]. (Fieldnotes, 2006)

Substances, Blessings and the Dead

Colloquial Lingala abounds in terms, both indigenous and imported, that describe the various forms of substantive personal power – *lupemba*, *nguya*, *mpifo*, *ngenge*, *dominance* and *onction*, to name but a few. It is clear than many of these terms are rooted in the *longue durée* of the Central African political tradition. Taking *lupemba* first, this is a quality much discussed with reference to musicians and to various others – like politicians or diamond dealers – who aspire to success in the world of bars, designer clothing and fast women. While *lupemba* is often glossed as success by informants (White 2004), this is perhaps insufficient to understand the full ramifications of the term. Informants listed various qualities from success to blessing, power and luck as the meanings of *lupemba*. Examining how the word is used in context, I would suggest that the notion of 'blessing' probably takes us the furthest.

As with blessing, one is said to 'give' *lupemba* – *kopesa lupemba*. There are many uses of the word that apparently pre-date the present association of the term with celebrity – one can ask for *lupemba* before an undertaking, particularly a journey. And in classic Central African fashion, one tends to ask for *lupemba* from a social elder. In this way, it fits into the broader category of blessings and curses, which lineage elders were, and to some extent still are, believed to be able to bestow on the young. Thus, after a period with a musical boss, musicians are said to 'take *lupemba*' – *kozua lupemba* – from the *président*, who is clearly in an elder/cadet type relationship with the rank-and-file musician.[9] Other examples take us deeper into the metaphysical complexities.

Just as Isaac gives his blessing to Jacob, so musicians will be heard saying things like 'Après cinq ans Koffi apes'ngai lupemba' – 'After five years Koffi gave me lupemba'. This sense of capacity bestowed on a musical 'cadet' by a musical 'elder' is very strong and is apparent even when the specific term *lupemba* is not employed:

Interviewer: You say you are the boss of Koffi, of JB [i.e. of all the popular musicians] ...

Kester: I am their chief in what sense? In the sense that the day I played the Olympia [in Paris], the first, the youngest of all the musicians who played the Olympia was Tabu Ley [famous musician from the generation before Kester]. He was the one who gave me power. He said 'With the power that is conferred on us, I hand to Emeneya [Kester's first name]'. Therefore I am the chief of all of them.

(Emeneya 2006, my translation)

The late Kester was the master of this kind of nonsense, but it is a nonsense that displays a clear cultural logic: Tabu Ley, the elder, has handed power to Kester.

Tshala Muana, an incredibly popular musician in her day who was the companion of Laurent Kabila and, when I interviewed her in 2011, an important music producer and head of the woman's league of the PPRD, had been awarded a customary office by the traditional authorities in her home province of Kasai Occidental. She said that they 'gave me *lupemba*' (*bapesa na ngai lupemba*). When I asked her as to what she meant by this, she indicated that this involved the ritual application of chalk to her eyes – a form of blessing common in the Central African tradition, which enables the initiate to 'see' witches (*ndoki*). This notion of a substance, held and passed on by elders, that allows one to 'see' a second powerful and dangerous world existing alongside this one is very common.

Informants originating from the province of Bandundu, where the specific word *lupemba* seems to originate, connected the term with white clay taken from a graveyard that lies in a village a few kilometres from the capital Kikwit. In this cemetery lie the remains of Kungu Pemba, a chief in the region who was said to have met with the whites when they first arrived in the region and performed some kind of exchange of mystical knowledge with them, which somehow invested in Kungu Pemba great powers over the destiny of the Congo. Those who wish to rule the country successfully must take earth from Kungu Pemba's grave, but, should you take this earth with a bad heart – 'na motema mabe' – you will die almost immediately. This, one informant said, is precisely what happened to Mobutu's first wife, Marie-Antoinette,[10] who had been rooting about at the grave-yard, up to no good.

One should also link *lupemba* with local notions of 'whiteness' more generally. Both De Boeck and White list 'whiteness' as one of the senses of *lupemba* and, beyond this, there is a pretty overwhelming case that, etymologically, they are related. *Mpemba*, from the root *vemba*, means white chalk or white porcelain clay in Kikongo, and one only needs to take a cursory glance at Central African ethnography to see that this is a substance freighted with meaning. Associated, among other things, with initiation, innocence (as in not guilty), the male principle and the dead (see, among many authors, Turner 1968; Vansina 1978; De Boeck 1994; MacGaffey 2000, 2009), *mpemba* is indeed the word for the land of the dead and for blessing in the languages of the lower Kongo. This becomes *bupemba* for the land of the dead in ChiLuba, further east (MacGaffey 2005: 203).[11]

White substances, particularly chalk or white clay, are often stored in sites that sacralize power, such as ancestral shrines. Such substances are also an essential element in the matter that fills *fétiche* (MacGaffey 1991). What underlies this is a series of connections between the dead and whiteness. Blessing, power, luck and other influences also very often come from the dead, perhaps via *fétiche*, so these qualities are often designated by the word *lupemba*, a term related to whiteness. And whiteness is just one strand in this dense set of connections.

Lupemba, being related to the idea of luck, is also heavily associated with ideas of success in the hunt. This plugs the concept into the idea of the hunt, an extremely important metaphor for capturing wealth and for the morality of division (De Boeck 1998). The 'forest' where the hunt takes place is, in addition, perceived as a kind of 'mystical elsewhere' linked to the dead (MacGaffey 1986). Whiteness is also associated with the white clay found in streams and, in general, spaces under or across water are associated with the dead. Many precolonial polities in Central Africa had origin myths about a migration from a land of the dead (see, for example, MacGaffey 2000), one that very often involved crossing a mystical river or emerging from a body of water. Various Lunda people trace their origins to a mystic river called Koola, while the Luba people are said to have emerged from Lake Upemba in Katanga (see MacGaffey 2000: 202).

Underlying these connections is a pervasive trope of *mpemba* – placing an empowering other-world in structural opposition to the world of the living. The moral valency of this world has always been dubious, but in the most recent, Pentecostal-inflected versions of this cosmology, *mpemba* is clearly satanic. In this modern version of the story, *mpemba* is called the 'deuxième monde'. Midday for the dead and for *ndoki* is our midnight, and their night is our day. The mists of the morning are their cooking fires. As the poet and musician Simaro Lutumba wrote: 'Tongo etani, ba ndoki bazonga ndako' – 'The day breaks, the witches return home' (Lutumba 1974/2000). Women who are barren in this world have several children in the other world (MacGaffey 1986: 49), while 'witch children' 'confess' to being adults with husbands and/or families on the other side (De Boeck and Plissart 2004: 151).

Just as the land of the dead may be 'the forest', which is opposed to the village where the living are found, so wild animals are often associated with *ndoki* and the dead. Thus, Werrason is known, among other things, as the *roi de la forêt* ('king of the forest') and *mokonzi na ba niama* ('chief of the beasts'), names that possess a sinister undertow and are also often associated with the customary chief. The bar that he owns and performs in is known as the Zamba Playa – the forest beach. Significant in this context is the way that Europe has been incorporated into this matrix. Europe, too, is frequently elided with the land of the dead. This can be directly stated (see, for example, MacGaffey 1986: 62; Bernault 2006) or implied, as in accounts where witches or powerful individuals travel to Europe in dreams or in mystical aeroplanes made from human body parts (De Boeck and Plissart 2004).

Another material/metaphorical opposition employed is between the land and the water. The dead are often said to be 'under water' and those using occult means in search of temporal success are often said to have 'plunged into water'. Pentecostal discourses that draw on this matrix claim that Mobutu placed Congo 'under water', replacing it with the demonic 'Zaïre'. Another story I was told stated that Bill Gates (I am unclear if this was the American billionaire or the Luba diamond dealer who has adopted this name) had 'plunged into water' in order to obtain his success. Likewise, success can be offered by tricking or trapping female spirits from the water, known as *mami wata*.

Dreams are the space of the dead. Dead people appear to the living in this medium, and the activities of *ndoki* are also made clear (Laman 1953–1968: 7). Thus, we can see that by never sleeping, or by sleeping only during the day, the musician Evoloko, whom we met earlier in this chapter, may hope to avoid the vengeance of the tricked *nganga*. Music is also a link to this other world; the spirit possession brought on by dancing was a sign of divine powers, and musical instruments were the voices of the dead. The custom of dancing at funerals, particularly through the night, is related to these precolonial connections.

This sense of capacities obtained from transcendent realms is even more powerfully illustrated in stories that speak of individuals using death to enhance their powers. Dona Beatriz, the leader of a religious movement in the early eighteenth century, 'died' every Friday, 'dining with God and pleading the cause of the blacks' (De Gallo, quoted in Thornton 1998); she then would rise again every Monday. In recent times the popular musician Pepé Kalle was said by one informant to have locked himself in his bathroom and died every day, travelling to Europe and visiting producers in this condition. According to the story, Pepé died[12] permanently when his wife, concerned about how long he was spending in the bathroom, broke in and, in her lamentations, somehow sealed off the pathway back to life.

The connection with the dead is sometimes linked to the belief that 'extraordinary' leaders may trade years of their own life in exchange for temporal success. One rather confusing story recounted to me about the veteran opposition politician Etienne Tshisikedi said that he had sold so many years of his life in return for mystic powers that he was 'already dead'. More typically, the extraordinary figure is said to have traded the lives of others, and the imagined locus of this sacrifice has generally been the lineage. As in the precolonial period, the sacrifice is often conceptualized as a form of eating – ingesting and thus taking on their vital substances, or offering these substances to other capacitating spirits from the other world.

Powerful individuals are commonly alleged to have asked underlings for a rooster, an act that is universally understood as the request for the sacrifice of a family member mystically transubstantiated into the bird (see also MacGaffey 1977). Sometimes animal 'familiars' are involved – as in the case of the crocodile discussed earlier. This trading of vital forces can extend as far as selling one's fertility or the possibility of having children. This is called 'selling the spine' – the spine in Central African medical theory being the site of fertility and of sperm. Such is the prevalence of this kind of belief that inferences are very often drawn about those who are wealthy but have no children. Thus, one of the directors of the state diamond-mining company MIBAS, who was known to be both very wealthy and childless, was commonly suggested to have 'sold his spine' (see also De Boeck 1998).

At the Zamba Playa, Heads Roll Towards an Awesome Individual

It is an evening in 2007 and I am in the *Zamba Playa* – 'forest beach' – the large open-air bar that plays home to Wenge Maison Mère. The audience is rough, demonstrative and loud. Fights break out, drunks try to rush the stage and the crowd cheers or boos various performances, saving its biggest cheer for Adjani, a drug-addled veteran of the *orchestre* who cannot remember the new dance steps but still sings like an angel. As the live performance comes to an end, a huge piece of board is brought on stage and images are projected onto it. First up comes a battle scene from a Hong Kong movie. This is a scene of hallucinatory violence. Divorced from all narrative, a *machette*-wielding ascetic dances through a field of belligerent unfortunates, severing a cornucopia of heads – heads that, sent spinning as they are cleaved from their bodies, are then caught on spikes. After ten minutes of carnage, the Hong Kong movie is cut and a Nigerian film appears on the screen. A Nigerian necromancer, his speech dubbed into Lingala, is directing a set of zombiefied adepts; glassy-eyed, each one heads for and climbs into an open, red silk-lined coffin. For the Kinois, Kung Fu epics relate to forms of masculinity based around fighting and physical prowess that are particularly associated with the poorest sections of the city's youth (see De Boeck and Plissart 2004; Pype 2007), who also make up the core of Wenge Maison Mère's support. Nigerian soap operas, which deal with ideas of witchcraft and accumulation, are immensely popular with a wide cross-section of the city and have become a staple of television schedules in Kinshasa.

One can make a link here between the films shown and elements of the precolonial imagery of rulership. In the Hong Kong film, the imagery of extreme violence could be seen as equivalent to the recurrent association made in precolonial artforms between the ruler and extreme violence.[13] This not untypical example of *Miimbi*, or praise poem, from the Yaka court shows a certain resemblance:

> The Nyaka was decapitated at the neck,
> In his breast the blood coagulated.

> (Swa-Kabamba 1997: 146)

The Nigerian film specifically evokes the notion that powerful individuals generate power (*kindoki* or cognate terms) via the occult sacrifice of certain individuals, in exchange for which they receive powers from the dead (MacGaffey 2000).

This interpretation receives a certain level of support from a drunk who approaches me as the Nigerian film draws to a close. The drunk has been pestering me long enough to know that I am from England. He shouts in my ear:

> *Mundele! Yebisa reine Elisabeth ke Werra eza terrible, bato nyoso wana bakufeli pona ye!*
> Whitey! Tell Queen Elizabeth that Werra is awesome [as in powerful], All those people are dying for him!

Thus, the loss of human life on the screen is interpreted as a mystical sacrifice that will increase the power of the man who commissions the act. The reference to Queen Elizabeth is also important. *La Reine d'Angleterre* was several times identified by informants as the 'traditional ruler' of England, a figure who was assumed to carry the same kind of metaphysical weight as the Central African *chef coutumier*. By implicitly positing a kind of equivalence between the onscreen necromancer and Werrason, and between Werrason and the traditional leader, all of whom draw power from the dead, the drunk makes explicit a series of connections that would have been made by much of the audience. Werrason, like other successful *présidents*, or indeed like the traditional elder, 'carries' a set of substances derived from occult sacrifice, substances that will have a bearing on the *orchestre's* popularity and upon the possibilities for accumulation that membership of the *orchestre* will afford.

Such conceptions appear to be an important aspect of how the Kinois think about power. In contemporary Kinshasa, as for nineteenth-century Bakongo peoples, the 'little people' are known as *mutu pamba*. The word *pamba* covers a semantic field that includes valueless, purposeless and also empty. The powerful, by contrast, are often referred to as *mutu munene* (big men) or *ya kilo* (heavy) – qualities that can be associated with a prominent belly, 'aspect' or, in the case of women, a big bum.[14] Several informants confirmed the connection between the political power of the women in the powerful rotating savings club of the 1970s, the *Moziki 100 kilos*, and the idea of their weighty bottoms. I have been told repeatedly that 'immoral' women, such as dancers in popular *orchestres*, will place a *magie* stock cube in their anus as part of some kind of magical ritual to grant a big bum. All of this implies, I think, that the small man, in contrast to the powerful, is perceived as an empty vessel. Thus, the body can at some level be perceived as an object, which in the case of the powerful individual is then 'animated' – rendered '"beautiful", "powerful", "strong", "attractive", "irresistible"' (Tonda 2005) – by certain substances.

This conception provides an explanation for why substances seen as emerging from within the person – such as breath or spittle – are also routinely associated with a kind of 'benediction'. To breathe – *kofula* – means something like 'to boost'. Hence, Werrason's praise name of *afula atala te* – 'he does not watch his breath' – can be translated as 'he gives of his encouraging forces freely' or 'he keeps no account of how he dispenses his vital capacities'. While blessings are only occasionally conveyed through spitting in contemporary Kinshasa, terms evoking this practice are still a part of general vocabulary; the most common term for blessing – *pambola* – appears originally to have meant 'to bless in spitting'.

In the case of the *président*, material goods obtained by subordinates are often seen as emerging from his person, either as actual 'blessings' themselves or as dependent upon the immaterial 'blessing' that the leader has dispensed. According to this view – often articulated in a 'front-of-stage' persona by rank-and-file musicians themselves – subordinate musicians have acquired all that they possess, including access to Europe and, by implication, a passport, thanks to the *président*'s abilities as a 'good giver'. One musician, pointing to the space of a modern Parisian studio, along with his designer clothes acquired during the trip and including, by implication, the French capital itself, which surrounded us, exclaimed, 'Tout ça grâce a *Phénomène*!' – 'All this thanks to *Phénomène*!' (*Phénomène Werrason* is another of Werrason's praise names.) The cars, clothes and consumer goods that musicians sometimes acquire are likewise frequently ascribed to the *lupemba* of the *président*, even if he has not directly been the source. In this context many of the enactments of affective ties performed for patrons have also turned inward. Musicians will address their *président* both as grateful cadet, in a kind of neotraditional language of praise, and increasingly also 'as women', in the language of romantic love that they use for other patrons (see Chapter 7). This is illustrated in *clips* put out by Koffi Olomide in 2007, which were included at the end of the DVD to his 'Maxi single' *Chocolat Chaud*:

Bolingo ngai na Quadra Kora Man naleli	My love for *Quadra Kora Man*[15] I cry!
	(Olomide 2006)

Audiences visibly appreciate such professions of deference, applauding declarations of humility and devotion from subordinate musicians when they are performed in concert and demanding of the *orchestre*'s new members that they will not show themselves 'ungrateful' like the defectors whom they are replacing. We should not overestimate the sincerity of these performances of deference – privately the rank-and-file musicians will often express resentment and frequently jump ship, but what is significant is that, even when the capacity of the *président* as 'good giver' is in dispute, the underlying ideology – that the extraordinary person is the source of wealth – is not disputed.

There is, as we have demonstrated, often considerable immorality associated with the acquisition of these capacitating substances. But this is tempered by the way in which the 'extraordinary individual' disperses the benefits. As MacGaffey observes, while 'the chief ... is supposed to "eat", he should also cause his followers to eat well' (2000: 138). Standing somewhat outside this are the Pentecostals, who reject the idea that their church leader trades in human life, though they will enthusiastically accuse others of such practices, including the leaders of other congregations.

Yet it is notable that the underlying ideas about value generation are still very similar. The generative capacity of the 'extraordinary individual' is believed to rely on access to capacitating substances derived from transacting with invisible worlds. For Kinshasa's Pentecostalized public sphere, the moral valence of material goods, and emotional and physical states, relates to the kind of invisible world with which one is transacting. Goods, or spirit possession, may come from *lola* (heaven) or from the demonic *deuxième monde* (see also De Boeck 2004; Pype 2006). Underlining this, terms such as *nguya* or *mpifo*[16] are routinely used to describe the extraordinary qualities of high-rolling politicians, diamond dealers, high-class prostitutes, wrestlers, gangsters and secular pop stars, but are also applied to Pentecostal pastors. And these are qualities that, in all cases, are channelled via the leader to the retinue. Indeed, while preaching, pastors will make throwing gestures and shout 'zwua nguya' – take *nguya* – at the congregation (Pype 2012), who in turn perform catching gestures.

These attributions of moral valence are crucial from a local point of view, but for the purposes of our analysis, they are less important. Some versions of this ideology seem to recognize a certain 'structural violence' in social relations, while others do not, but they all participate in a more central kind of misrepresentation, in that it is the person, dissociated from a wider set of socioeconomic relationships, who is cast as the source of value. This leads to notions of debt towards gatekeepers, which, though sometimes confusing to outsiders, is characteristic of this mode of production.

Myths and Ideological Dominance

The previous section has sketched in some elements of a mythic/symbolic nexus. Having spent so much time evoking this mythic nexus, it is tempting to conclude, with Lévi-Strauss, that myths think people – a kind of cultural software that programmes authority and obedience. But this is not the argument being made. Power is a fragile edifice and without a continuous investment in ideological labour by the powerful, underlings will tend to interpret social relations in ways that are favourable to their own interests. These subaltern interpretations generally draw on exactly the same mythic nexus as employed by the rulers, and there is generally little inherent in the myths themselves to prevent them from doing this. As various authors point out (see, for example, Turner 1968; Patterson 1982), myths generally have the potential to be understood in multiple ways and inspire diverse conclusions – and, as such, are not in themselves sufficient explanation for social obedience.

Most of the myths presented in the previous section relate in some way or other to the powerful person. The conception of the individual revealed here is very different from the self-owning 'possessive individual' of liberal theory. Some (for example, Strathern 1988) have argued that in places where this kind of possessive individual subject does not exist, there is simply no way for locals to think about an individual's right to his or her own labour and, by extension, no concept of alienation.

But this argument, at least when applied to Central Africa, appears to confuse 'possessive individualism' with the idea of the individual *tout court*. While the conception of the individual on display here is very different from the possessive individual subject, there is an extensive and highly charged vocabulary for thinking about personal authorship and the morality of division. This brings us back to the central argument of this chapter. Those who are able to depict themselves as the generators of value will accede to resources as of right. Given that this relies on depicting others as incapable of producing value – representing them as literally worthless – it is often possession of this imputed capacity for generation that is *itself* the most prized possession. There is nothing innate in any ideology that renders such interpretations simple to establish. Dominant classes must both spend and kill to establish their image as generators of value and to depict others as worthless. Retaining control of these ideologies of generation is not a one-off event either – it requires ceaseless investment.

Some of these themes are illustrated in the social context of the song 'Amour Intérêt' by Ferre Gola,[17] which was included on an album made in 2004 by a group of musicians who had split from Wenge Maison Mère and who called themselves Les Marquis de Maison Mère. Members of Les Marquis had deserted Werrason after a well-publicized dispute over the division of funds in the *orchestre*, which was discussed in the last chapter. Many of the young stars felt that the *président* was unwilling to share the profits they were making in a proper or equitable way. In this extract, the metaphor of the hunt is drawn upon. As we alluded to above, success in the hunt and the morality of division afterwards were metaphysically charged activities in precolonial Central Africa. By clearly stating that it is they, and not others, who have felled the game, the Marquis de Maison Mère (in Gola 2004) challenges the right of others to alienate their creative labours. Serge Mabiala sings of how it was 'likonga ngai', 'his spear' that brought down monkeys, his arrow that even felled a buffalo, but when others were left to divide this bounty, they 'sabotaged him'.

Other more everyday metaphors (for the Kinois) also allude to the fact that those who create value should see the benefits of their labour:

> *Bakabolaka Manga te soki mobuki ekiti te*
> They don't divide up mangoes if the thrower has not climbed down [i.e. the one who climbed the tree to get them]
>
> (D'Eté 2004)

If such voices 'from below' are less often heard in Kinshasa today, at least in the media, this is in part because of the ceaseless investment by gatekeepers in ideological labour.

This then is the theory of charismatic fetishism – where the backstage appropriation of ideological and material labour allows the appropriator to draw upon *longue durée* Central African notions of the person and present himself as generative. Yet, in creating a fetish around the person of particular appropriators, this investment also creates a wider ideology sustaining a system of power relations.

Political Figures

While we have focused on the *président d'orchestre*, such attributions of value are not restricted to music or the cultural sphere, but are the common feature of authority. We have seen various examples of this – Tshatsho Mbala, 'Saddam Hussein' Mobutu, Figuero and other prominent big men. The most curious and extraordinary example of this is Mobutu himself, who, despite leaving office with GDP per capita in real terms at less than twenty per cent of what it had been at independence (Exenberger and Hartman 2013: 31), is still often remembered by the Kinois as a wealth creator. 'Tango ya Mobutu tosakana ya mbongo!' – 'In Mobutu's time we played with money' – as one market trader put it to me.

In economic terms, things have not got much better for the majority of Kinois since the fall of Mobutu, and it is of course possible to explain such representations in terms of nostalgia. But I think there are fundamental reasons for the perception of Mobutu as wealth creator. Many of the people I encountered who made such comments were far from positive about aspects of Mobutu's legacy. One clearly identified political opponent of Mobutu, who had passed his life in poverty during the thirty years of Mobutu's rule and who expressed support for the regime of President Kabila, nevertheless said to me: 'It must be recognized that Mobutu made people rich.' He went on to describe how: 'Mobutu gave money to those close to him and they dispersed it among those close to them and so forth.'

As De Boeck (1996) notes, Mobutu was a master at representing his theft as a kind of gift, and he drew heavily on music and dance to add plausibility to the notion of himself as a generative source. Similar patterns can be observed in the way in which many important figures in the contemporary political scene are regarded. To take an example from the regional government in Kinshasa, we can see how the appropriation of both ordinary funds and ideological labour allows theft to be represented as individual munificence.

Ignace's Story: Bringing it in and Giving it out in Kinshasa

Ignace, who had been unemployed since he left university, got a job working for the revenue service. A prominent figure in the regional government gave a speech to the young recruits. He told the young men that their financial worries were over and that, given their new financial status, they should remember to 'use protection' in the numerous sexual encounters to which this new wealth would lead. All the young recruits cheered, went to bars, bought beers on credit and began to seek the life previewed in this motivational speech. Twelve months on, Ignace had been paid only seven months of his pitiful (one hundred and fifty dollars a month) salary. At Christmas, the governor added five frozen chickens and a small bag of rice to the salary. Other branches of the service were paid half their salary and given one chicken between four people.

In some comparatively wealthy parts of town, people will pay the revenue inspectors a bribe to keep away tax bills, and this can lead to a reasonable, though not excessive, income for certain units of tax collectors, although, in line with our analysis in Chapter 5, such income will lead to serious penalties unless various gatekeeper figures are given an important share. But in the poorer districts of Kinshasa – like Masina, where Ignace works – people have no money to give and often threaten to kill anyone who appears to be assessing the property for tax. In this context Ignace touches base at the tax office a few times a month – just enough to receive his salary on the occasions when it is paid.

Income and property taxes have always been a fairly minimal part of the state's budget, but one can be certain that top officials have access to considerable resources. And these resources are not employed to carry out the conventional functions of government. While I was in Kinshasa in 2010, I attended a performance of the Orchestre Zaiko Langa Langa in an open-air bar in Bandal. Not only was the concert free, but food and beer had been laid on – all at the expense of the prominent official mentioned earlier. The musicians inserted *mabanga* for the man at every possible moment and he was seen sitting with Jossart, the *président* of Zaiko. Journeys around the capital by this official are accompanied by hordes of people. And when they came to Matete (where Ignace lives), most of Ignace's family joined in, shouting praise names and offering adulation in the hope of a few stray dollars.

One should not overestimate the extent to which people are fooled, or the kind of claims we are making here for the political effectiveness of fetishism. People frequently enact wildly insincere performances, seeing adulation as a kind of job (Geenen 2009). And without violence as a central implement of power, the system would collapse. Nevertheless, relations of production are not simply sustained by violence, and the kind of charismatic fetishism we have discussed here is another essential element in sustaining the status quo. Some individuals notable for their largesse – like Moise Katumbi, governor of Katanga, or, to a lesser extent, André Kimbuta, governor of Kinshasa (both of whom are keen music patrons) – do seem to inspire genuine enthusiasm. But on the whole, I would say that, at a systemic level, the effect of this kind of fetishism is less to render politicians popular and more to render the unpopularity of the ruling class incoherent – impressing the fetishistic theory of value on consciousness. Retinues often deplore the behaviour of, say, *présidents d'orchestres*, diamond dealers or politicians in much the same way as the Blairite and Brownite factions of Britain's Labour Party may have deplored the behaviour of investment bankers, but concluded, ultimately, that these individuals were the generators of wealth.

Theorizing the 'Fetish' in Africa and Elsewhere

Our presentation has drawn on notions of fetishism drawn from Marx. But the theory presented here is far from identical to Marx's, and in many particulars it contradicts his original theory. At the same time, other uses of the word 'fetishism' are quite common in a Central African context, both within and beyond the academy. With this in mind, I think it may be helpful to return to this wider body of theory, and to compare and contrast our findings with more established writings.

In his oft-cited essay 'The Banality of Power and the Aesthetics of Vulgarity in the Postcolony', Achille Mbembe describes the 'common daily rituals that ratify the *commandement*'s own institutionalisation in its capacity as a fetish' (Mbembe 1992: 5). One senses that Mbembe is describing something new and important about the operation of power in Central Africa, but there is much that is not clear (or not clear to me) in his article. In what way is the notion of fetish being used here? Is it in the Freudian or Marxist sense? Or is it in the local sense – that is, as having to do with powerful objects within a ritual complex? Or is it being employed in some new or synthetic sense? And what is the relationship of all this symbolic and corporeal domination to political economy?

Joseph Tonda (2005) attempts to answer some of these questions by constructing an ambitious theory that links ideas about fetishism developed by Marx, Freud and Bourdieu to local notions of the *fétiche*. Central to Tonda's analysis is the notion of *la violence du fétichisme/la violence de l'imaginaire*. Somewhat similar to the description found in Tsambu-Bulu (2004), where the 'violence' discussed goes well beyond the physical,[18] Tonda examines 'imaginative violence' in detail – local ideas about magic and human sacrifice that are related to physical violence, where cosmetics or clothes are thought of as 'weapons' to overpower adversaries, while the pillage of commodities can be conceptualized as rape. I draw on many of the insights that flow from this manner of theorizing violence, as proposed in different ways by Tsambu-Bulu and Tonda. But the local obsession with hidden forms of mystical violence, while it may reflect some awareness of structural issues, is in fact central to ideologies that systematically hide exploitative economic relations. My suggestion has been to understand this process via a modified version of Marx's theory of 'commodity fetishism'.

Attempts to use or develop the theory of commodity fetishism are complicated by the mischievous nature of *Capital* itself, and in discussing this work one runs the risk of a po-faced dissection of what was meant as a playful discussion. *Capital* was itself meant as a critique of the then-current forms of economic thought, and Marx seems to take most pleasure in taunting 'bourgeois science' (Wolff 1988; Sperber 2013). Nevertheless, I think there are real limitations to Marx's theory, which are worth discussing, even at the risk of seeming to be a killjoy.

The first of these limitations concerns the European theorizations of the fetish on which Marx drew. This is a problem that is brought out in a rather apt fashion by the regional focus of this book. As Pietz (1985, 1987, 1988) has shown, the word 'fetish' comes from the medieval Portuguese *feitiçaria*,[19] which in early modern Portugal meant minor forms of witchcraft. As the Portuguese extended their trading empire into Atlantic Africa, the terms *feitiço* and *feitiçaria* were used to refer to the variety of charms and ritual practices that they encountered and that were sometimes used to mediate trade between Africans and Europeans in the expanding Atlantic commerce, notably with the Kingdom of Kongo (Pietz 1985).

As both Thornton (1984) and Pietz argue, the sixteenth- and seventeenth-century Portuguese saw the use of fetishes as a sign that Africans lacked 'true religion', but this was not incorporated into a wider ideology of innate African inferiority. By the end of the seventeenth century, however, Protestant-inspired objections to idolatry are shading into a wider Enlightenment critique. Such critiques dwell on the chance nature of the objects of worship – 'chance trifles' and 'natural curiosities' (Pietz 1988: 106). The worship of material objects and of 'chance trifles' was to be contrasted with the abstract and universal mind of 'civilized man'. This stress on the fetish as the mark of a primitive mindset, characterized by the trifling and the particular, and incapable of abstraction, was adopted by the early sociologists and anthropologists like Comte or Tylor, on whom Marx draws directly.

As Pietz's essay shows, Enlightenment discourses about fetishes were a kind of rhetorical counterpoint to the development of modernist ideas about science and the relationship of matter to mind. In this rhetoric, African ideas about objects and intentionality were cast as the binary opposite of European ones. The reality was of course much more complex – Central African political cosmology does contradict European ideas about the mind–body split, but this is not the simple confusion of objects with living people. Rather, these Central African theories have tended to see both ritually important objects *and* powerful people as vessels, which are then animated by powerful forces/substances from the dead. In this way, powerful chiefs in the nineteenth century and ritually important charms were often viewed as functionally equivalent. Both emerged at nodes in the commercial network and were presumed to 'eat' nocturnal victims, in order to accumulate power and offer blessing and protection to the wider polity (MacGaffey 2000). I believe that such ideas are still important today, and understanding how they 'play out' in the modern setting forms an important element of our presentation in this chapter.

It is true that Marx's use of the term 'fetishism' is an ironic inversion of these then-current theories about the progression of man from the primitive past (see also MacGaffey 1977). It is, Marx tells us, *modern* society where fetishism is truly pervasive, and this fetishism is permitted by our own inability to deal with the greater abstraction found in a market society – mistaking the products of our labour for magic objects. Yet while he subverts the casual assumptions of superiority in the early anthropologists, Marx also makes certain assumptions about ancient and modern that are almost as problematic. His discussion of the commodity posits a divide (taken from Aristotle) between barter, use value and 'natural exchange' on the one hand and the market, exchange values and fetishism on the other. Commodity fetishism is supposed not to occur under other economic configurations, and serfs and assorted 'Asiatics' and 'ancients' are said to have clearly perceived the social nature of production (Marx 1867/1961: 76). Western Marxist disciples, such as Lukacs or Adorno, who fuse Marx's fetishism with Weberian notions of rationality, accentuate still further the importance of this kind of epochal change to the theory. But as we noted in the Introduction and in the previous chapter, this kind of divide between a modernity characterized by instrumental rationality versus a past characterized by affect or the spirit of the gift has been extensively and effectively discredited (Bloch and Parry 1989; Graeber 2011).

Also somewhat discredited are Marx's ideas about 'primitive common property', which rely on inaccurate characterizations of the non-Western world (particularly India) current in the nineteenth century (see Anderson 1974a; Donham 1990. Because of this, Marx's attempts to look at fetishism in a comparative and historical fashion are thoroughly contradicted by twentieth-century scholarship (Bloch

and Parry 1989; Donham 1990). Contra Marx, a weight of scholarship
has shown that forms of exploitation and mystification of labour very
similar to what Marx calls fetishism are abundantly present in noncapitalist situations (see, for example, Josephides 1985; Bloch 1989;
Donham 1990).

Taussig (1980, 1993) tries to argue that this fetishism is of a different order – according to this version of events, the fetishization
on the periphery actually presents a critique of exchange value. But
even in the Andean literature on which Taussig draws for some of
his material, there would seem to be ample evidence for the continuity in fetishistic practices that treat the 'fertility' of mines, buses and
butchers' shops in remarkably similar ways to fields and mountains
(see Harris 1989; Tassi 2008). More to the point, such continuities in
'fetishization' are also apparent in the Congo/Zaïrean case, where, to
take a similar example, the productivity of fields, but also diamond
mines and human beings, is seen as augmented by blessings from
elders[20] or by mystical sacrifice (see De Boeck 1998; Mbiki 2008).

Some of Marx's discussion, then, is untenable in the light of subsequent scholarship, but the central element of this theory retains a
great importance. In *Capital*, Marx performs a kind of anthropological analysis of the circulation of money and commodities. His analysis shows that, examined close up, these essential and apparently
familiar elements of a capitalist economy are in fact 'very queer ...
abounding in philosophical niceties and theological subtleties' (Marx
1867/1961: 71). Underneath Marx's heavily ironical tone, we can see
that the major effect of this 'metaphysics' of capital serves to misattribute value. The idea that capital produces value 'as ... a pear tree
produces pears' (Marx 1895/1991: 516) clearly gives legitimacy to
the dominance of those who have capital over those who sell their
labour. This illusion of generation, created by 'fetishized' capital,
casts a fecund shimmer over the ruling class's division of resources.

The term 'commodity fetishism' is widely used by Marx and
others, but Marx makes it clear that it is in capital itself – represented
by its adherents as 'money which begets money' or 'portion fruc-
tifiante de la richesse' (1867/1961: 15, 523) – that fetishism is most
entrenched and most central to capitalism's self-understanding (see
also the discussion in vol. 3: Marx 1895/1991). Elaborating on Marx's
insight, I want to suggest that it is this idea of generation that is most
central. Capital is the most fundamental form of wealth in the capitalist system because it is regarded as *generative wealth*. Extending
Marx's original conception, I suggest that elements of this fetishization are found in all social systems. Moreover, we can argue that the

most valued form of wealth in any mode of production is that which is seen as generative.

Indigenous Central African theories predominantly attribute this kind of 'generative' quality not to capital or other commodities, but to the *person* of the powerful. This ideology depicts the person of the 'big man' as generative of wealth, divorced from the relations of production that have underwritten his largesse; not the 'capital fetishism' that Marx discusses, but certainly an analogous process, which I have termed a 'charismatic fetish'. This especial emphasis on the super-animate qualities of the powerful *person* relates to the specific elements of this mode of production – some elements of which we have explored in this chapter. As I argued, the super-animate, generative shimmer given off by the patron via the potlatch makes a divorce of social reproduction from wider relations of production plausible. In this way, those who control exchange are depicted as those who generate value.

Fetishism, Ideological Labour and the Charismatic Individual

In sum, then, Marx believes that 'fetishism' – mystification of the product of labour – is generated by the abstract nature of capitalist market relations. The peasant, so the story goes, can see that the pig that gets eaten by the lord is a product of his labour. The industrial worker – enmeshed in a nexus of specialized and long-distance productive relations – cannot. This sounds plausible, but we have seen that, in fact, all societies are inclined to misattribute value and that in all stratified societies, ruling classes rely on this kind of misattribution in order to justify their disproportionate access to resources. This mystification happens in 'simple', agrarian communities as much as in 'complex', industrial ones. Just because the castle where the pig was eaten was visible from the hovel where the swineherd lived, we should not assume that the swineherd always saw this theft for what it was.

This being the case, it is likely that fetishization occurs not because of social abstraction, but because of an ideological effort by dominant classes. On this understanding, most people have a strong inclination to think about the production and distribution of resources in ways favourable to their own interest. It is only with a considerable investment of time and effort that they can be persuaded to see things differently. Thus, the forms of fetishism that underwrite contemporary capitalism, like those that underwrote feudalism, or the lineage mode of production, etc. rely on an investment by the powerful in ideological labour – be it in advertising or in building cathedrals.[21]

In our introduction we discussed the idea of ideological labour – forms of communicative and aesthetic production that could not be reduced to units of 'socially necessary labour time' because of their particular and sensuous character. As our discussion above indicates, mystifying the sources of value is essential to the perpetuation of any stratified society,[22] and ideological labour is a crucial element in this mystifying of the sources of value. But this ideological labour is itself alienated from its producers. For most of the value created by ideological labour accrues not to the labourer – the cameraman, the musician, the master builder or the journalist – but to persons elsewhere in the system. To return to a concrete example from the society under discussion, music patronage links the emotion and the sensuality generated by rank-and-file musicians, and attributes it to the patron and to the *président d'orchestre*. The great surge of goods, delivered in a context of music and dance, lends an emotional plausibility to ideas that these patron's persons are mysteriously generative. The emotions thus appropriated go to work on behalf of the economically powerful, not on behalf of their creators.

Some of these 'charismatic' gatekeeper figures do have their own aesthetic skills – indeed, some are surely *maestros* in the art of self-presentation. But this should not detract from the very considerable degree of path dependence in the production of 'charisma'. By this I mean that such personal skills can only confer significant amounts of authority where a requisite level of resources has already been accumulated – resources that may include ideological labour as well as access to more conventional means of production. Above this threshold, the effects of personal charm or social adroitness held by the individual gatekeeper will become magnified, feeding off the shimmer cast by the ideological labours of others and by the attributions of power invited by the display and dispersal of prestige goods. Below this threshold, personal charm is more likely to have a limited effect. Indeed, it is likely to be constantly undercut by the persistent tendency, found in all social systems, to dishonour social subordinates – the primordial act of alienation that robs subordinates not simply of the value produced by their labour, but also of the very belief in their capacity to produce value. Hence the constant repetition that social inferiors are children, boys, juniors, cadets, small, empty, valueless and without purpose.

It is worth noting that this is an explanation for a dominant ideology that does not posit any very great degree of strategic awareness, or class unity, or elaborate forms of coordination among dominant classes. This kind of fetishization is invested in primarily because it is satisfying to the individual rather than because of a coordinated plot to 'reproduce the system'. In performing the potlatch, the things 'given off' by the patron include joy, luck, love, attractiveness, a sense of munificence and generosity. These are obviously desirable things and require us to posit no elaborate political theory on the part of the ruling class to explain decisions to invest in them. The backstage appropriations that underwrite these investments do rely on a minimal sense of class interest – gatekeepers rely on other gatekeepers, using them as their 'go to' individual, and it is via this kind of solidarity that surpluses are regularly extracted from retinues (see Chapter 5). But it is not hard to see how the repeated investment in the potlatch, taken cumulatively, does reproduce an ideology that sustains a wider set of unequal productive relations. While the details would differ, many of the points made here would apply to other ideological systems.

An Afterword on 'Neopatrimonialism' and Systemic Mystification

I have shown that there is a misrepresentation that attributes value to those who have in fact appropriated it. I have argued that the potlatch – the display and dispersal of prestige goods and the expenditure on various kinds of performance – is key to this mystification. There is a strong intuition that such appropriations are also connected to the economic stagnation of the DRC. I believe such an intuition is, ultimately, correct. But we need to be careful about how we make the argument, it is much more common for an erroneous set of connections to be made between this distribution of resources by corrupt patrons and wider economic conditions.

First, there is no doubt that, at an individual level, some people are made poorer by the very act of potlatch. In Chapter 6, we saw that some *mikiliste* would be richer today if they had 'bought fewer shoes and started more shops'. I think we could widen this to include some other groups. Had the *bana Lunda* wanted, or been able, to use their money in ways that better corresponded with capitalist ideas of 'saving' or 'investment', they would, *as individuals*, be better off today.

A second point is that appropriation *in itself* is unlikely to be the cause of economic stagnation. Marx argued that capitalism depended on an original act of theft, and many observers of African politics note, correctly, that the misappropriation of funds is not unique to African elites. Nor is the strong imperative to distribute resources over a personal network particularly African. Many countries – Indonesia and Italy are two recent examples – have economies that have grown dramatically without a public life premised on the divorce of individual and office, that is, in systems that would be characterized as *neopatrimonial*. And even in those countries like Britain where this divorce may have happened, the divorce seems to have occurred *after* the takeoff of economic growth, not before (see also Trapido 2015).

Many accounts have wanted to link these two points and have thus argued that if elites were more inclined to save money rather than disperse resources on their retinues or on 'shining', then African societies would be richer in aggregate terms (see, for example, Bayart 1993; Warnier 1993; Chabal and Daloz 1999; Hyslop 2005). Such ideas have powerful roots in our own cultural understandings of wealth and poverty – ideas proposed, or at least articulated, by Weber and, before him, Adam Smith. Both these thinkers saw in the 'principle of frugality' the origin of national enrichment (Buchan 2007: 107; on the cultural roots of European economic theory, see also Gudeman and Rivera 1990). With this intellectual baggage, it is easy to cast the joyous, open-handed African gatekeeper/*patrimoine* as the opposite of Weber's careful, anxious Protestant. But I believe that such accounts of African economic affairs are themselves labouring under an illusion. Like the Congolese themselves, such scholars are captivated by the theatre of dispersal and the figure of the charismatic *patrimoine*. As a result of this fascination, they miss the real destination of most wealth and thus misidentify the real causes of economic stagnation.

Most wealth is not dispensed over a retinue or even spent on personal consumption – the important gatekeepers in the DRC hand out only a fraction of what they steal. As I have argued elsewhere (Trapido 2015), it is more plausible to attribute the failure of accumulation to the fact that retinues are too weak to insist that resources remain in circulation within the local economy. In this context, some gatekeeper figures do accumulate very significant amounts, which they send offshore, from whence they are invested in other more promising locations. And, beyond even this, most wealth is passed to non-Congolese economic actors, both directly in deals that enrich the outside buyer more than the seller and indirectly in the fact that money stored in tax havens is reinvested in other, richer parts of the world.

Successive studies by Boyce and Ndikumana (1998, 2011) have shown that the scale of capital flight as a percentage of GDP is significantly higher in Africa than in the rest of the world. As they state:

> the comparison of accumulated capital flight to accumulated external debt suggests that Zaïre was in fact *a net creditor to the rest of the world*, exporting more capital than it imported. The difference, of course, is that while the external debt is a public liability bequeathed to the new government of Congo, the external assets built up through capital flight are strictly private. (Boyce and Ndikumana 1998: 202, emphasis added)

And yet in 1997, the new regime was bequeathed debts of more than thirteen billion dollars owed to various creditors by Mobutu. This money lent to the regime was, of course, immediately reshipped abroad, and the people who were left with a debt never got to spend it.

It is not only, or even primarily, the Congolese who misrepresent how their money is created and dissipated. The forms of theatre that allow these acts of global misdirection are less aesthetically pleasing than Congolese music and, unlike the claims made by Kinois power-brokers, they are in no way redeemed by an underlying admission of their own ridiculousness. But they are very effective.

Notes

1. The son of Simon Kimbangu and, until his death, the spiritual leader, which is to say the incarnation of the holy spirit, of the main branch of the Kimbanguist Church.
2. True or not I cannot say, but this belief is often offered as an etymology for the name Mai-Mai/Mayi-Mayi, which is applied to, or used by, various rebel groups both in the 1960s and now. The cry Mai-Mai ('Water-Water') was supposed to turn bullets to water.
3. Or at least during highly sustainable forms of crisis.
4. There are innumerable reasons why Sam might have been denied a visa, but he suspected that there was someone in the French Embassy who had an agreement with the former *président* to sabotage his applications. Sam eventually got a visa.
5. Felix Wazekwa is a Congolese musician who contributed many songs to both Papa Wemba and Koffi Olomide before the relationship broke down in acrimony. He has since become a successful musician in his own right.
6. Thorton (2003), speaking of the Catholic Church in the seventeenth-century lower Congo, tells a story of a woman who with each sin she confesses expels a scorpion from her mouth. But when she arrives at her one greatest sin, she is unable to confess,

and all the other scorpions jump back into her mouth and take up residence in her belly once more.

7. *Ndoki* are 'witches' – people who have been initiated into a kind of looking-glass society of flesh-eating night workers, seen as immoral rather than – like *Mfumus*, 'chiefs' or *ngangas* – merely ambiguous.

8. The story was told to me many times in more or less the same form and this version represents something of an amalgam. Evoloko lived in Europe for several years, including periods in London and in Brussels. 'No really, he never sleeps', informants repeated. 'He was always the last one up in the *nganda* [bar]'. The story has gained such currency that Evoloko is used as a term for those who don't sleep – I have several times heard mothers refer to children who will not go to bed as 'Evolokos'.

9. Musicians will be heard saying things like 'Après cinq ans Koffi apes'ngai lupemba' – 'After five years Koffi gave me *lupemba*'.

10. An ominous name for a tyrant's wife, Marie-Antoinette kept it despite her husband's drive to make ordinary Zaïrois change their names to 'authentic' African names. She is often said to have been a restraining influence on *Le Guide*.

11. *Lu* is a common noun class prefix in many western Bantu languages, shifting to *Bu* further east (MacGaffey 2009). While I have not encountered the precise word *lupemba* in the historical literature, I have seen reference to *luhemba* – as white chalk to go inside an *nkisi* – and to *lugemba* – as blessing and white chalk (MacGaffey 1991: 13) – where *gemba* and *hemba* are dialect variants of *mpemba* (MacGaffey, personal communication, 2009).

12. It should be said that Pepé Kalle appeared to be morbidly obese and is just as often said to have died of a heart condition.

13. Werrason is also linked to the forest. One of the overlapping sites of the dead. Probably his most durable praise title is *Roi de la Fôret* and he is often referred to as *de la Fôret* – of the Forest – while his bar, where the rehearsal takes place, is the *Zamba Playa* – literally 'forest beach' (see Tsambu-Bulu 2004 for discussion of the Forest in rivalries between *orchestres*).

14. The swollen belly of malnutrition is often said to be involved in accusations of witchcraft against children.

15. One of Koffi's praise titles. He has won four Kora awards (African music awards).

16. *Mpifo* may once have designated a senior in a lineage or clan – clearly a related quality, where age and social weight were so closely associated. See Vansina 1978: 115.

17. Though the particular couplets quoted are sung by Serge Mabiala and may have been improvised by him.

18. Yet it is very different from Bourdieu's 'symbolic violence', where the subject is unaware of the attack.

19. Rather like the Spanish *hechiso* or the English 'hex'.

20. For example, UNITA would force local Mbangala customary leaders to bless the local diamond mines to make them fertile (see Mbiki 2008: 134–6).

21. Indeed, most of the subsequent interpretations of Marx's theory of fetishism (see, for example, Adorno (2002) or Swain (2012)) simply assume a major contribution to the fetish by the 'culture industry', not even noticing that this is somewhat at odds with Marx's original theory.

22. Save in those examples – rare in occurrence and limited in duration – where domination is maintained purely by violence.

CONCLUSION

Throughout the chapters of this book, we have studied the relationship between aesthetics, performance, ideologies of the extraordinary individual, and wider political-economic concerns. Another recurrent motif has been the connection between this nexus and various forms of historical continuity and change. In this final chapter I will review the evidence I have presented and the conclusions to which I have come. During this study I have drawn on a great many works, but obviously I have found certain authors and certain theoretical formulations particularly helpful. In this conclusion I will, then, also try and relate my work to this literature, underlining where my book may contribute or extend various fields of knowledge.

Modes of Production

This study has acknowledged and incorporated the work of scholars (Bloch and Parry 1989; Graeber 2011) who point out that money, markets and instrumental behaviour are often ancient, and that capitalist economies often float on underlying forms of solidarity. Nevertheless, I have argued against the current fashions in social theory and have put forward the view that there is a strong epochal divide between capitalist and noncapitalist societies. Drawing on the idea of the 'mode of production', I have proposed that in places where capitalism is not dominant, people face significantly different social imperatives.

Wolf describes a mode of production as the 'political-economic relationships that underlie, orient and constrain interaction' and – when used comparatively – as a concept that 'calls attention to major variations in political economic arrangements' (Wolf 1997: 80–81). In this book, the idea of a mode of production has been helpful to me in conceptualizing the prevalence of closure and scarcity within the political-economic area under study and in theorizing the importance that points of articulation with a wider world take on in this context. Inevitably, some of the convictions underpinning this theoretical approach are themselves beyond the scope of this book – that (against the arguments of those such as Bayart (1993)) such economic 'closure' of the Congolese economy is largely externally imposed and that (against a very widespread line of argumentation, perhaps most prominently put forward by Castels (2000: 83–120)) Central Africa remains strategically relevant to the global economy in various ways that are not well measured by volumes of trade or in flows of 'information'.

While the Dupré 'lineage mode of production' or anything like it was destroyed, this book suggests that the dominance of the capitalist mode was both weak and intermittent. In the moments when capitalism was at its weakest, other social formations, with some resemblance to precolonial systems, began to appear. We have shown that articulations with other political-economic systems, notably that of Western Europe, were crucial to processes of social reproduction in Kinshasa. Implicitly, also, we have shown that those who, at various levels, are able to effect this articulation reproduced a set of political-economic arrangements that are not themselves capitalist. Trying my best to sidestep the vast question of what it now means to 'be' capitalist, it seems to me apparent that for much of the time, the set of economic behaviours and prevailing political-economic constraints in operation here were radically different, even if capitalism is understood in fairly heterodox terms.

Capital, Wealth and the Person

I have shown how a considerable 'wealth in things' circulates in the systems of transnational exchange here examined – designer clothes, dollars, cars, etc. – some of which could be understood to operate as currency, or in quasi-currency-like terms. But we can say that while much of this 'wealth in things' has been moderately successful as a medium of exchange, it has been less successful as a store of value. Crucially, banking was a largely alien concept to almost all of my informants, and this wealth in things – including the large stockpiles of dollars (held by diamond dealers, for example) – has not 'played a role in the credit and debit systems which underlie capitalism' (Guyer 1995: 5). In this account we have shown that the considerable wealth in things has, in the final analysis, been a kind of prop – essential but nonetheless an adjunct – to performances designed to establish the value of persons, and it is persons who act as the primary 'asset' (see also Leach 1954; De Boeck 1999; Graeber 2001).

In this context, the cultural industries, including popular music, are geared towards proclaiming the extraordinary personal qualities of individual patrons. I have argued that, via emotional and performative consumption, destruction and dispersal of goods, qualities that appear as 'shining', 'charisma' or 'singularity' are established. These performances are highly reliant upon, and are often dispersed through, the medium of music. In so doing, I have made particular use of Guyer's (1991) account, which, following Kopytoff (1987), uses the notion of objects and people passing through various value registers, attaining, at the top end, a total 'singularity'. Guyer (1993: 256–7) stresses how 'valued work' was a way of 'singularising the producer'. While Guyer recognizes that the system entailed the radical disposability of persons at the bottom of value scales, she perhaps underemphasizes how much the creation of an aura of personal distinctiveness at the top was tied to the harsh exploitation of subordinates at the bottom and to a violent interaction with capitalism (Harms 1981; Vellut 2004). Most of all, Guyer makes little allusion to the ways in which exchange, ritual and performance may have attributed value and what she calls 'authorship' to the powerful and removed it from the weak. By contrast, this book has emphasized how notions of 'singularity' produced by various kinds of labour very often accrue to figures other than the producer. Guyer states that the object of 'realization' 'was persons, not fetishised commodities or currencies' (1993: 257). This book has argued, using the figure of the *président d'orchestre* as a particular example, that the 'extraordinary person' is just as likely to be fetishized as any other form of asset.

Ideas of shining, singularity, charisma or *lupemba* conceal or otherwise mystify access to resources – resources of the interior, political rents and access to aid or migrant dollars based on fraud. However, material resources on their own are not enough, and the power or success of a patron depends upon performative and aesthetic considerations in the dispersal of this largesse. Yet even here, a kind of transfer takes place, from subordinate performers to *présidents d'orchestres* and from performers in general to the patrons/local big men who sponsor their performances. In attempting to theorize this appropriation, we have drawn the works of Mbembe (1992) and Tonda (2005) and have adapted the Marxist concept of fetishization so as to apply it to persons as well as things.

If Guyer's (1993) discussion of 'singularity' recapitulates some of the flaws I detected in other discussions of personal extraordinariness, at other points her discussion supplies further evidence for the critique of charisma included in Chapter 8. For she shows how the production of personal 'singularity' has long been a 'routine' aspect of power relations, emerging from the systems of currency, exchange and ritual fines, and in the centuries of interaction between capitalism and local modes of production. This is an argument that, if true, destroys the notion of charisma in anything like the Weberian sense (i.e. as a revolutionary force opposed to routine), but it also challenges the accounts of those like Worsley (1970) who have seen upsurges in 'charismatic' leadership on the colonial fringe, as a consequence of short-lived 'millenarian' crises. Millenarian hypotheses are further weakened by evidence from accounts such as those of MacGaffey (2000) and Dupré (1985), which show how, over centuries of Central African involvement with the global economy, attributions of 'extraordinary' occult powers have repeatedly emerged at 'nodes in the commercial networks' (MacGaffey 2000: 82). While such attributions clearly relate to real violence – violence that *is* related to the demands of an expanding world economy – the durability of such representations must raise certain doubts over the status that should be given to 'millenarian capitalism' as an explanatory factor in theories of the occult (Comaroff and Comaroff 2001).

Imaginative Internationalism, Narcissistic Localism

Many authors have argued that earlier Central African representations of whites have associated them with ancestors, and Europe with the land of the dead (Fernandez 1982; MacGaffey 2000; Bernault 2006). To what extent these representations persist is difficult to assess in the material I have gathered, but – as various authors before me have noted (e.g. Friedman 2004; Gandoulou 1989, 1989b; Tipo-Tipo 1998) – Europe is clearly a highly mythologized destination for the Congolese. Countries, like persons, are placed on a value scale and, notwithstanding the huge upsurge of nationalism in recent years, the Kinois perceive clearly that theirs is a *faux mboka* – a 'false' country – and that they themselves are the *mutu pamba* – the insignificant or 'empty' persons – of the global order. The West and its products – *mikili* – are linked to the *mundele* and to his power, and thus, for musicians and migrants, access to Europe is legitimating. In the case of Congolese *orchestres*, we have seen how tours of Europe grant them a gloss of internationalism. Most of all, Europe is perceived as the source of fantastic largesse, and it is the source of the prestige goods that are so central to rituals of social reproduction. Thus, we see that while there is a certain acuity in their geopolitical diagnoses, the Congolese representation of elsewhere is part of a fiercely local set of social struggles. Yet, for all the obsession with Europe and despite the fetishistic desire that drives many Kinois to do almost anything to get to the rich North on almost any terms, it seems that in the final analysis, access to Europe is valued for the success it enables in Kinshasa.

For what has emerged from this research is that, ultimately, the real theatre of social reproduction for the Congolese is Kinshasa. This is not to downplay the role of Europe in these transnational performances or to diminish the importance of my fieldwork in Paris. But what is striking is that while so much of the raising of funds, production and performance was undertaken in Europe, it was almost all intended for a Kinois 'stage'. Musicians design and imagine their works playing in the bars of Kinshasa. And, in spite of the fact that a recording has been made in Paris and that the only plausible consumer market for the record is also in Paris, it is to Kinshasa that musicians will depart for promotional campaigns. Within the context in which they operate, this is perfectly rational – all Congolese music fans, including migrants in Paris, will only listen to and, at the level of patronage, 'invest' in the kinds of music they believe to be 'of' and popular in Kinshasa. Producers in Europe will spend hand over fist on 'clips' so that the albums they have sponsored will receive television airplay in Kinshasa, a town where a quarter of the population has insufficient money to feed itself every day. Needless to say, much of this is quite fanciful – musicians long forgotten by the Kinois and producers with no knowledge of the market will spend extraordinary sums trying to access the media in Kinshasa. As we saw in Chapter 2, this image of Kinshasa as the 'source' of emotion and creativity is also somewhat misleading. In recent years the networks of producers and musicians found in Europe have been a source of finance, but also of creativity and new ideas in Congolese music.

Production and Reproduction

The idea of 'reproduction' used here has drawn on the studies of the French Marxists, notably Meillasoux (1960) and Rey and Dupré (1980). In these studies, control of exchange by elders gave control of the demographic reproduction of lineages that, in these agrarian societies, granted control of the surpluses produced by 'cadets'. In these accounts, as in earlier studies of exchange in Africa, there is a sense of exchange goods as tokens within reasonably stable systems of value. Mary Douglas, describing the uses to which raffia cloth was put among the Lele (1968), famously resorts to an analogy with the rationing coupon. Yet subsequent scholarship has shown that the monetary history of West and Central Africa is far from stable (see Harms 1989; Guyer 1995; Dupré 1995). This evidence makes the social efficacy of exchange systems a 'problem to be explained rather than a premise to be assumed' (Guyer 1993: 245). This book has proposed that the aesthetic and performative aspects of exchange present one plausible mechanism for how this explanatory gap might be filled. In Chapter 2 we saw how an unstable exchange threshold was carved out by a group of quasi-marginal youths, using designer clothes, music, dance and oratory to create an aura of value.

Looking at accounts of the political tradition in the Congo Basin, it is apparent that music is frequently present at moments of exchange. Events such as funerals, where slaves would be killed, imported items destroyed or put beyond circulation and lavish prestations made to the lineage, were saturated with music (Laman 1953–68; Dupré 1985). Likewise, the forms of therapeutic cult association such as Lemba (Janzen 1982) that played an important role in maintaining social distinctions were totally enmeshed with music and – indeed – the prohibitive costs of hiring musicians was one of the ways in which the disadvantaged could be excluded from such cults. Likewise, the connection between music and political economic articulation has clear historical roots. Central to the political content of praise singing was the aural mapping of mythical migration routes undertaken by the clan. Descent was constructed around the shifting content and ownership of such narratives, while the places listed on migration routes were constantly rewritten to reflect differing balances of power and to construct alliances that granted access to a coastal trade and prestige goods (Dupré 1985; MacGaffey 2000, 2005; Thornton 2003).

While we have argued for the significance of recording such continuities, this book has also pointed to the considerable discontinuities concerning social reproduction. The incredible emphasis on music and performance in Kinshasa today is perhaps even more striking to the observer because the relationship between control of social reproduction and to the control of surpluses is much more complex than in the basically agrarian world of nineteenth-century lower Congo. Perhaps linked to this, ideologies of marriage and the lineage appear to have weakened somewhat and more diffuse notions of 'wealth in people' have gained a certain prominence.

This is not to say that the appropriation of surpluses has suddenly become irrelevant – elites in Kinshasa draw an important secondary income from tithes on the general population, reaping extensive protection money for intervening in disputes, skimming the cream from various informal fines, etc. Moreover, Kinshasa is a site of articulation through which all sorts of resources must pass. I do not think it unduly conspiratorial to assert that the recurrent potlatch expenditure by elites in Kinshasa, notable since the time of independence (see La Fontaine 1970; Biaya 1996), is related to the strategic importance of the city.

Nevertheless, one should not crudely map such strategic considerations onto social actors. For most individuals involved, and especially migrants, the wild spending we have described seems to have dissipated social efficacy almost as often as it reinforced it. Where music has been deployed in a formal political context, e.g. in campaign songs written for elections in Kinshasa or Brazzaville, it is hard to quantify quite what form or degree of persuasion this affects. But at a general level, we can state that the present ruling class is hugely unpopular in Kinshasa and the most notable immediate consequence of such campaign songs was a surge of anger by the Kinois, and Kinois migrants, against the musicians who performed them. In less formal contexts, potlatch spending does seem to have granted tangible social and political gains, but it seems more convincing to say that actors were motivated by a desire to access valued emotional states rather than by a search for an abstract quality known as 'power'. Yet even this formulation still polarizes matters in an unsatisfactory way. As we argued in Chapter 6, emotional states such as love or joy are often culturally construed as substantive powers.

The fact that sites of exchange and articulation such as Kinshasa also emerge as sites of performance points to the fact that socially dominant groups must reproduce not only political-economic relations, but also the set of emotional dispositions that make social success on their terms desirable. As we have seen in Chapter 5, the powerful cannot always direct such processes from on high, but their political-economic dominance is a very serious advantage, both in terms of accessing such emotions themselves and controlling the access of others. And it is here that the greatest political effect of such performances lies – in associating a set of economic forms with a set of emotional states. In so doing, music has rendered emotionally plausible the idea that the wealthy (or the merely flush) are the source of joy and must be courted to ensure social reproduction.

BIBLIOGRAPHY

Adorno, T.W. 2002. *Essays on Music: Theodor W. Adorno; Selected, with Introduction, Commentary, and Notes by Richard Leppert*, new translations by Susan H. Gillespie. Berkeley: University of California Press.

Allen, L. 2004. 'Music and Politics in Africa', *Social Dynamics: A Journal of African Studies* 30(2): 1–19.

Anderson, B. 1990. *Language and Power: Exploring Political Cultures in Indonesia*. Ithaca: Cornell University Press.

Anderson, P. 1974a. *Passages from Antiquity to Feudalism*. London: Verso.

———— 1974b. *Lineages of the Absolutist State*. London: Verso.

Ansoms, A., and S. Marysse (eds). 2011. *Natural Resources and Local Livelihoods in the Great Lakes: A Political Economy Perspective*. Basingstoke: Palgrave Macmillan.

Appadurai, A. 1996. *Modernity at Large: Cultural Dimensions of Globalization*. Minneapolis: University of Minnesota Press.

Asad, T. 1972. 'Market Model, Class Structure and Consent: A Reconsideration of Swat Political Organisation'. *Man*, 7(1), new series, 74-94.

Bakhtin, M. 1965/1993. *Rabelais and His World*. Translated by Hélène Iswolsky. Bloomington: Indiana University Press.

Balandier, G. 1961. 'Phénomènes sociaux totaux et dynamique sociale', *Cahiers Internationaux de Sociologie* 30: 23–34.

Barbalet, J.M. 1998 *Emotion, Social Theory and Social Structure*. Cambridge: Cambridge University Press.

Barber, K. 1987. 'Popular Arts in Africa', *African Studies Review* 30(3): 1–78

———— 1995. 'Money, Self-Realization and the Person in Yoruba Texts', in J. Guyer (ed.), *Money Matters: Instability, Values, and Social Payments in the Modern History of West African Communities*. Portsmouth, NH: Heinemann/James Currey, pp 205–223.

———— 1997a. 'Preliminary Notes on Audiences in Africa', *Africa: Journal of the International African Institute* 67(3): 347–62.

———— 1997b. 'Introduction', in K. Barber (ed.), *Readings in African Popular Culture*. Bloomington: Indiana University Press, 1997, pp. 1–12.

———— 2007a. 'When People Cross Thresholds', *African Studies Review* 50(2): 111–23.

———— 2007b. *The Anthropology of Texts, Persons and Publics*. Cambridge: Cambridge University Press.

Barber, K., and C. Waterman. 1995. 'Traversing the Global and the Local: Fuji Music and Praise Poetry in the Production of Contemporary Yoruba Popular Culture', in D. Miller (ed.), *Worlds Apart: Modernity through the Prism of the Local*. London: Routledge, pp. 240–262.

Bayart, J.-F. 1993. *The State in Africa: The Politics of the Belly*. London: Longman.

———— 2000 'Africa in the World: A History of Extraversion', *African Affairs* 99(395): 217–68.

Bayart J.-F., and J.-P. Warnier. (eds). 2004. *Matière à Politique: le Pouvoir, les Corps et les Choses.* Paris: Karthala

Bazakana, P. 'Tabu Ley Raconté par le Journaliste Bazakana', *Afriquechos.ch.* 20 February 2014. Retrieved 1 August 2016, from http://www.starducongo.com/Tabu-Ley-raconte-par-le-journaliste-Bazakana_a9188.html.

Bazenguissa-Ganga, R. 1999. 'The Spread of Political Violence in Congo-Brazzaville', *African Affairs* 98(390): 37–54.

———— 2005. *Democratic Republic of Congo (Congo-DRC) and Republic of Congo (Congo) Country Study.* ESRC Centre on Migration, Policy and Society, Oxford: COMPAS.

Bazenguissa-Ganga R., and J. MacGaffey. 2000. *Congo-Paris: Transnational Traders on the Margins of the Law.* Oxford: International African Institute in association with James Currey.

Berger, J. 1975. *Ways of Seeing.* London: Penguin.

Bernault, F. 2006. 'Body, Power and Sacrifice in Equatorial Africa', *Journal of African History* 47: 207–39.

Biaya, T.K. 1996. 'La Culture Urbaine dans les Arts Populaires d'Afrique: Analyse de l'Ambiance Zaïroise', *Canadian Journal of African Studies/Revue Canadienne des Études Africaines* 30(3): 345–70.

———— 1997. 'Kinshasa: Anomie, "ambiance" et violence', in G. Hérault and P. Adesanmi (eds), *Jeunes, Culture de la Rue et Violence Urbaine en Afrique/Youth, Street Culture, and Urban Violence in Africa,* Ibadan: IFRA, pp.329–378.

Bilakila, A. N. 2004. 'The Kinshasa Bargain', in T. Trefon (ed.), *Reinventing Order in Congo: How People Respond to State Failure in Kinshasa.* London: Zed Books, pp. 20–32.

Blackburn, R. 1997. *The Making of New World Slavery: From the Baroque to the Modern, 1492–1800.* London: Verso.

Bloch, M. 1989. 'The Symbolism of Money in Imerina', in M. Bloch and J. Parry (eds), *Money and the Morality of Exchange.* Cambridge: Cambridge University Press, pp. 165–90.

Bloch, M., and J. Parry 1989. 'Introduction', in M. Bloch and J. Parry (eds), *Money and the Morality of Exchange.* Cambridge: Cambridge University Press, pp. 1–32.

Blom Hansen, T., and O. Verkaaik. 2009. 'Urban Charisma: Everyday Mythologies of the City', *Critique of Anthropology* 29(1): 5–26.

Bohannan, P. 1959. 'The Impact of Money on an African Subsistence Economy', *Journal of Economic History* 19(4): 491–503.

Bourdieu, Pierre, 1977. *Outline of a Theory of Practice.* Translated by Richard Nice. Cambridge: Cambridge University Press.

Boyce, J.K., and L. Ndikumana, 1998. 'Congo's Odious Debts: External Borrowing and Capital Flight in Zaire', *Development and Change* 29: 195–217.

———— 2011. *Africa's Odious Debts: How Foreign Loans and Capital Flight Bled a Continent.* London: Zed Books.

Breckenridge, K. 2000. 'Love Letters and Amanuenses: Beginning the Cultural History of the Working Class Private Sphere in Southern Africa, 1900–1933', *Journal of Southern African Studies* 26(2): 337–48.

Brenner, P. 1977. 'The Origins of Capitalist Development; A Critique of Neo-Smithian Marxism', *New Left Review* I(104): 25–92.

Buchan, J. 2007. *Adam Smith and the Pursuit of Perfect Liberty.* London: Profile.

Carey, J. 1992. *The Intellectuals and the Masses: Pride and Prejudice among the Literary Intelligentsia, 1800–1939.* London: Faber.

Chabal, P., and Daloz, J.-P. 1999. *Africa Works: Disorder as Political Instrument.* Oxford: International African Institute/James Currey.

Cole, J. 2009. 'Love, Money, and Economies of Intimacy in Tamatave, Madagascar', in J. Cole and L.M. Thomas (eds), *Love in Africa,* Chicago: University of Chicago Press, pp. 109–34.

Comaroff, J., and J.L. Comaroff. 1993. 'Introduction', in J. Comaroff and J.L. Comaroff (eds), *Modernity and its Malcontents: Ritual and Power in Postcolonial Africa*. Chicago: University of Chicago Press, pp. xi–xxxi.

———— 1999. 'Occult Economies and the Violence of Abstraction: Notes from the South African Postcolony', *American Ethnologist* 26(2): 279–303.

———— 2001. *Millennial Capitalism and the Culture of Neoliberalism*. Durham, NC: Duke University Press.

Cooper, F. 1981. 'Africa and the World Economy', *African Studies Review* 24(2/3): 1–86.

———— 2000. 'Africa's Pasts and Africa's Historians', *Canadian Journal of African Studies Revue Canadienne des Études Africaines* 34(2): 298–336.

———— 2001. 'What is the Concept of Globalization Good for? An African Historian's Perspective', *African Affairs* 100(399): 189–213.

———— 2002. *Africa since 1940: The Past of the Present*. Cambridge: Cambridge University Press.

Coplan, D. 1997. 'Eloquent Knowledge: Lesotho Migrant's Songs and the Anthropology of Experience', in K. Barber (ed.), *Readings in African Popular Culture*. Bloomington/Oxford: Indiana University Press/ James Currey, pp. 29–39.

Davis, M. 2006. *Planet of Slums*. London: Verso.

De Boeck, F. 1994. 'Of Trees and Kings: Politics and Metaphor among the Aluund of Southwestern Zaire', *American Ethnologist* 21(3): 451–73.

———— 1996. 'Postcolonialism, Power and Identity – Local and Global Perspectives from Zaire', in R. Werbner and T. Ranger (eds), *Postcolonial Identities in Africa*. London: Zed Books, pp. 76–106.

———— 1998. 'Domesticating Diamonds and Dollars: Identity, Expenditure and Sharing in Southwestern Zaire (1984–1997)', *Development and Change* 29: 777–810.

———— 2004. 'On Being Shege in Kinshasa: Children, the Occult and the Street', in T. Trefon (ed.), *Reinventing Order in Congo: How People Respond to State Failure in Kinshasa*. London: Zed Books, pp. 155–73.

De Boeck, F., and M. Plissart. 2004. *Kinshasa Tales of the Invisible City*. Tervuren/Ghent: Royal Museum for Central Africa/Vlaams Architectuurinstituut.

De Heusch, L. 2002. *Du Pouvoir: Anthropologie Politique des Sociétés d'Afrique Centrale*. Nanterre: Société d'ethnologie.

De Herdt, T. 2002. 'Democracy and the Money Machine', in *Zaire Review of African Political Economy* 29 (93/94): 444–62.

De Herdt, T., and S. Marysse. 1996. *L'Économie Informelle au Zaïre: (Sur)vie et Pauvreté dans la Période de Transition*. Paris: L'Harmattan.

De Witte, L. 2001. *The Assassination of Lumumba*. London: Verso.

Devlin, L. 2007. *Chief of Station, Congo: a Memoir of 1960–67*. New York: Public Affairs.

Dibango, M. 1995. *Trois Kilos de Café: Autobiographie*. Paris: Seuil.

Donald, L. 1997. *Aboriginal Slavery on the Northwest Coast of North America*. Berkeley: University of California Press.

Donham, D. 1990. *History, Power, Ideology: Central Issues in Marxism and Anthropology*, Berkeley: University of California Press.

Douglas, M. 1968. *The Lele of the Kasai*. London: International African Institute.

Dupré, G. 1995. 'The History and the Adventures of a Monetary Object of the Kwele of the Congo', in J. Guyer (ed.), *Money Matters: Instability, Values, and Social Payments in the Modern History of West African Communities*. Portsmouth, NH/London: Heinemann/ James Currey, pp. 77–96.

Dupré, G., and P.P. Rey. 1980. 'Reflections on the Relevance of a Theory of the History of Exchange', in H. Wolpe (ed.), *The Articulation of Modes of Production: Essays from Economy and Society*. London: Routledge & Kegan Paul, pp. 63–131.

———— 1982. *Un Ordre et sa Destruction*. Paris: Collections Mémoires.

_____ 1985. *Les Naissances d'une Société: Espace et Historicité chez les Beembé du Congo.* Paris: ORSTOM.

Engelke, M. 2007. *A Problem of Presence: Beyond Scripture in an African Church.* Berkeley: University of California Press.

Englebert, P. 2003. 'Why the Congo Persists Sovereignty, Globalisation and the Violent Reproduction of a Weak State', *Queen Elizabeth House Working Paper WPS95*, February.

Englebert, P., and J. Ron. 2004. 'Primary Commodities and War: Congo Brazzaville's Ambivalent Resource Curse', *Comparative Politics* 37(1): 61–81.

Ewens, G. 1994. *Congo Colossus: The Life and Legacy of Franco and OK Jazz.* North Walsham: Buku Press.

Exenberger, A., and S. Hartman 2013. 'Extractive Institutions in the Congo, Checks and Balances in the *Longue Durée*', in E. Frankema, and F. Buelens (eds), *Colonial Exploitation and Economic Development: The Belgian Congo and the Netherlands Indies Compared.* Abingdon: Routledge, pp. 18–41.

Fabian, J. 1990. *Power and Performance: Ethnographic Explorations through Proverbial Wisdom and Theatre in Shaba, Zaire.* Madison: University of Wisconsin Press.

_____ 1997. 'Popular Culture in Africa: Findings and Conjectures', in K, Barber (ed.), *Readings in African Popular Culture.* Bloomington: Indiana University Press, pp. 18–28.

Faligot, R., and J. Guisnel, (eds). 2006. *Histoire Secrète de la Ve République.* Paris: Découverte.

Fardon, R. 1995. 'Introduction: Counterworks', in *Counterworks: Managing the Diversity of Knowledge: 4th Decennial Conference, ASA Decennial Conference Series.* London: Routledge, pp. 1–23.

Fardon, R., and G. Furniss (eds). 2000. *African Broadcast Cultures: Radio in Transition.* Oxford: James Currey.

Faveri, S. 2013. *Making Do in* la Cité, *Inventiveness in the Face of Economic Insecurity*, unpublished paper.

Fernandez, J.W. 1982. *Bwiti: An Ethnography of the Religious Imagination in Africa.* Princeton: Princeton University Press.

Foucault, M. 1979. *Discipline and Punish: the Birth of the Prison.* Harmondsworth: Penguin Books.

Frankema, E., and F. Buelens (eds). 2013. *Colonial Exploitation and Economic Development: The Belgian Congo and the Netherlands Indies Compared.* Abingdon: Routledge.

Frankfurt, H.G. 2005. *On Bullshit.* Princeton: Princeton University Press

Freedberg, D. 1989. *The Power of Images: Studies in the History and Theory of Response.* Chicago: University of Chicago Press.

Freund, B. 2013. 'Class Politics', in D. Anderson and N. Cheeseman (eds), *Routledge Handbook of Politics in Africa.* London: Routledge, pp. 83–94.

Ferguson, J.G. 2002. 'Of Mimicry and Membership: Africans and the "New World Society"', *Cultural Anthropology* 17: 551–69.

Friedman, J. 2004. 'The Political Economy of Elegance: An African Cult of Beauty', in J. Friedman (ed.), *Consumption and Identity.* London: Routledge, pp. 167–89.

Friedman, K.E. 1991. *Catastrophe and Creation: The Transformation of an African Culture.* Philadelphia: Harwood Academic Publishers.

Gandoulou, J.-D. 1989a. *Au Cœur de la Sape: Mœurs et Aventures des Congolais à Paris.* Paris: L'Harmattan.

_____ 1989b. *Dandies à Bacongo: le Culte de l'Élégance dans la Société Congolaise Contemporaine.* Paris: L'Harmattan.

Gardener, L. 2013. 'Fiscal Policy in the Belgian Congo in Comparative Perspective', in E. Frankema and F. Buelens (eds), *Colonial Exploitation and Economic Development: The Belgian Congo and the Netherlands Indies Compared.* Abingdon: Routledge, pp. 130–52.

Geenen, K. 2009. '"Sleep Occupies No Space": The Use of Public Space by Street Gangs in Kinshasa', *Africa: Journal of the International African Institute* 79(3): 347–68.

Geschiere, P. 1997. *The Modernity of Witchcraft: Politics and the Occult in Postcolonial Africa,* trans. P. Geschiere and J. Roitman. Charlottesville: University Press of Virginia.

Giddens, A. 1991. *Modernity and Self-Identity: Self and Society in the Late Modern Age.* Stanford: Stanford University Press.

Ginsburg, F.D., L. Abu-Lughod, and L. Brian. 2002. *Media Worlds: Anthropology on New Terrain.* Berkeley: University of California Press.

Gluckman, M. 1963. 'The Magic of Despair', in M. Gluckman, *Order and Rebellion in Tribal Africa.* London: Cohen and West, pp. 137–45.

Gondola, C.D. 1997a. *Villes Miroirs: Migrations et Identités Urbaines à Brazzaville et Kinshasa, 1930–1970.* Paris: L'Harmattan.

———— 1997b. 'Popular Music, Urban Society and Changing Gender Relations in Kinshasa, Zaire', in Maria Grosz-Ngaté and Omari H. Kokole (eds), *Gendered Encounters, Challenging Cultural Boundaries and Social Hierarchies in Africa.* New York: Routledge, pp. 65–84.

———— 1999. 'Dream and Drama: The Search for Elegance among Congolese Youth', *African Studies Review* 42(1): 23–48.

Graeber, D. 2001. *Toward an Anthropological Theory of Value: The False Coin of Our Own Dreams.* New York: Palgrave.

———— 2011. *Debt: The First 5,000 Years.* New York: Melville House.

Gudeman, S., and A. Rivera. 1990. *Conversations in Colombia: The Domestic Economy in Life and Text.* Cambridge: Cambridge University Press.

Guyer, J.I. 1993. 'Wealth in People and Self-Realization in Equatorial Africa', *Man* 28(2): 243–65.

———— 1995. 'Introduction: The Currency Interface and its Dynamics', in Jane Guyer (ed.), *Money Matters: Instability, Values, and Social Payments in the Modern History of West African Communities.* Portsmouth, NH/London: Heinemann/James Currey, pp. 1–33.

———— 2004. *Marginal Gains: Monetary Transactions in Atlantic Africa.* Chicago: University of Chicago Press.

Habermas, J. 1992. *The Structural Transformation of the Public Sphere: An Inquiry into a Category of Bourgeois Society,* trans. T. Burger and F. Lawrence. Cambridge: Polity Press.

Hannerz, U. 1997. 'The World in Creolization', in K. Barber (ed.), *Readings in African Popular Culture.* Bloomington: Indiana University Press, pp. 12–17.

Harris, M. 1974. *Cows, Pigs, Wars and Witches.* New York: Random House.

Harris, O. 1989. 'The Earth and the State: Sources and Meanings of Money in Northern Potosi, Bolivia', in M. Bloch and J. Parry (eds), *Money and the Morality of Exchange.* Cambridge: Cambridge University Press, pp. 232–68.

Harms, R.W. 1981. *River of Wealth, River of Sorrow: The Central Zaire Basin in the Era of the Slave and Ivory Trade, 1500–1891.* New Haven: Yale University Press.

Hilton, A. 1983. 'Family and Kinship among the Kongo South of the Zaire River from the Sixteenth to the Nineteenth Centuries', *Journal of African History* 24(2): 189–206.

Hirsch, J.S., and H. Wardlow (eds). 2006. *Modern Loves: The Anthropology of Romantic Courtship & Companionate Marriage.* Ann Arbor: University of Michigan Press.

Hunt, N.R. 1991. 'Noise over Camouflaged Polygamy, Colonial Morality Taxation, and a Woman-Naming Crisis in Belgian Africa'. *Journal of African History* 32(3): 471–94.

———— 1999. *A Colonial Lexicon, of Birth Ritual, Medicalization, and Mobility in the Congo.* Durham, NC: Duke University Press.

Hyslop, J. 2005. 'Political Corruption: Before and after Apartheid', *Journal of Southern African Studies* 31(4): 773–89.

International Organization for Migration. 2006. *Mapping Exercise DR Congo, London November 2006.* London: IOM UK.

James, D. 2011. 'The Return of the Broker: Consensus, Hierarchy and Choice in South African Land Reform', *Journal of the Royal Anthropological Institute* 17(2): 318–38.

Janzen, J. 1982. *Lemba 1650–1930: A Drum of Affliction in Africa and the New World.* New York: Garland Publishing.

Janzen, J., and W. MacGaffey. 1974. *An Anthology of Kongo Religion: An Anthology of Texts from Lower Zaire.* Lawrence: University of Kansas Press.

Jankowiak, W.R. (ed.). 2008. *Intimacies: Love and Sex across Cultures.* New York: Columbia University Press.

Jewsiewicki, B. 1992. 'Jeux d'Argent et de Pouvoir au Zaïre: la "Bindomanie" et le Crépuscule de la Deuxième République', *Politique Africaine* 46: 55–70.

——— (ed.). 2003. 'Introduction', in B. Jewsiewicki (ed.) *Musique Urbaine au Katanga: de Malaika à Santu Kimbangu.* Paris: L'Harmattan, pp. 1–20.

Josephides, L. 1985. *The Production of Inequality: Gender and Exchange among the Kewa.* London: Tavistock.

Kalb, D. 2013. 'Financialization and the Capitalist Moment: Marx versus Weber in the Anthropology of Global Systems', *American Ethnologist* 40: 258–66.

Keane, W. 2007. *Christian Moderns, Freedom and Fetish in the Mission Encounter.* Berkeley: University of California Press.

Kopytoff, I. (ed.). 1987. *The African Frontier: The Reproduction of Traditional African Societies.* Bloomington: Indiana University Press.

La Fontaine, J.S. 1970. *City Politics: A Study of Leopoldville, 1962–63.* Cambridge: Cambridge University Press.

Laman, K.E. 1953–68. *The Kongo.* London/Uppsala: Kegan Paul/Uppsala Universitet.

Larkin, B. 2008. *Signal and Noise: Media, Infrastructure, and Urban Culture in Nigeria.* Durham, NC: Duke University Press.

Leach, E. 1954. *Political Systems of Highland Burma: A Study of Kachin Social Structure.* Cambridge, MA: Harvard University Press.

Leavitt, J. 1996. 'Meaning and Feeling in the Anthropology of Emotions', *American Ethnologist* 23(3): 514–39.

Lukacs, G. 1923/1967. *History and Class Consciousness,* trans. R. Livingstone. London: Merlin Press.

——— 1937/1981. *The Historical Novel,* trans. H. Mitchell and S. Mitchell; introduction by Fredric Jameson. Lincoln, NE: University of Nebraska Press.

Luttman, V. 1998. 'Papa Wemba Mwana Molokai'. Retrieved 1 August 2016 from http://www.aozj17.dsl.pipex.com/wembaindex.html.

MacFarlane, A. 1979. 'Reviewed Work(s): The Family, Sex and Marriage in England 1500–1800 by Lawrence Stone'. *History and Theory* 18(1): 103–26.

MacGaffey, W. 1977. 'Fetishism Revisited: Kongo "Nkisi" in Sociological Perspective', *Africa: Journal of the International African Institute* 47(2): 172–84.

——— 1983. *Modern Kongo Prophets: Religion in a Plural Society.* Bloomington: Indiana University Press.

——— 1986. *Religion and Society in Central Africa: The BaKongo of Lower Zaire,* Chicago: University of Chicago Press.

——— 1991 *Art and Healing of the Bakongo, Commented by Themselves: Minkisi from the Laman Collection/Kikongo Texts Translated and Edited by Wyatt MacGaffey.* Stockholm: Folkens Museum-Etnografiska.

——— 2000. *Kongo Political Culture: The Conceptual Challenge of the Particular.* Bloomington: Indiana University Press.

——— 2005. 'Changing Representations of African History', *Journal of African History* 46(2): 189–207.

——— 2009. Email on the subject of mpemba/lupemba

Macpherson, C. 1964. *The Political Theory of Possessive Individualism from Hobbes to Locke.* Oxford: Oxford University Press.

Martin, P. 1986. 'Power, Cloth and Currency on the Loango Coast.' *African Economic History*, (15): 1–12.

—— 1995. *Leisure and Society in Colonial Brazzaville*. Cambridge: Cambridge University Press.

Marx, K. 1852/1970. 'The Eighteenth Brumaire of Louis Bonaparte', in K. Marx and F. Engels, *Selected Works*. London, Lawrence & Wishart pp. 96–166.

—— 1859/1970. 'Preface to the Critique of Political economy', in K. Marx and F. Engels, *Selected Works*. London, Lawrence & Wishart, pp. 180–84.

—— 1867/1961. *Capital: A Critical Analysis of Capitalist Production, Volume 1*, trans. S. Moore and E. Aveling. Moscow: Foreign Languages Publishing House.

—— 1895/1991. *Capital: A Critical Analysis of Capitalist Production, Volume III*, with introduction by E. Mandel, trans. D. Fernbach. London: Penguin.

Marx, K., and F. Engels. 1846/1998. *The German Ideology: Including Theses on Feuerbach and Introduction to the Critique of Political Economy*. Amherst: Prometheus Books.

—— 1970. *Selected Works*. London: Lawrence & Wishart.

Mauss, M. 1924/1990. *The Gift: The Form and Reason for Exchange in Archaic Societies*, trans. W.D. Halls. London: Routledge.

Mbembe, A. 1992. 'The Banality of Power and the Aesthetics of Vulgarity in the Postcolony', *Public Culture* 4 (2): 1–30.

—— 2006. 'Variations on the Beautiful in Congolese Worlds of Sound', in S. Nuttall (ed.), *Beautiful Ugly: African and Diaspora Aesthetics*. Durham, NC: Duke University Press, pp. 60–93.

Mbiki, D.D. 2008. *L'Épopée du Diamant du Sang en Afrique, un Creuseur Zairo-Congolais à Lunda Norte*. Paris: L'Harmattan.

McNeill, F. 2012. 'Making Music Making Money, Informal Music Making Production and Performance in Venda, South Africa', *Africa: Journal of the International African Institute* 82(1): 92–110.

Meintjes, L. 2003. *Sound of Africa! Making Music Zulu in a South African Recording Studio*. Durham, NC: Duke University Press.

Meagher, K. 2006: 'Cultural Primordialism and the Post-structuralist Imaginaire: Plus ça Change', *Africa : Journal of the International African Institute* 76(4): 590–97.

Meillasoux, C. 1960. 'Essai d'Interprétation du Phénomène Economique dans les Sociétés Traditionnelles d'Autosubsistance', *Cahiers d'Etudes Africaines* 4: 38–67.

Merlier, M. 1962. *Le Congo de la Colonisation Belge à l'Indépendance*. Paris: Maspero.

Meyer, B., and Geschiere, P. 1999. 'Introduction', in B. Meyer and P. Geschiere (eds), *Globalization and Identity: Dialectics of Flow and Closure*. Oxford: Blackwell, pp. 1–16.

Miers, S., and I. Kopytoff. 1977. *Slavery in Africa: Historical and Anthropological Perspectives*. Madison: University of Wisconsin Press.

Miller, D. 1992. 'The Young and the Restless in Trinidad: A Case of the Local and the Global in Mass Consumption', in R. Silverstone, and E. Hirsch (eds), *Consuming Technologies: Media and Information in Domestic Spaces*. London: Routledge, pp. 92–102.

—— 1995. 'Introduction: Anthropology, Modernity and Consumption', in D. Miller (ed.), *Worlds Apart: Modernity through the Prism of the Local*. London: Routledge, pp. 1–22.

—— 1998. *A Theory of Shopping*. Cambridge: Polity Press.

Monnier, L., B. Jewsiewicki and G. De Villers (eds). 2001. *Chasse au Diamant au Congo/Zaïre*. Paris: L'Harmattan.

Mpengo-Mbey, S. 2004. 'Les Congolais à Londres', *Grands Lacs* 37: 12–13.

Mpisi, J. 2003. *Tabu Ley 'Rochereau': Innovateur de la Musique Africaine*. Paris: L'Harmattan.

Mufuta, P. 1969. *Le Chant Kasàlà des Lubà*. Paris: Julliard.

Muir, E. 1997. *Ritual in Early Modern Europe*. Cambridge: Cambridge University Press.

Multi Media Congo. 2007. 'Exclusivité : Céléo réaffirme Son Attachement à Werrason'. Retrieved 1 August 2016 from http://www.digitalcongo.net/article/44591.

Ndaywel é Nziem, I. 1998. *Histoire Générale du Congo: de l'Héritage Ancien à la République Démocratique*. Paris: Duclot.

Niehaus, I. 2002. 'Bodies, Heat, and Taboos: Conceptualizing Modern Personhood in the South African Lowveld', *Ethnology* 41(3): 189–207.

Nyamnjoh, F., and J. Fokwang. 2005. 'Entertaining Repression: Music and Politics in Postcolonial Cameroon', *African Affairs* 104(415): 251–74.

Nzongola-Ntalaja, G. 1970. 'The Bourgeoisie and Revolution in the Congo', *Journal of Modern African Studies* 8(4): 511–30.

_____ 2002. *The Congo from Leopold to Kabila: A People's History*, London: Zed.

Onyumbe, T. 1982. 'Nkisi, Nganga et Ngangankisi dans la Musique Zaïroise Moderne de 1960 à 1981', *Zaïre-Afrique* 169: 555–66.

_____ 1983. 'Le Thème de l'Argent dans la Musique Zaïroise Moderne de 1960 à 1981', *Zaïre-Afrique* 172: 97–111.

_____ 1984. 'La Femme Vue par l'Homme dans la Musique Zaïroise Moderne de 1960 à 1981', *Zaïre-Afrique* 184: 229–43.

_____ 1985a. 'L'Amour dans la Musique Zaïroise Moderne de 1960 à 1981', *Zaïre-Afrique* 197: 427–39.

_____ 1985b. 'Le Mariage dans la Musique Zaïroise Moderne de 1960 à 1981', *Zaïre-Afrique* 198: 491–502.

Omasombo, J. (ed.). 2009. *Biographie des Acteurs de la Troisième République*. Louvain: MRAC/CEP/CEDAC.

Parry, J. 1986. 'The Gift, the Indian Gift and the "Indian Gift"', *Man* 21(3): 453–73.

Patterson, O. 1982. *Slavery and Social Death: A Comparative Study*. Cambridge, MA: Harvard University Press.

Pietz, W. 1985. 'The Problem of the Fetish, I', *Anthropology and Aesthetics* 9: 5–17.

_____ 1987. 'The Problem of the Fetish, II', *Anthropology and Aesthetics* 13: 23–45.

_____ 1988. 'The Problem of the Fetish, IIIa: Bosman's Guinea and the Enlightenment Theory of Fetishism', *Anthropology and Aesthetics* 16: 105–24.

Pinney, C. 2001. 'Piercing the Skin of the Idol', in C. Pinney and N. Thomas (eds), *Beyond Aesthetics: Art and the Technologies of Enchantment*. Oxford: Berg, pp. 187–200.

Povinelli, E.A. 2006. *The Empire of Love: Toward a Theory of Intimacy, Genealogy, and Carnality*. Durham, NC: Duke University Press.

Prunier, G. 2009. *From Genocide to Continental War: The 'Congolese' Conflict and the Crisis of Contemporary Africa*. London: Hurst.

Pype, K. 2006 'Dancing for God or the Devil, Pentecostal Discourse on Popular Dance in Kinshasa', *Journal of Religion in Africa* 36(3–4): 296–318.

_____ 2007. 'Fighting Boys, Strong Men and Gorillas: Notes on the Imagination of Masculinities in Kinshasa', *Africa: Journal of the International African Institute* 77(2): 250–71.

_____ 2009. '"We Need to Open Up the Country": Development and the Christian Key Scenario in the Social Space of Kinshasa's Teleserials', *Journal of African Media Studies* 1(1): 101–16.

_____ 2012. *The Making of Pentecostal Melodrama: Religion, Media and Gender in Kinshasa*. Oxford: Berghahn Books.

Raeymaekers, T. 2010. 'Protection for Sale? War and the Transformation of Regulation on the Congo-Ugandan Border', *Development and Change* 41(4): 563–87.

Reddy, W. 2001. *The Navigation of Feeling: A Framework for the History of Emotions*. Cambridge: Cambridge University Press.

Reno, W. 1998. *Warlord Politics and African States*. Boulder: Lynne Rienner Publishers.

Rey, P.P. 1971. *Colonialisme: Néo-colonialisme et Transition au Capitalisme; Exemple de la Comilog au Congo-Brazzaville*. Paris: F. Maspero.

_____ 1973. *Les Alliances de Classes*. Paris: F. Maspero.

Ringel, G. 1979. 'The Kawkiutl Potlatch: History, Economics, and Symbols', *Ethnohistory* 26(4): 347–62.

Rousseau, J.J. 1762/2006. *Du Contrat Social, ou Principles de Droit Politique*. Paris: Librio.

Rowlands, M., and J.-P. Warnier. 1988. 'Sorcery, Power and the Modern State in Cameroon', *Man*, 23(1): 118–32.

Roth, C. 2002. 'Goods, Names, and Selves: Rethinking the Tsimshian Potlatch', *American Ethnologist* 29(1): 123–50.

Sang'Amin, K. G. 1989. *Les Spectacles d'Animation Politique en la Republique du Zaïre*. Louvain-la-Neuve: Cahiers du Theatre.

Schatzberg, M. 1980. *Politics and Class in Zaire: Bureaucracy, Business, and Beer in Lisala*. New York: Africana.

Schoepf, B., and Engundu, W. 1991. 'Women's Trade and Contributions to Household Budgets in Kinshasa', in J. MacGaffey (ed.), *The Real Economy of Zaire: The Contribution of Smuggling and Other Unofficial Activities to National Wealth*. London; James Currey, pp. 124–138.

Scott, J. 1969. 'Corruption, Machine Politics, and Political Change', *American Political Science Review* 63(4): 1142–58.

_____ 1990a. *Weapons of the Weak: Everyday Forms of Peasant Resistance*. Delhi: Oxford University Press.

_____ 1990b. *Domination and the Arts of Resistance: Hidden Transcripts*. New Haven: Yale University Press.

Schama, S. 1989. *Citizens: A Chronicle of the French Revolution*. London: Penguin.

Shakespeare, W. 1641/2001. *The Tempest*. Oxford: Oxford University Press.

Shaxson, N. 2007. *Poisoned Wells: The Dirty Politics of African Oil*. New York: Palgrave Macmillan.

_____ 2012. *Treasure Islands: Tax Havens and the Men Who Stole the World*. London: Vintage.

Sperber, J. 2013. *Karl Marx: A Nineteenth-Century Life*. New York: Liveright.

Stearns, J. 2011. *Dancing in the Glory of Monsters: The Collapse of Congo and the Great War of Africa*. New York: Public Affairs.

Stewart, G. 2001. *Rumba on the River: A History of the Popular Music of the Two Congos*. London: Verso.

Stoller, P. 1984. 'Sound in Songhay Cultural Experience', *American Ethnologist* 11(3): 559–70.

_____ 1995. *Embodying Colonial Memories: Spirit Possession, Power, and the Hauka in West Africa*. New York: Routledge.

Stone, L. 1990. *The Family, Sex and Marriage in England, 1500–1800*. London: Penguin.

Strathern, M. 1988. *The Gender of the Gift: Problems with Women and Problems with Society in Melanesia*. Berkeley: University of California Press.

Sumata, C. 2001. *L'Économie Parallèle de la RDC: Taux de Change et Dynamique de l'Hyperinflation au Congo*. Paris: Harmattan.

_____ 2002. 'Migradollars and Poverty Alleviation in the Congo', *Review of African Political Economy* 29(93–94): 616–19.

Swain, D. 2012. *Alienation: An Introduction to Marx's Theory*. London: Bookmarks.

Swa-Kabamba, J.N. 1997. 'The "Mbiimbi", a Panegyrical Dynastic Poem of the Yaka, and its Principal Characteristics', *Research in African Literatures* 28(1): 141–58.

Tassi, N. 2008. 'Living Languages, Representation and Alterity in Urban Andean Settings', Ph.D. dissertation. London: University College London.

Taussig, M.T. 1980. *The Devil and Commodity Fetishism in South America*. Chapel Hill: North Carolina University Press.

_____ 1993. *Mimesis and Alterity: A Particular History of the Senses*. New York: Routledge.

Taylor, C.C. 1999. *Sacrifice as Terror: The Rwandan Genocide of 1994*. Oxford: Berg.

Tchebwa, M. 1996. *Terre de la Chanson: la Musique Zaïroise, Hier et Aujourd'hui*. Louvain-la-Neuve: Duculot.

Thomas, N. 1991. *Entangled Objects: Exchange, Material Culture, and Colonialism in the Pacific.* Cambridge MA: Harvard University Press.

Thompson, E.P. 1978. *The Poverty of Theory, or, An Orrery of Errors,* London: Merlin Press.

Thornton, J. 1984. 'The Development of an African Catholic Church in the Kingdom of Kongo, 1491–1750', *Journal of African History* 25(2): 147–67.

———— 1998. *The Kongolese Saint Anthony: Dona Beatriz Kimpa Vita and the Antonian Movement, 1684–1706.* Cambridge: Cambridge University Press.

———— 2003. 'Cannibals, Witches, and Slave Traders in the Atlantic World', *William and Mary Quarterly* 60(2): 273–94.

Tipo-Tipo, M. 1995. *Migration Sud/Nord: Levier ou Obstacle?: les Zaïrois en Belgique.* Brussels/ Paris: Institut Africain-Cedaf/L'Harmattan.

Tilly, C. 1999. *Durable Inequality.* Berkeley: University of California Press.

Tollens, E. 2004. 'Food Security in Kinshasa: Coping with Adversity', in T. Trefon (ed.), *Reinventing Order in Congo: How People Respond to State Failure in Kinshasa.* London: Zed Books, pp. 47–64.

Tonda, J. 2005. *Le Souverain Moderne: le Corps du Pouvoir en Afrique Centrale.* Paris: Karthala.

Trapido, J. 2005. 'Stones in Paradise', MA dissertation. London: University College London.

———— 2015. 'Africa's Leaky Giant', *New Left Review* 92: 5–40.

———— 2016. 'Potlatch and the Articulation of Modes of Production: Revisiting French Marxist Anthropology and the History of Central Africa', *Dialectical Anthropology.* (40) 3: 199–220.

Trapido, J., and L. Tsambu-Bulu. 2007. 'Du stade des Martyrs au Palais omnisport de Paris-Bercy', *Histoire Urbaine en Afrique Centrale: Lieux, Regards et Espaces. Nouvelles Méthodologies dans l'Historiographie des villes, 19 September 2007.* Kinshasa: Centre des Etudes Politiques.

Trefon, T. 2004a. 'Introduction: Reinventing Order', in T. Trefon (ed.), *Reinventing Order in Congo: How People Respond to State Failure in Kinshasa.* London: Zed Books, pp. 1–20.

———— 2004b. *Ordre et désordre à Kinshasa: Réponses Populaires à la Faillite de l'Etat.* Tervuren/ Paris: Royal Museum for Central Africa/L'Harmattan

———— 2007. *Parcours Administratifs dans un Etat en Faillite: Récits Populaires de Lubumbashi (RDC).* Paris: L'Harmattan.

———— 2011. *Congo Masquerade: The Political Culture of Aid Inefficiency and Reform Failure.* London: Zed Books.

Tsambu-Bulu, L. 2004. 'Musique et violence a Kinshasa', in T. Trefon (ed.), *Ordre et Désordre à Kinshasa: Réponses Populaires à la Faillite de l'Etat.* Tervuren/Paris: Royal Museum for Central Africa/L'Harmattan, pp. 93–111.

———— 2005. 'Epure d'un Développement de l'Industrie du Disque Congolaise par le Mécénat Privé', *Revue Africaine des Médias* 13(2): 36–67.

———— 2010. 'Sociétés d' Élégance', unpublished paper.

Tshimanga Mbuyi, C. 2012. 'Evolution de la Pauvreté en Republique Democratique du Congo', in S. Marysse and J.O. Tshonda (eds), *Conjunctures Congolaises, chroniques et analyses de la RD Congo en 2011.* Paris: L'Harmattan, pp. 143–69.

Turino, T. 2000. *Nationalists, Cosmopolitans and Popular Music in Zimbabwe.* Chicago: University of Chicago Press.

Turner, T. 2007. *The Congo Wars: Conflict, Myth, and Reality.* London: Zed Books.

Turner, V. 1968. *The Drums of Affliction: A Study of Religious Processes among the Ndembu of Zambia.* London: International African Institute in association with Hutchinson University Library for Africa.

UN-HABITAT. 2008. 'The State of African Cities: A Framework for Addressing Urban Challenges in Africa'. Nairobi.

Urry, J. 2000. *Sociology beyond Society: Mobilities for the 21st Century.* London: Routledge.

Van Woudenberg, A. 2006. 'Dairy: Congo', *London Review of Books* 28(20): 33–35.

Vangu-Ngimbi, I. 1997. *Jeunesse, Funérailles et Contestation Socio-Politique en Afrique: le Cas de l'Ex-Zaïre*. Paris: L'Harmattan.

Vansina, J. 1978. *The Children of Woot: A History of the Kuba Peoples*. Madison: University of Wisconsin Press.

Vaughan, M. 2009. 'The History of Romantic Love in Sub-Saharan Africa: Between Interest and Emotion', *Raleigh Lecture on History British Academy, 26th February*. London.

Veblen, T. 1899/2001. *Theory of the Leisure Class*. London: Random House.

Vellut, J.-L. 2004. 'Réflexions sur la Question de la Violence dans Afrique Central', in P.M. Mantuba-Ngoma (ed.), *La Nouvelle Histoire du Congo: Mélanges Eurafricains Offerts à Frans Bontinck*. Paris: L'Harmattan, pp. 269–87.

Verhaegen, B. 1966. *Rebellions au Congo*. Brussels: Centre de recherche et d'information socio-politiques.

Warnier, J.-P. 1993. *L' Esprit d'Entreprise au Cameroun*. Paris: Editions Karthala.

_____ 2004. 'Pour une Praxéologie de la Subjectivation Politique', in J.-F. Bayart and J.-P. and Warnier (eds), *Matière à Politique : le Pouvoir, les Corps et les Choses*. Paris: Karthala, pp. 7–33.

_____ 2007. *The Pot-King: The Body and Technologies of Power*. Leiden: Brill.

Waterman, C.A. 1990. *Jùjú: A Social History and Ethnography of African Popular Music*. Chicago: University of Chicago Press.

Weber, M. 1968. *On Charisma and Institution Building: Selected Papers*. Chicago: University of Chicago Press.

White, R.W. 1999. 'Modernity's Trickster: "Dipping" and "Throwing" in Congolese Popular Dance Music', *Research in African Literatures* 30(4): 156–75.

_____ 2002. 'Congolese Rumba and Other Cosmopolitanisms', *Cahiers d'Études Africaines* 42(168): 663–86.

_____ 2004. 'The Elusive Lupemba, Rumours about Fame and (Mis)fortune in Kinshasa', in T. Trefon (ed.), *Reinventing Order in Congo: How People Respond to State Failure in Kinshasa*. London: Zed Books, pp. 174–91.

_____ 2008. *Rumba Rules: The Politics of Dance Music in Mobutu's Zaire*. Durham, NC: Duke University Press.

Wolf, E. 1956. 'Aspects of Group Relations in a Complex Society: Mexico', *American Anthropologist* 58: 1065–77.

_____ 1997. *Europe and the People without History*. Berkeley: University of California Press.

Wolff, R.P. 1988. *Moneybags Must Be So Lucky: On the Literary Structure of Capital*. Amherst: University of Massachusetts Press.

Worsley, P. 1970. *The Trumpet Shall Sound: A Study of 'Cargo' Cults in Melanesia*. London: Paladin.

Young, C. 1965. *Politics in the Congo: Decolonization and Independence*. Princeton: Princeton University Press.

_____ 1966. 'Post-independence Politics in the Congo', *Transition* 26: 34–41.

Young, C., and T. Turner. 1985. *The Rise and Decline of the Zairian State*. Madison: University of Wisconsin Press.

Zelizer, V. 2005. *The Purchase of Intimacy*. Princeton: Princeton University Press.

Song List

Amisi, R. 1996. 'Didi Kinuani', *Ziggy*. Paris: Galaxie Productions.

Bel, M. 2006. 'Yamba Ngai', *Boya Ye/Ba Gerants ya Mabala, 84/85*. Paris: Syllart/Genidia.

Bitshou, C. 1970. 'Infidelité Mado' *Madeline, Franco et l'Ok Jazz*. Paris: Sonodisc.

Boyibanda, M. 1974/2000. 'Zando ya Tipo Tipo', *Franco et le T.P. OK Jazz 1972/1973/1974*. Paris: Sonodisc.

Boziana, B. 1988. 'Canon ya Mofude', *Anti-Choc*. London: Sterns/Aswe.

Brain, A. 2014. 'Brazzos & Petit Pierre: Making Indépendance Cha-Cha', ONU MAG #7. Retrieved 30 August 2016 from https://www.youtube.com/watch?v=vl0xRNbl5d8.

Cheacaine, L. 1977/1998. 'Sala lokola Lutadilla', *Bomba, Bomba Mabe +Mbongo*. Paris: Sonodisc.

D'Eté, J. 2004. 'Ecole', *Miracles*. Paris: Simon Music.

Djanana, D. 1986/1998. 'Mbuma Elengi', *Choc Stars Riana/Zikondo*. Paris: P.A.V. Mayala.

Emeneya, K. 1980/1996. 'Dembela', *Ndako ya Ndele, Kester Emenaya et Viva la Musica*. Paris: Sonodisc.

———— 1982/2008a. 'Sans préavis', *Les Meilleurs Succes de Victoria Eleison Vol 1*. Paris: Veve/Mayala/FBD

———— 1982/2008b. 'Okosi ngai mfumu', *Les Meilleurs Succes de Victoria Eleison Vol 1*. Paris: Veve/Mayala/FBD

———— 1984/2008. 'Mobali ya ngenge', *Les Meilleurs Succes de Victoria Eleison Vol 2*. Paris: Veve/Mayala/FBD

———— 1991/2008. 'Ngonda' *Djo Kester/Ngonda*. Paris: P.A.V. Mayala

———— 2006. 'Kester Emeneya' (interview). Retrieved 1 August 2016 from http://uk.youtube.com/watch?v=lbs4tbsUPAY.

———— 2007. 'King Kester Emeneya: Weston' (interview) Retrieved 1 August 2016 from http://www.youtube.com/watch?gl=GB&hl=en &v=SSyKqyjle2w&feature=related.

Evoloko 'Joker' (Atshuamo). 2005. 'Eliyo', *Les Meilleurs Succes de Langa Langa Stars Vol 4*. Paris: Veve/Mayala/FBD.

Franco, L.M. 1977/1995. 'Bandeko Ngai ya Mibale Basundoli Ngai', *Souvenirs de l'Un Deux Trois*. Paris: AM.

Gentamicine. 2006. 'Kipe ya yo!', *Kipe ya Yo!* Paris: Ndiaye

Gola, H.F. 2004. 'Amour intérêt', *Miracles*. Paris: Simon Music

———— 2007. '365 Jours x 2', *Sens Interdit*. Paris: DRTV.

Ipupa, Fally. 2006a. 'Associé', *Droit Chemin*. Paris: Obouo Music

———— 2006b. 'Liputa', *Droit Chemin*. Paris: Obouo Music

'King Richard'. 2005. *Maisha Park*, 4, Ricardo Productions: Paris.

Ley, T. 1970/1997. 'Mokolo nakokufa', *Le Seigneur Rochereau a L'Olympia*, Paris: Syllart..

———— 2007. 'Kaful Mayay', *The Voice of Lightness: Congo Classics 1961–1977, Disc 2 Tabu Ley Rochereau*. London: AMG.

———— 2007b. 'Mongali', *The Voice of Lightness: Congo Classics 1961–1977, Disc 2 Tabu Ley Rochereau*. London: AMG.

Lotin, Eboa 2008. 'Chaud Lapin', *Temps Presents*. Paris: Duo D'Enfer.

Lutumba, S. 1974/2000. 'Mabele', *Franco et le T.P. OK Jazz 1972/1973/1974*. Paris: Soneca.

———— 1977/1998. 'Mbongo', *Bomba, Bomba Mabe +Mbongo*. Paris: Sonima

Massela, D. 1994. 'Tempête du désert', *Wenge Musica, les Anges Adorables volume 1*, Sonodisc CD 8801.

Mpiana, J.B. 1996. 'Bana Lunda', *Feux de l'Amour*. Paris: Simon Music.

———— 2008. 'Zadio', *Quelle est ton Probleme ?* Paris: Ndiaye.

———— 2011. 'Mpunda', *Soyons Sérieux*. Paris. Obouo Music.

Olomide, Koffi. 1978/1998. 'Synza', *Viva la Musica and Papa Wemba*. Paris: Ngoyarto NG0108.

———— 1991. 'Ngobila', *Ngobila*. Paris: FDB 300061.

———— 2004. *Monde Arabe*. Paris: Sonima.

———— 2006. 'Chez Ntemba', *Danger de Mort*. Paris: Sonima.

———— 2007. Bonus from the DVD/Maxi single, *Swi*. Paris: Diego Music.

———— 2008a. 'BB gout', *Bord ezanga kombo*. Paris: Diego Music.

———— 2008b. 'Ikea', *Bord ezanga kombo*. Paris: Diego Music.

Prince, P. 1982/2008. 'Sango ya mabala commission', *Les Meilleurs Succes de Victoria Eleison Vol 1*. Paris: Veve/Mayala/FBD.

Sukami, T. 1978/2005. 'Pachalabran', *Zaiko Langa Langa Les Immortels*. Paris: Wendoo Music B0025BBIHG.

Wemba, P. 1995. 'Kaokokokorobo', *Pole Position*. Paris: Sonodisc CDS 8815

_____ 1977/1998. 'Mère supérieur', *Viva la Musica and Papa Wemba*. Paris: Ngoyarto NG0108.

_____ 1985/2000. 'Beau Gosse Ya Paris', *Beau Gosse Ya Paris*. Paris: Ngoyarto.

_____ 2001. 'Proclamation', *Le Meilleurs Succes de Papa Wemba 1983–1984* (2 volumes). Paris: Éditions Mayala FDB300094/95.

_____ 1982/2004. 'Matebu', *Papa Wemba, Mwana Molokai, the First 20 Years*. London: Sterns.

Wendo, A.K. and H. Bowane. 1948/1996. In: *Marie-Louise Ngoma, The Early Years, 1948–1960*. Frankfurt: Popular African Music.

Wenge Musica BCBG. 1994. *Kala yi Boeing*. Paris: Ngoyarto.

_____ 1996. *Pentagone*. Paris: Simon Music.

Wenge Maison Mère 2009. 'Techno-Malewa'. Retrieved 1 August 2016 from http://www.youtube.com/watch?v=4qxEoR-9Kfg.

Werrason, N.N. 1995. 'Tshasho Mbala', *Pleins Feux!!!* Paris: Saga SG960003.

_____ 2004. 'Na touche', *Tegmoignage*. Paris: Sonima SMCD1645.

Werrason, N.N., and B.C. Kalonji. 2002. 'Ma Personnalité', *A la Queue Leu Leu (Koyimbi ko)*. Paris: Sonima.

INDEX

DISLOCATIONS

General Editors: August Carbonella, *Memorial University of Newfoundland, Don Kalb, University of Utrecht & Central European University, Linda Green, University of Arizona*

The immense dislocations and suffering caused by neoliberal globalization, the retreat of the welfare state in the last decades of the twentieth century, and the heightened military imperialism at the turn of the twenty-first century have raised urgent questions about the temporal and spatial dimensions of power. Through stimulating critical perspectives and new and cross-disciplinary frameworks that reflect recent innovations in the social and human sciences, this series provides a forum for politically engaged and theoretically imaginative responses to these important issues of late modernity.